AT HOME

IN

THE

WORLD

Also by Michael Jackson

Ethnography
The Kuranko
Allegories of the Wilderness
Barawa, and the Ways Birds Fly in the Sky
Paths Toward a Clearing

Fiction
Rainshadow
Pieces of Music

Poetry
Latitudes of Exile
Wall
Going On
Duty Free

AT HOME

IN

THE

WORLD

Michael Jackson

Duke University Press *Durham and London 1995*

© 1995 Duke University Press
All rights reserved
Printed in the United States of America on acid-free paper ∞
Typeset in Berkeley Medium by Tseng Information Systems
Library of Congress Cataloging-in-Publication Data
appear on the last printed page of this book.

FOR FRANCINE

After all, what would be the value of the passion for knowledge if it resulted only in a certain amount of knowledgeableness and not, in one way or another and to the extent possible, in the knower's straying afield of himself? There are times in life when the question of knowing if one can think differently than one thinks, and perceive differently than one sees, is absolutely necessary if one is to go on looking and reflecting at all. People will say, perhaps, that these games with oneself would better be left backstage; or, at best, that they might properly form part of those preliminary exercises that are forgotten once they have served their purpose. But, then, what is philosophy today—philosophical activity, I mean—if it is not the critical work that thought brings to bear on itself? In what does it consist, if not in the endeavor to know how and to what extent it might be possible to think differently, instead of legitimating what is already known?—Michel Foucault

ACKNOWLEDGMENTS

To the Warlpiri people, who accepted my wife and me into their communities, I owe an intellectual and personal debt. Although I use pseudonyms to protect the identity of those whose experiences, voices, and Dreamings permeate the pages of this book, I am aware that disguising names neither effaces identity nor writes off debts. Like many anthropologists today, I reject the idea that the rationale of our intellectual endeavor is the discovery of "the one and only truth about the world." Fieldwork provides a heightened awareness of what is and is not humanly possible. Its goal is, to some degree, to work out a modus vivendi among people whose cultural values are radically different, to show that human beings *can* coexist in "an atmosphere of tolerant solidarity." In this sense, anthropology is a form of experimentation and critique in which the anthropologist and his or her culture figure as focal subjects. Method becomes a question of making a virtue out of what others have historically had to do as a matter of necessity—finding a way across cultural divides and social barriers, enlarging horizons, learning new languages, living rather than paying lip service to a pluralistic ethos, attempting to move beyond the received opinions which conventionally condemn human beings to isolation from one another in the name of essential difference. In writing this account of my experience among the Warlpiri I have striven to communicate something of these imperatives, and at the same time convey crucial Warlpiri concerns to those of my own culture who remain oblivious or indifferent to the struggle of tribal peoples in modern nation states. In this measure I hope that this book may reciprocate the goodwill of those who received me, a stranger, so generously into their world. I gratefully acknowledge members of the Lajamanu and Yuendumu councils and all those Warlpiri individuals who helped me and my wife in the course of our research. I am particularly indebted to Jimmy Robertson Jampijinpa, Shorty Ray Rose Japaljarri, Ian Jimmy Jangala, Abie Jangala, Joe Long Jangala, Paddy Nelson Jupurrurla, Harry Nelson Jakamarra, Henry Cook Jakamarra, Teddy Morrison Jupurrurla, P. B. (*kumunjayi*) Japanangka, and Cecil Johnson Japangardi, who worked closely with me in every aspect of my fieldwork. When I first went to Central Australia in 1989, Petronella Morel and Jim Wafer helped me get my bearings. I owe Robert Hoogenraad thanks for photocopying a Warlpiri dictionary for me at short notice. During my association with the Central Land Council, Angus Green was unstinting in his assistance and advice. Both my wife and I owe a great deal to his friendship and support. Finally, I would like to record my gratitude to the College of Arts and Sciences, Indiana University, which provided funds for fieldwork in Central Australia in 1989, 1990, and 1991, and for a return visit to Lajamanu in 1994.

AT HOME

IN

THE

WORLD

ONE

Most serious thought in our time struggles

with the feeling of homelessness.

—Susan Sontag

==

This book is about the experience of home. It is a record of a journey in search of what it means, in the late twentieth century, to be at home in the world. The journey took me to Central Australia, where I did ethnographic fieldwork in 1990 and 1991, but the philosophical and personal impulse to write this book has been with me for a long time, nurtured by years of living outside the country where I was born and raised, by experiences working among the homeless in London, and by what I have seen of the impact of migration, dispossession, and loss in the lives of people in Europe, West Africa, America, and the antipodes. Yet it would be a mistake to locate the origins of this book in one particular moment or one particular place, because personal experience is always foreshadowed and fated by imperatives that belong to our shared history and common humanity. This is why, when I embarked upon this project, I knew I would have to walk away from the familiar. Only with the advantage of distance could I hope to throw into relief the ways in which, in John Berger's telling phrase, "we live not just our own lives but the longings of our century."

Ours is a century of uprootedness. All over the world, fewer and fewer people live out their lives in the place where they were born. Perhaps at no other time in history has the question of belonging seemed so urgent. Since the end of the Second World War, millions of men and women have migrated from the impoverished countries of the south to cities of the industrialized north because they see no future for themselves at home. They sell their labor and hope to return to vil-

1

lages where they will become heroes. As with the homeless of metropolitan Europe and the United States, census enumerators can never accurately count their number.

"I'm not counted, so I guess I don't exist," said James Gibb, a forty-year-old Vietnam veteran, who spends a lot of time riding the New York subway.

"We don't count for society," said another homeless man. "It's like we're just fleas on a dog."

As if one has to be numbered to be known.

These days, the dispirited comments of the migrant worker, the refugee, the street kid, the vagrant, are metaphors for something we all feel. The quarter we drop into the panhandler's Styrofoam cup on a freezing January afternoon betokens our own mood of estrangement, even when we are well-housed and well-heeled.

Perhaps it is the pace of historical change that makes a mockery of any expectation that one might ever live, as W. B. Yeats put it, "like some green laurel / Rooted in one dear perpetual place." Home, observes Salmon Rushdie, "has become a scattered, damaged, hydra-various concept in our present travails." Certainly, it is difficult now to find anywhere that abets the illusion that one's own world is also *the* world. Edward Said describes exile as "the unhealable rift forced between a human being and a native place, between the self and its true home." For a lot of people this describes the state of the world.

Yet homelessness isn't always experienced as a mutilation of one's life, an insurmountable sorrow.

In 1917, the poet Blaise Cendrars, having lost his right arm in the war, returns to the 5th arrondissement in Paris. He is a changed man. So too is the old quarter. Some of the street names are different, Saint-Séverin has been stripped bare, la place Maubert is bigger, rue Saint-Jacques has been widened.

This is the neighborhood where the twenty-year-old poet exchanged his Swiss birth name for the sobriquet Cendrars, assuming a French identity and being born to poetry. Now, ten years on, rather than mourn the changes, he celebrates them—in a poem from *Au coeur du monde*—as expressions of the liberating spirit of modernity. It is the first time he has written a poem with his left hand:

> Je porte un visage d'aujourd'hui
> Et le crâne de mon grand-père
>
> C'est pourquoi je ne regrette rien
> Et j'appelle les démolisseurs

Foutez mon enfance par terre
Ma famille et mes habitudes
Mettez une gare à la place
Ou laissez un terrain vague
Qui dégage mon origine

Je ne suis pas le fils de mon père
Et je n'aime que ma bisaïeule
Je me suis fait un nom nouveau
Visible comme une affiche bleue
Et rouge montée sur un échafaudage
Derrière quoi on édifie
Des nouveautés des lendemains*

The word "home" is shot through with ambiguity. "To be rooted," wrote Simone Weil, "is perhaps the most important and least recognized need of the human soul." But isn't it also true that we often feel an equally strong need to uproot ourselves and cross the borders that conventionally divide us? According to Freud, "the dwelling-house was a substitute for the mother's womb." He forgot to mention that it can also be a tomb.

In 1950 the Australian anthropologist Kenneth Read was on a patrol in an area of the Eastern Highlands of New Guinea where people had never before seen a white man. One morning, as Read and his companions were breaking camp, a young boy from the village approached them. Using gestures, he made it clear that he wanted to return with them to the place they had come from. The boy was perhaps thirteen or fourteen. He spoke no language but his own. Yet he was prepared to throw in his lot with these outsiders and undertake a journey, Read wrote, "immeasurably greater than the distance involved, virtually a transition from one world to another." Even though the terrors of the unknown were mitigated by a kind of visionary opportunism (since, to have any hope of becoming a leader in one's natal village, a man had to brave the hazards of the outside world and seek out the power and wealth said to exist only in alien lands), this "leap through time," Read notes, "took a measure of courage and a degree of foresight almost

---

* I wear a face for today/and the skull of my grandfather/It's why I have no regrets/and call out to the demolition gangs/raze my childhood to the ground/my family and my customs/build a railway station there instead/or leave some waste ground/to erase my origins/I am not the son of my father/I love only my grandfather/I gave myself a new name/as legible as a blue and red/poster pasted on the scaffolding/behind which they are dreaming up/innovations for the days to come.

impossible to comprehend." Did the boy, Susuro, whose new name was an affectionate diminutive of the name of his adopted village, ever succeed in his aspirations? Thirty years after leaving "The High Valley" Read went back. Old acquaintances told him that Susuro had remained in Susuroka for several years, growing to manhood there and working from time to time in a nearby township. He then returned home. Of Susuro's subsequent fate, all Read could learn was that he was dead, killed by sorcery among his own people.

Thomas Wolfe made famous the phrase "You can't go home again." For him the words were filled with the forlorn realization that we cannot reverse time, cannot retrace our steps along a certain road and expect to experience ourselves as we were when we first walked down it. But Susuro's story suggests an outlook pervaded less by nostalgia than a yearning to open oneself up to the world at large. It brings to mind the famous anecdote about Diogenes, who, when asked the name of his hometown, replied, "the world."

Susuro's story also reminds us that history has made go-betweens of us all, and that anthropology is itself a product of an age of trespass and travel, a world in which frontiers no longer contain those born within them. Crossing erstwhile boundaries in order to transmute local into global knowledge, anthropology has usurped the restive role which the German Romantic poet, Novalis, accorded philosophy: the urge to be at home everywhere. There may be something heroic about this, as Susan Sontag suggests. Rather than be oppressed by the intellectual vertigo of living without determinate borders, one celebrates the possibilities that are opened up for understanding oneself in otherness.

This is how I understood the journey I embarked upon. Much had been written on the subject of home and homelessness in the Western world, but what of the experience of home elsewhere? By going to Aboriginal Australia, I hoped to explore the ways in which people created and sustained a sense of belonging and autonomy when they did not build or dwell in houses, and house was not synonymous with home.

This search for what it is to be at home in the world entailed another: I wanted to develop a style of writing which would be consonant with lived experience, in all its variety and ambiguity.

Nowadays, one must have recourse to art and literature if one is to keep alive a sense of what hard science, with its passion for definitive concepts and systematic knowledge, often forgoes or forgets.

The painter who dispenses with framing in order to reunite the field of artistic vision with the space of the world, or the composer who breaks down the boundaries between what is deemed music and noise (I am thinking here of John Cage*), find a natural ally in the philosopher who, aware that concepts never cover the fullness of human experience, sees the task of description as more compelling than that of explanation.

John Berger writes: "If every event which occurred could be given a name, there would be no need for stories. As things are here, life outstrips our vocabulary."

Theodor Adorno called this the untruth of identity, by which he meant that concepts plunder but never exhaust the wealth of experience. Life cannot be pressed into the service of language. Concepts represent experience at the cost of leaving a lot unsaid. So long as we use concepts to cut up experience, giving value to some things at the expense of others, we inhibit our sense of the plenitude of Being. We gain some purchase on the world, to be sure, but claiming that our concepts contain all that can be usefully said about experience, we close off the possibility of critique. It is only when we cease trying to control the world that we can overcome our fixation on the autarchy of concepts.

It is because no word is able to contain the moods of a moment, or capture what Gerard Manly Hopkins called "things counter, original, spare, strange," that writers approach the world so tortuously and obliquely, using "inept metaphors and obvious periphrases" to draw attention to a subject they are unwilling to name. It is their way of recognizing that life eludes our grasp and remains at large, always fugitive. Like a forest in which there are clearings. Like a forest through whose canopy sunlight filters and falls.

A hundred years ago William James observed: "Our fields of experience have no *more* definite boundaries than have our points of view. Both are fringed forever by a more that continuously develops . . . and supercedes them as life proceeds." But many of us are intolerant of indefinite things which overflow boundaries and plunge us into the confusing stream of direct experience. We tend to single out ex-

---

*John Cage asks: "Which is more musical, a truck passing by a factory or a truck passing by a music school?" It is one way of underscoring the need for a musically open-minded "attitude that is non-exclusive, that can include what we know together with what we do not yet imagine."

periences which we can handle, with which we are comfortable, with which we can live. Other experiences go by the board, thrown back into a world we repudiate as Other and try to forget. So we set more store by nouns than the words that conjoin them. "We ought to say a feeling of *and,* a feeling of *if,* a feeling of *but,* and a feeling of *by,* quite as readily as we say a feeling of *blue* or a feeling of *cold.* Yet we do not: so inveterate has our habit become of recognizing the existence of the substantive parts alone, that language almost refuses to lend itself to any other use."

Perhaps the fault lies with the English language. Many of the words we think of as stable nouns should really be called verbs, in as much as they refer to fleeting things. The Hopi language is more natural in this sense, classifying lightning, stormcloud, and flame as verbs because they are transitory. In Nootka, you don't say "house," but "it houses," or "a house occurs" because, for the Nootka, houses are impermanent.

Sometimes, the places where we feel most at home are like nouns in sentences. We are comforted by the way they appear to be sealed off from the world, complacent in their own definition. But sometimes it is imperative to unsettle that sense of being housed, to risk oneself in the world, to recognize the power of verbs, prepositions, and copulas.

"To approach experience," writes John Berger, "is not like approaching a house."

I left the United States in the dead of winter and flew to New Zealand on my way to Sydney.

It was an odd experience arriving home, and thinking about home, when I had been living away from my native country for so many years.

There is a Maori saying that for as long as a person lives on the land or returns regularly to it, a fire burns there (*ahi ka*). But if you go away and do not return, the fire goes out (*ahi mataotao*). Hardly a year had gone by without my visiting family and friends in New Zealand, but, like many antipodeans of European descent, I had an ambivalent relationship with my homeland. You feel estranged from your European roots yet cannot identify wholeheartedly with the indigenous culture of the land. You live betwixt and between, uneasy about your origins, unsure of where you stand, in two minds about your identity and allegiance.

The quandary is, of course, rooted in the problem of how indigenous and European cultures can coexist. The Maori are the *tangata whenua,* people of the land. Others are guests, strangers, interlopers.

Perhaps it is the land which holds the answer.

Whata ngarongaro he tangata, toitu he whenua (human beings pass away, while the land remains), goes the Maori adage.

Certainly, it is always the land I think of when I think of New Zealand. In winter, rainclouds scudding over indelibly green hills. In summer, the smell of dry grass and river water. The blueness of the mountains in the south.

In Auckland I rented a car and drove to Coromandel. I wanted to look up old friends who lived on a commune near Waikawau Bay.

The asphalt road shimmered in the heat and the air smelled of lupins. It had been a long time since I had experienced the exhilaration of the open road, and snatches of Walt Whitman kept running through my head.

> Done with indoor complaints, libraries, querulous criticisms,
> Strong and content I travel the open road . . .
>
> From this hour I ordain myself loos'd of limits and
>   imaginary lines,
> Going where I list, my own master total and absolute,
> Listening to others, considering well what they say,
> Pausing, searching, receiving, contemplating,
> Gently, but with undeniable will, divesting myself of
>   the holds that would hold me . . .
>
> Now I re-examine philosophies and religions,
> They may prove well in lecture-rooms, yet may not prove at all
>   Under the spacious clouds and along the
>   Landscape and flowing currents . . .

Along the narrow Coromandel road, gnarled pohutukawas clung to embankments of yellow clay. Dishevelled shags roosted on black rocks. The stench of the sea filled my nostrils.

My first morning at the commune I woke at first light and went for a run along the beach. Oyster catchers and plover skittered away. The sand was slicked with pale blue, like the slip smoothed under a potter's hand.

I kicked off my running shoes, stripped naked, and walked into the sea. It washed around my ankles and gouged a hollow under my heels. I hesitated. The water was cold, the beach deserted. I looked out beyond the breakers for telltale signs of a rip, wondering vaguely who would come to my assistance if I got into difficulties. I felt foolish and vulnerable. Then, as another wave began to break, I ran forward and plunged in. It knocked the breath out of me, but my trepidation vanished and I struck out for the horizon.

TWO

Ubi bene, ibi patria (Your home is where

they treat you well)

—*Latin proverb*

Sydney: February 1990. On one side of Caroline Street is a row of run-down terrace houses. On the other side is a vacant lot surrounded by a corrugated iron fence. LOVE IS A DRUG says the graffiti. A fire is burning on the corner of the street. Some Aboriginal people are standing around the fire, swigging beer from cans. Not many cars drive down Caroline Street. Many non-Aborigines call the neighborhood an Aboriginal ghetto. They will tell you it is not a safe area and ask you what on earth you're doing down there. Cab drivers refuse to take you farther than the top of the street. They earbash you with accounts of Aboriginal kids breaking taxi windows with volleys of stones.

I am walking toward the railway station at Redfern. An Aboriginal bloke is walking ahead of me. He keeps glancing back over his shoulder. Whenever he sees a taxi coming he steps out onto the road and tries to flag it down. Four cabs drive past without stopping. One swerves dangerously close to where he is standing. Angrily he yells after it, "Fuck you!"

There is a lot of anger in Caroline Street.

A woman is sitting on the front step of the house next door. She is shouting drunkenly down the street, "Ya cunt, ya fuckin' cunt, lockin' me outta me own house like a fuckin' mongrel dog!" Her abuse seems vaguely directed at the men standing around the fire at the street corner. A tall man with his shirt hanging out starts walking back down the street toward her. The woman clambers to her feet and waits for him to approach. She is still bawling abuse. When the man walks up to her she spits the abuse straight into his face. "Ya cunt!" The man

9

Australia

cuffs her hard and she falls to the ground. She crawls along the foot-path, among fragments of glass, then climbs to her feet and calls him a dead cunt. The man has a half-empty wine bottle in his left hand. He breaks it over the woman's head. She falls to her knees, bleeding from the gash in her skull. "Doesn't hurt me," she says.

In January, the police set up a surveillance position on the TNT towers, overlooking Redfern. Using high-powered telescopes and bin-oculars, they spied on the Aboriginal community. In the early hours of February 8, a Tactical Response force of the Sydney police raided houses in Caroline, Eveleigh, Lawson, Hugo, and Louis Streets. Doors were smashed in with sledgehammers. People woke in panic to find police in riot gear pointing shotguns at their faces. The police claimed to be searching for illegal drugs and stolen goods. For the people of

Redfern it was another act of racial harrassment. Tonnette Simpson described how police threatened her husband and two-year-old son with a pistol before arresting her. "They just smashed down the door and there were eight police in my bedroom," she said. "My two-year-old son ran to his dad because he was scared and I thought: 'Oh, my God, this gun is going to go off!'" A spokesman for the Aboriginal Legal Service called the raid "typical of the police's South African–style fascist and Gestapo tactics." Another resident said, "They broke into our homes like animals."

Days of unremitting rain. The harbor water bloated like a carcass. The smell of brine and decaying seagrass. I am reading a book called *The Lost Children,* based on interviews with thirteen men and women of Aboriginal descent who, as young children, were taken from their parents and placed in state homes or adopted into white families. Their stories are typical of 100,000 others. People whose fate was decided by an official government policy to assimilate Aborigines into white Australian society.

Aboriginals had allegedly lost their culture. The popular stereotype was of black people living in makeshift camps overrun by drunks, dogs, dirt, and disease. To put an end to this degradation and hasten assimilation, it was decreed that Aboriginal children be taken from their parents and raised as whites. According to the Adoption Act, the child's Aboriginal identity ceased to be a legal fact. Adopting parents were encouraged to erase whatever they knew of their child's past so the child could never discover anything about his or her origins.

In 1980 an Aboriginal corporation called Link-Up was founded. Its aim was to reunite Aboriginal adults who had been fostered, adopted, or institutionalized as children. *The Lost Children* was edited from interviews with some of the men and women who had made this painful journey home.

One thing struck me again and again in these interviews. These children had grown up feeling they were were different. For many of them it was a long time before they had a word for this difference, before they learned they were Aboriginals. It fitted the feeling of unworthiness and lovelessness they had felt from the start. To be of Aboriginal descent was to be made to feel ashamed. Pauline McLeod's foster parents told her that Aboriginals were lazy, got drunk, and went walkabout. She was told that her natural parents had abused her, which is why she had been taken away. Nancy De Vries's foster parents would point to Aboriginals in the street and say, "Look at them, aren't they dirty, aren't they awful." Whenever she got into trouble she was told it was because she "was an Aboriginal, bad, lazy." These children were only ever reminded of their backgrounds in order to be stigmatized. At the same time they became increasingly aware that their adoptive identities were facades. Because they were black they could never really be white; by the same token, they could never really be intelligent, acceptable, or good. They were therefore driven to seek their identity through the very world they had been denied: the shadowy and disparaged world of Aboriginality. Because this world was defined as a negation of white, middle-class values, the raw material from which these children had to shape their lives was slag and detritus and dross. Each person would experience his or her life as a movement "through many negatives to what I am."

Looking back, Nancy De Vries said:

> I think it's important that people realise that these kids that were taken away from their families, separated from their culture, their identity, had to put up with dreadful, dreadful things. How many of us have survived sane I don't know, and I realise why so many of us have died through alcohol. I was lucky, as I grew up, that alcohol never agreed with me. Instead of the slow death of alcohol I tried the quick death of pills or hanging. I always tell people I cut my wrists here cutting a jam tin, because it's very embarrassing admitting that I tried to commit suicide. I tried to kill myself. I was lonely. I was unhappy. I wanted my mother, I wanted my identity, I felt cheated, I wanted to be me.

Nancy De Vries was ten when she first ran away from home. She remembers one time going to the Registry of Births, Deaths, and Marriages "trying to find out who I was and where I came from." At age fifteen Rick McLeod ran away from home for the first time, something his foster father would later, unforgiveably, call his "going walkabout." When Sherry Atkinson was fifteen she left home leaving this note: "Thank you for everything you've done, I'm sorry I'm not the perfect daughter that you want me to be but I have to find out who my mother is and my family is and where I come from. Don't come looking for me because it won't change anything."

For a long time Aboriginality kept its taint and stigma. These people did not find the family, the community, the acceptance which would prove the stereotype pernicious and false. They had been taught to think they were nothing but the persons they were said to be. They existed only as objects under the judgmental gaze of whites. They knew no other names but the names they were given.

It is hard to reconstrue such definitions, to make such names your own. In West Africa people took up the words their oppressors used to deprecate them. They "gathered them from the mud," a black poet said, "in order to wear them with pride." This was the genesis of "negritude."

Sartre comments: "Negro, yes, and dirty nigger, if you like; but by tearing your words, your concepts, away from you and applying them to myself in full sovereignty, by laying claim to that nature you scorn but whose originality you cannot avoid recognizing, I recapture the initiative, I dare to think about myself, I personalize myself against you, and I become that permanent indignity—the self-conscious other."

In Australia, this transformation was far more arduous. People had first to reject the culture in which they had been raised, before they could recover the culture from which they had been torn. You could run away from home, to be sure, but it would take half a lifetime before you found a home to which to run.

With the help of Link-Up, a lot of Aboriginals have been reunited with their natural parents. The reunions are inevitably nerve-racking. Often people have grown up being told their parents were dead. Some parents cannot overcome the shame and guilt at having let themselves be persuaded or duped into giving up their children for adoption. And men and women must face the reality that the people who bore them and are their flesh and blood are also strangers. But sometimes acceptance is almost immediate, as in Pauline McLeod's case. "It was great to see Mum. She was very special. I was scared because I didn't know what would happen. They were so nice, so kind. They accepted me for what I was. It was beautiful. And I really did feel I didn't have to act, I didn't have to fight for love. I was home. It was one of the most relieving feelings I ever had. I felt comfortable with them, I really did . . . It was great to be where I really belonged . . . and I thought 'Yeah, I'm home, I'm really home.'"

Looking back, there is always bitterness. These Aboriginal children grew up with a sham identity born of pretended kinship. Acceptance was never unconditional. Affection was faked. Their color, names they were called at school, the sense they got of having despicable origins, all conspired to make them rank outsiders. After their homecomings people felt awkward, but at least they could let go the sham. "I didn't have to pretend any more," said Pauline McLeod. Paul Cremen observed that it was immaterial to him that there were dilapidated houses, broken windows, and overgrown yards in the Aboriginal community to which he returned. What mattered were the people. "They don't have to live any pretensions," he said. "They don't have to keep things for appearance sake."

There is also regret about the life one was denied—heritage, home, family, community, unconditional love. "I just feel like I've really been cheated, cheated bad of my life," says Sherry Atkinson. And Alicia Adams: "They never told us where we came from or who our people were, and it's too late, now, to tell us. If they had told us earlier it would have been different. But now it's been ruined."

A lot of people speak of something "missing" in their lives. Jeanette Sinclair describes it as a hole you walk around with that nothing can ever completely fill.

In his autobiography, *A Bastard Like Me,* the Aboriginal activist, Charles Perkins, remembers what it was like growing up on an Aboriginal reserve on the edge of Alice Springs. It was a segregated world in which "part-Aboriginal people were nobodies, nothing. They did not belong to anyone." Charlie was made to feel "scum" and "unwanted" in the white town, and was kept from ever meeting his tribal kin. "I always had the feeling that there was a gap, something missing in me. I think a lot of part-Aborigines feel that there is something wrong, something missing in them, and the pieces are not fitting into place."

Reading books like *The Lost Children* and *A Bastard Like Me,* I began to realize how much was missing in the lives of white Australians too—the immense gap there is in our understanding of Aboriginals as people.

The most difficult thing for whites is to break the habit of categorizing Aboriginal people. It hardly matters whether we denigrate them as Stone Age remnants, romanticize them as New Age sages, or pity them as victims. Definition is itself at the roots of racism: the way we reduce the world to a word, and gag the mouths of others with our labels. One man put it very succinctly: "Amongst ourselves we are *people*: whites turn us into Aborigines." The great empty spaces in our knowledge of Aboriginal people get filled with the noise of our wildest imaginings and settled with our fears.

William James had this to say about the way we polarize "us" and "them": "All narrow people *intrench* their Me, they *retract* it,—from the region of what they cannot securely possess. People who don't resemble them, or who treat them with indifference, people over whom they gain no influence, are people on whose existence, however meritorious it may intrinsically be, they look with chill negation, if not with positive hate. Who will not be mine I will exclude from existence altogether; . . . such people shall be as if they were not."

In Australia's bicentennial year a book was published called *After 200 Years: Photographic Essays of Aboriginal and Islander Australia Today*. The photographs are all by Aboriginal photographers. Several of the photos were taken at a place called Nyirrpi in Central Australia. One photo showed Nyirrpi itself—a handful of tin houses in the middle of a spinifex plain. It was an "outstation," a new community on traditional land to which people had moved after living more than a generation in a settlement 163 kilometers away. There were photos of smiling women and laughing children. "Here we are now, back in our own country, Nyirrpi," reads the caption by Charlie Jampijinpa Gallagher. "The reason we shifted was because of family getting drunk and so we didn't want to live at Yuendumu . . . We've come back to our family's country, our grandfather's country, to live in this country, my own country, my father's country, father-in-law's, grandmother's and mother's country, so our children can grow up here. The children will mind this country. There are lots of children growing up here."

It was the photos of Nyirrpi that drew me to Central Australia. I wanted to experience firsthand a society such as Charlie Jampijinpa described, where to be housed was not necessarily to be at home, where home meant being with one's kinsmen in one's own country, and land was the root metaphor for freedom.

My wife and I walked for hours through now-familiar Sydney streets, planning our trip to the red center. At dusk the rumble of trains. A silver can of Resch's Pilsener on a window ledge. At first light the din of traffic, an ambulance siren, a eucalypt branch scraped across an iron roof. Waves of uncertainty swept over me when I thought about the desert, its remoteness, openness, and otherness.

One morning we were sitting at a pavement table outside the Mali café in Crown Street. There was a cabinetmaker's shop next door. The smell of the sawed jarrah planks stacked in the shop doorway made me think of Kabala, in northern Sierra Leone, and the mixture of trepidation and exhilaration I had felt when I went there for the first time.

THREE

I think of two landscapes—one outside

the self, the other within.

—Barry Lopez

Someone I met in Sydney said that Alice Springs was the ugliest town in the world. But I hardly noticed the town. I was looking up at the quartzite escarpment of the Western Macdonnells, inhaling the dry air of the desert. Inwardly, I was celebrating something I had all but forgotten—arid places are where I feel most at home.

I ambled through the town like any other visitor, looking at Aboriginal art in the Papunya Tula gallery, browsing through books on Aboriginal culture in the Arunta bookshop.

What struck me about the Aboriginal people I saw in the street was the way they walked. Whites moved singly and lineally toward their destinations, pressed for time, giving no ground. Aborigines dawdled, sauntered, strolled, idled. They circulated in groups. Eddies or whorls in a stream.

At dusk I set out on a walk along the broad, sandy bed of the Todd river. Aborigines were sitting in circles under the big river gums, drinking cans of Victoria bitter or casks of Coolabah wine. Several Aboriginal men drifted past me. Shocks of coal-black hair, eyes like anthracite in shadowy faces. They smelled of woodsmoke, booze, and the earth.

I crossed the causeway, moving further up the creek. A police van was driving slowly along the riverbed, lurching over sandy ridges, dropping into shallow depressions. The van stopped and two cops got out. They walked up to a group of Aboriginal men. The men resembled a circle of black firestones. The cops said something to the drinkers, then took up positions on either side of one of the men, grabbed a handful of his jersey, and hauled him to his feet. The drinker was made to stumble toward the van. Without a protest he was pushed into the cage. His fingers clutched the mesh window, his face in darkness. The cops returned to the circle of drinkers. Another man was extracted like a rotten tooth and hauled away to the van. When they had taken five men the cops drove off up the creek where other Aborigines were sitting under the gums.

A woman in a filthy blue cardigan and cotton skirt tottered toward me, crying out in a hoarse voice. She fell into a heap on the sand and began pummelling her forehead with her fists. Her hands fell. She snatched at the hem of her dress as she cried out. Her body rocked to and fro as she voiced her distress and confusion. She looked through me. She looked into nowhere.

I left the creek bed and strolled along a street that seemed to lead away from the town. A white jogger ran past. A white couple walked out of their driveway with a dog scampering and bounding ahead of them. They looked through me too.

There was a sandy track that wound into a landscape of rock and spinifex. I followed it until I was clear of the town. A flock of green budgerigars flew up from the scrub. I stood for a while, listening to the silence, overwhelmed by the vividness of a ghost gum against rust-colored rocks. It was easy to understand the Aboriginal belief that children were born of a place as well as of human parents, that each person is an incarnation of a landscape. But what of the men and women camped in the riverbed? Where, for them, was home?

In Central Australia, many Aboriginal people have, through land rights legislation enacted in the 1970s, regained rights in perpetuity over traditional lands. Given the traumatic history of their encounters with white miners, pastoralists, welfare administrators, and government officials, it is not surprising that Aboriginal people nowadays work hard to assert and protect their autonomy. In dealing with whites they want to negotiate from a position of strength, and expect to call the shots. But Aboriginal people still need legal, economic, and bureaucratic support in dealing with mining corporations, reclaiming traditional land, and securing government aid. This support is provided by an organization called the Central Land Council.

Francine and I knew that if we were going to live in a desert community there would have to be some kind of quid pro quo. So we approached the Central Land Council and asked if there was any anthropological research we might usefully do.

We were assigned the task of studying the social impact on Warlpiri people of a gold mine at a place in the Tanami desert known as The Granites. Francine was to research the experiences and views of Warlpiri women; I would work with the men. To ensure that my fieldwork on home did not conflict with Warlpiri interests, I signed a legally binding agreement with the CLC, giving the organization the right to read and, if necessary, censor anything I wrote for publication on the basis of my research.

We left Alice Springs on the birthday of Shakespeare and Shirley Temple. For several weeks I had worked in the Alice Springs Public Library, reading ethnographies by Baldwin Spencer and F. Gillen, W. E. H. Stanner, T. G. H. Strehlow, Géza Roheim, Basil Sansom, Nicholas Peterson, Robert Tonkinson, Nancy Munn, Fred Myers, M. J. Meggitt, Nancy Williams, Diane Bell, A. P. Elkin, and C. and R. Berndt in preparation for my own fieldwork. Now the time had come to turn from reflection, and plunge into the real world.

Our first stop was to be Yuendumu, where we had enrolled for a week-long intensive course in Warlpiri.

The dirt road was the color of rust. It ran straight toward the horizon and melted into the sky. Looking back, we could see nothing for dust. To the south, in the hammering heat of the afternoon, a plain of porcupine spinifex and drab mulga stretched away toward the slabs and wedges of the Stuart Bluff Range.

There was no detail, that first day driving into the desert, that I thought so insignificant that I should not make a record of it. The yellow road signs peppered with .22 calibre bullets: FLOODWAY, BORE, GRID. Hawks flapping around the carcass of a red kangaroo. The shredded truck tires beside the road. The wuthering of the wind.*

We had been told to expect the worst at Yuendumu—potholed streets, gutted houses, rusting car bodies, rubbish, and red dirt. But we experienced the place as neither oppressive nor alien.

We strolled around in the dusk. Women were drifting toward humpies in the West Camp, carrying plastic bags of store-bought supplies. Young men ambled past and murmured wary greetings. In the shadows of casuarinas, we made out groups of people sitting around fires. Sometimes a TV set, as anomalous as a cube of ice, illuminated the

---

*In Warlpiri, the wind's wuthering is also described onamatopoeically: *wuurrwuurr wangkami.*

faces of children. We heard guttural and minatory voices in the darkness, and a snatch of song as a woman lulled a baby to sleep.

Our language course was at the local school. We sat crammed into tiny chairs behind tiny desks while the teacher-linguist unfurled brown paper drawings and urged the class to chorus the Warlpiri words for kangaroo, dog, man, woman, child, fireplace, firewood, meat, delicacy, and vegetable food. Then we learned the words for settlement, camp, hearth, and home.

Ngurra: homeplace, camp, hearth, country.
Ngurra wardingki: place of origin.
Yirraru kanpa nyinami: longing for your home (literally your sitting place).
Yirraru-jarrimi karnarla ngurraraku: I am homesick (for my camp).

Clearly, location was an index of social identity. In Yuendumu, for instance, people from different parts of the country live in different quarters. Those in the West Camp hail from country to the west of the settlement, and people in the South Camp from country to the south. Cardinal points are also used where we would use left and right, so that a Warlpiri person might tell you to move closer to a fire by saying "Move west!"

More verbs. "In Warlpiri," said the teacher, "*nyinami* means both 'to sit' and 'to be.' For example, *ngurrangkalipa nyinami,* means literally 'where your kinspeople are sitting,' which is to say 'your homeplace.'"

This metaphorical connection between existence and the earth may be universal. All over the world, people objectify their sense of being and belonging in images of place. Among the Kuranko, for instance, neighbors are known as *siginyorgonu,* literally "people with whom one sits." In German the word for property, *besitzen,* is derived from the verb "to sit upon," a possible allusion to the fact that human beings are "sitting animals" whose specialized anatomy enables us to define territorial rights through squatting or sitting. This is why we speak of the seat of power, and why in so many societies stools, chairs, and thrones are made symbols of authority. Warlpiri people sometimes refer to themselves by saying "*Walyangka karnalu nyina,*" which means, "We sit on the ground." To be with Warlpiri you must be prepared to sit with them and live, as they do, on the ground. In 1957, after her first few months in Yuendumu, the anthropologist Nancy Munn decided to move out of her house and set up camp among the Warlpiri. It was, she noted, "the most important single factor in establishing a satisfactory role for me in my work . . . Men constantly remarked on my new living quarters (a tent), pointing out that I now lived 'on the ground' as did the Walbiri."

On the second day, we were introduced to the intricacies of the Warlpiri section system.

Every Warlpiri person belongs to one of eight named groupings or "subsections." In Aboriginal English these are called "skin groups" and "skin names." Women's names begin with "N." Men's names begin with "J."

Napaljarri	Napangardi	Nakamarra	Nungarrayi
Japaljarri	Japangardi	Jakamarra	Jungarrayi
Napurrurla	Nangala	Napanangka	Nampijinpa
Jupurrurla	Jangala	Japanangka	Jampijinpa

Warlpiri children often called in to see us at the house where we were staying. They would wander in unannounced, poke among our provisions, ask for food, and explore the rooms, enviably free of the idea that a house might be considered a private place. Sometimes the older girls would sit with Francine and search through her hair for lice. Always they would ask, "What is your skin name?" And we would have to confess we had none. Accordingly, no one knew what to make of us or how we might be fitted into their social universe.

Our language teacher had the assistance of a Warlpiri friend. It was Kay Napaljarri who undertook to show us how social relationships were reckoned in terms of the subsection system. The simplest way of getting the gist of it was for us to pretend to be Warlpiri. So Kay assigned everyone in the class a skin name.

Francine was given the name Napanangka. I became Jupurrurla, because a Napanangka is normally married to a Jupurrurla.

Now that we had Warlpiri names the kids who came by in the evenings could relate to us. "Napanangka," one girl exclaimed, laughing and throwing her arms around Francine's waist, "you are my daughter!" This was because the girl's skin name was Nampijinpa, and the mother of a Napanangka is usually a Nampijinpa. This placed me in somewhat of a quandary, because the girl was therefore my mother-in-law, a person whom, according to Warlpiri convention, I had to avoid.

Playing with skin names helped us understand how they worked as a kind of shorthand for a far-reaching social order in which every person was related to every other person in a determinate way. For example, because I was Jupurrurla all other Jupurrurlas were my "brothers." All Napanangkas were my classificatory "wives." Because a Jupurrurla's father is always Jakamarra, I regarded all other Jakamarras as "fathers." And because Jakamarras normally marry Napaljarris, I related to Napaljarris as "mothers." And so forth.

With the language course behind us, Francine and I were impatient to begin fieldwork. But fieldwork cannot be willed into happening. Inevitably, it proceeds by fits and starts. Anxieties and doubts beset you, no matter how good your language skills, how thorough your background reading, how extensive your ethnographic experience in other cultures. This is because the savoir faire on which your social survival and sense of self-worth depend stems not from any abstract understanding but from direct familiarity with a body of practical knowledge which informs every aspect of everyday life and *can only be acquired gradually through trial and error.* At first you are reduced to a state of childlike naïveté, completely at the mercy of people around you, dependent upon them for guidance, information, and, above all, acceptance as a human being. Even if you are fortunate enough to enlist the help of a sympathetic and knowledgeable informant, much of your time is spent coming to terms with ambiguous gestures, mystifying silences, and unspoken protocols. Through inept questioning and endless guesswork you struggle to get your bearings, seeking an underlying pattern which will render everything comprehensible and clear. But there are no short cuts. Understanding is a product less of your methodology than your mastery of basic social skills. And this demands time and perseverance.

Because we were working under the auspices of the Central Land Council, most Warlpiri were eager to help us. And we were lucky in Yuendumu to have the assistance of Sam Brown Jakamarra.

Sam is bilingual and had worked for the CLC before. He had been a key witness at land-claim hearings in the Warlpiri area, and was used to making his culture intelligible to whites. When we explained our brief to him, Sam taped a translation so we would be able to play it to people wherever we travelled. Sam knew the kind of data we had to collect, but more important he was responsive to our need, as strangers, for acceptance, and our interest in the invisible signatures of the land.

With Sam's assistance, I interviewed men who traced their descent to the country around The Granites or had links to that country through various ancestral travelling tracks known as Dreamings. These links through descent and Dreamings gave these men rights to hunt in that country and obliged them to look after its sacred places. Nowadays, the links also bestowed rights to royalty dollars from gold mined at The Granites.

I am sitting in the shade of a casuarina tree, talking to an old man who was born at The Granites and remembers the white men who came there in the 1930s. The old man sits in half lotus. The soles of his feet are cracked and calloused. His two fighting boomerangs are laid on the ground beside him. His beard is grizzled. He is wearing a dirty shirt and shorts, a battered Stetson.

I ask the old man about the country in which he was raised, the country he calls home.

Sam explains: "We call the country mother."

"Is that because it nurtures and nourishes like a mother?"

"*Yuwayi* (yes)," says Sam. "The mother gives everything, like the land. A woman gives birth on the ground, always on the ground. So when you think of where you were born you think of the country." In the past, a newborn baby was rubbed with ash to help darken the body and strengthen the spirit.

"Do you have to give anything to the country in return?"

"You have to look after it," Sam says, explaining that the Warlpiri verb *nyangunyangu-manilipa* implies caring for or watching over someone. It could be a child, a wife, or a sacred site. "Or," he added, "you could say *warrawarra kanyilipa* (to care for, to nurture)."

That afternoon, a group of women cleared the ground outside the Women's Centre. Then, with white feathers in their headbands, they sat clumped together, painting each other's upper arms, breasts, and faces with ground ochers. At the Sports Centre, where I went with Sam to watch a video of a recent town meeting, I heard the hoarse, nasal drone of the women's voices merging with the wind.

Sam set up the video player and monitor on a desk. We sat on broken chairs. The cement floor was covered with red dust and scraps of paper. The graffiti on the wall was made up of a motley of famous names—Michael Jackson, Duran Duran, Cliff Richard, Iron Maiden, Bob Marley, Dire Straits, Led Zeppelin—and scores of cryptic love notes. *K. Martin onlie one loves no sluts here. Don't love Celestial Marshall OK Mother Fucker 1989.*

The women's intoning came and went. I hesitated to ask Sam what the women were doing, but he seemed to read my mind. The women were preparing to travel to Alice Springs, he said, where they would try to persuade the Northern Territory health minister not to grant a liquor license to the owner of the Napperby Creek Cattle Station. For Warlpiri women, the battle against alcohol abuse can only be won by keeping their communities dry. A liquor outlet at Napperby Creek, only 100 kilometers from Yuendumu would be disastrous. But their voices would probably go unheard. It was rumored that the owner of Napperby Creek had close ties with the royal family and it was unlikely that his application for a liquor license would be denied.

We settled to watching the video. It was called *Yuendumu Workshop: What do we do to make Yapa strong again?* It documented a meeting that had taken place a few weeks before to air grievances over the way some whites in Yuendumu had caused dissension in the community, trying to impose their views on local people, undermining the town council. The video had been made by Francis Kelly Jupurrurla who ran the Warlpiri Media Association at Yuendumu.

"What do people mean when they speak of a strong community?" I asked Sam. "Do they mean strong leadership?"

"No, not really. It means being independent of government control."

Sam explained how the community had recently solved the problem of petrol-sniffing among local kids. The kids had been shamed in front of the community—held across forty-gallon drums and publicly thrashed. Those responsible for the delinquent kids had had to promise that they would take proper care of them. Petrol-sniffing ceased to be a problem.

"But you don't see that on TV," Sam said ruefully. "You only see Aboriginal kids sniffing petrol and getting into trouble. Aboriginal people are always made out to be problems that only white people know how to remedy."

On the way back to his house, Sam asked if I'd like to drive out of town and see something of the country. I asked if Francine could come with us. Of course, Sam said; he would bring his wife and daughter along as well.

Sam sat beside me in the Toyota, guiding me through a maze of dirt tracks, past the airstrip, and out onto the road. He used the flat of his hand to signal directions. A short chopping motion meant keep going. Waving his hand to one side meant that I should turn. They were the same hand signals people used when hunting.

23

Sam signalled for me to stop and back up. Something in the scrub had caught his eye.

It took me a long time to discern the two pine saplings half-hidden in the mulga.

"Whitefella trees," Sam said, obviously mystified at how they had come to be growing there.

The road dropped into a dry creek bed.

"Mission Creek," Sam said. "People used to camp here." He waved his hand toward the rocky hills in the north. This was Wakulpa, a special place for him. But of his initiatory travels he said nothing. Instead, he told me about two white miners who died near there, one of thirst and one of TB. Warlpiri people looked after them at the last, and buried them when they died.

"When did that happen?"

"Long time ago."

Sam pointed to a row of low hills directly ahead. He said, "That is where the *kardiya* (whites) tracked down the *yapa* (blacks) who killed that old man, Brooks."

"The Coniston killings?"

"Yuwayi."

It happened in 1928, at Coniston Station, seventy kilometers east of Yuendumu. An old dingo hunter, Fred Brooks, was axed to death by two Warlpiri men, probably because Brooks was sleeping with the wife of one of them and had kept her longer than the husband had bargained for. Whites immediately organized punitive raids, and over the next few weeks more than 100 Warlpiri men, women, and children were indiscriminately murdered.

I stared at the hills. Were these my Dreamings that Sam was so nonchalantly introducing to me? Stories I had to acknowledge as mine? I was aware that I still tended to think categorically. I was white. Sam was black. Therefore he belonged to those who were killed and I belonged to those who did the killing.

We drove on in silence as far as the turnoff to Vaughan Springs where Sam gestured for me to turn south.

Vaughan Springs was a whitefella name, Sam said. The place was properly called Pikilyi. He had been born there sometime around 1944. His mother died not long afterward. His father worked as a handyman on the station. Every winter they travelled south and east as far as the Siddeley Range in search of wild tobacco. The men sun-dried the tobacco, tied it into bundles, and traded it with people in the north for artifacts and spears. Sam remembered these as the good times, walking 20–25 miles in a day, gathering food on the way, going ahead with the older men to find water or dig soakages. Of the hard times, Sam said nothing.

We stopped on the deserted road. The sun was close to the horizon. Spinifex pigeons fluttered up from the dry grass.

Sam's wife dragged a crowbar from the back of the Toyota, and she and Francine headed off into the mulga to hunt for goannas. I wandered down the road with Sam and his small daughter. Sam was looking around as we walked, reading the ground.

"A kangaroo here," he said, "chased by a dingo."

I was reminded of when Sam and I went to the school that morning, looking for someone we wanted to interview. At the library, Sam had opened the door and called out, "Anybody there?" When no one answered, I had started to move on, but Sam had said, "He must be here somewhere, here's his tracks." In the trampled dirt he had picked out traces of the footprints of the man we were looking for. Sam hadn't appeared to be scrutinizing the ground at all.

"Is it possible to read people's faces the same way that you read tracks?" I asked.

"Yuwayi."

I felt an odd kinship with Sam. Perhaps it was because we were alone together in the middle of an apparently empty landscape. Perhaps the feeling was born of gratitude, because he had shared details of his life with me, a comparative stranger. I told him about the book I had read in Sydney, of the photos of Nyirrpi.

"Nyirrpi is not far from Vaughan Springs," Sam said. "We could go there anytime."

"We have to go to Lajamanu for a while," I said. "Maybe we can go to Nyirrpi some other time."

The night before we headed north, we camped at a place called Ngarliyikirlangu, not far from Yuendumu.

As the sun got lower in the sky, the great granite boulders of Ngarliyikirlangu glowed as if they had absorbed heat from a fire.

I spaded a clear space in the spinifex and unrolled our swags. Francine unloaded supplies. Then, before darkness overtook the landscape, I set off to climb the huge rock behind us.

From the top, I looked out over an unbroken plain of spinifex and withered mulga. The boulders threw thimbles of shadow over the terra-cotta earth.

Sam had told me that Ngarliyikirlangu was a sacred site, but I had no notion what inner meanings found expression in the immense stones, tumbled like petrified eggs over the plain. Yet I knew from ethnographic reading that the shadow line between the embodied and the intangible, between surface appearance and underlying reality, was fundamental to the Aboriginal worldview. Fred Myers speaks of a distinction between the immediately visible world and the Dreaming—a noumenal dimension of Being out of which everything emerges, in which all life forms are steeped, but which people must be taught to see. Thus understood, the Dreaming resembles the idea of the unconscious—that "landscape of shadow" which psychoanalysis construes as an abyssal region of the mind, but in other traditions of thought, figures as a region in *space* encompassing the unknown and the inscrutable. Psychoanalysis also shares the Warlpiri view that dreams may give people access to the things which lie beyond ordinary awareness. Most pertinent, however, is that both traditions exemplify a universal human assumption that the visible world is grounded in the invisible.* Even scientific thought—allegedly more rational than hermeneutic, religious, or primitive thought—participates in the view that truth is elusive, cryptic, and concealed, and can only be uncovered through techniques possessed by a specialist elite.

Flies whined and buzzed, crawling into my eyes. A hot blustery wind flipped the pages of my notebook against my hand as I wrote down details of the day's events. When it became too dark to write, I clambered down the rock face and walked back to our camp. The sky was changing from lilac to indigo, and Orion and the Southern Cross were already visible.

That night we cooked a spinach risotto, and boiled a billy can of tea made from the wild lemongrass that scents the air at Ngarliyikirlangu.

Our ten days of fieldwork in Yuendumu had exhausted us. But at places like Ngarliyikirlangu you are instantly replenished. It is partly because you are surrounded by an empty land. When the sun sets, the flies stop buzzing. There is nothing to do but sit and listen to the silence. Life is stripped of everything superfluous. All that matters are the bare essentials: water, food, a fire, a cleared space to sleep under the stars.

*John Dewey observes: "The visible is set in the invisible; and in the end what is unseen decides what happens in the seen; the tangible rests precariously upon the untouched and ungrasped. The contrast and the potential maladjustment of the immediate, the conspicuous and focal phase of things, with those indirect and hidden factors which determine the origin and career of what is present, are indestructible features of any and every experience."

> The crumpled flame of a mulga fire
> a cicada incessant in the grass
> the stony silence of the night . . .

I turned in early, but found it hard to sleep. I watched Orion and the Pleiades disappear in the west as Scorpio rose in the east, like a shallow dish scooping up the inky water of the sky.

The night wind fanned my face. The fire guttered out. I lay on my back and looked straight up into the vertiginous vault of the heavens. Sagittarius. The Milky Way turning on its hidden axis. The whole sky wheeling in steadfast silence. I felt as if I were floating. Rather than lying on the ground looking up, I was suspended in space looking down and out into the depths of the sky. I felt dizzy and exposed, a kind of agoraphobia, I guess, born of a lifelong habit of living indoors.

How ironic, that in such an undisturbed landscape one should be unsettled by the absence of walls!

FOUR

A house is a good thing. You can lock it up

and go and live anywhere you like.

—*Walter Pukatiwara*

⸻

When I first saw it, the country around Lajamanu reminded me of the sea. Unbroken horizons under cloudless skies, and the boundless sea blue of eucalypts. It goes without saying that Warlpiri perceive the country quite differently.

In the 1950s they were forcibly trucked to this place which did not belong to them. Whites called it Hooker Creek. People asked, how can you make yourself at home on someone else's land? Many rolled up their swags and walked into the desert, heading back to their own country hundreds of miles to the south. Some died in the terrible heat. Others returned to erstwhile camps on cattle stations or near the gold and wolfram mines where they had worked occasionally for rations of flour, sugar, and tea. The white bosses said they were no longer welcome there, the old era was over, they should return to the government settlement and change their ways.

During the period which Warlpiri refer to as the "welfare time," various managers tried to talk them into abandoning polygamy and giving up their ceremonial life. They were told they should live in houses, change their diet, send their children to school, cultivate vegetable gardens, work to timetables, and settle down. Hooker Creek became little more than a work camp, a "total institution" for assimilating Aborigines into the dominant white culture.

It was our first night in Lajamanu. Kids were crowding into our caravan, pushing and shoving, demanding to know our names. The girls were searching for lice in Francine's hair. A small boy was fingering the lines on my face, asking what had caused such scars. Canned food, clothes, and books were scattered everywhere, covered with red dirt.

In the end, the only way of getting the kids out of the caravan was for us to leave it. We walked across the football oval toward the main street. Most of the kids drifted off into the darkness, though a few still dogged our heels, grabbing at our hands and asking where we were going.

The headlights of a vehicle came up behind us. We half turned, blinded by the beam. The vehicle slowed and the driver shouted something in our direction. In the gloom I could see nothing of his face.

"Who are you?" he called. Then, as if any reply of mine could only confirm something he already knew, he announced that he was Pincher Jampijinpa, the most important man in Lajamanu. I should come and see him in the morning and explain what I was doing in the settlement.

Jampijinpa slammed the Toyota into gear and drove off. For a moment the headlights panned over the disgruntled faces of people sitting outside their houses. A mangy dog limped along the fenceline. Then the children reached for our hands, drawing us back on to the road.

"That was my father," a girl said to Francine.

In the following weeks, I saw Pincher almost every day. He would come to the caravan and call my name: "Jupurrurla!" I was always glad of his company and thankful for the chance to make a start on my research, even though Pincher's sardonic responses to my questions made me less and less confident that I would ever understand who was who in relation to The Granites mine. Pincher's main concern seemed to be one of letting me know that he was a man of importance and knowledge, and that I should be on my guard against other men who would tell me all kinds of cock and bull stories if it was to their advantage.

If Pincher did not come looking for me, I would walk past his house in the hope he would invite me to sit with him.

There was usually a mob of people at Pincher's place, sitting around a smoldering fire in the yard, playing cards. I would stand a little way off, waiting to be asked over, which is the Warlpiri custom. If people can't be bothered with you, they ignore you. Such directness can take a little getting used to.

Melville Is.

Darwin

Katherine • Barunga

Victoria River Downs• Daly Waters

Top Springs
Buchanan Hwy
Pigeon Hole• Montejinni • Dunmara

Kalkaringi
Daguragu • Wave Hill • Newcastle Waters
Cattle Creek

N O R T H E R N

Lajamanu
Winnecke Cr.

T A N A M I
D E S E R T

Tennant Creek

Tanami T E R R I T O R Y

The Granites
Lander R.

Tanami Road

Warrabri

Willowra

Stuart Highway

Mt. Singleton
Mount
Doreen
Ti Tree

Barrow Creek

Lake
MacKay

Yuendumu

Mount Wedge

HARTS RANGE

Mt. Liebig
Blanche Tower
Haasts Bluff
Papunya
Glen
Helen
MACDONNELL RANGES
Hermannsburg
Areyonga

Alice Springs

0   100 mi.
0   150 km.

Elevation >2000 ft.

PETERMANN RANGES
Mt. Olga
Ayers
Rock

Finke
R.

jmh

Northern Territory, Australia

One day Pincher beckoned me over. He spread out a grimy pink blanket and we sat beside the fire facing each other.

Pincher had a red bandanna tied across his forehead. His hair was disheveled, and he had not shaved for several days.

"Jupurrurla," he said, "I want some paints."

"What kind of paints?"

"You buy them at the shop. Red one, white one, yellow one, that's all."

"When do you want them?"

"Anytime."

"I could go and get them now."

"Yuwayi."

When I returned an hour later with the tubes of acryllic paint, Pincher gestured for me to follow him into his house.

The house was more of a storeroom than a dwelling. Some rags were strewn about on the concrete floor, and a faucet was dripping into a grimy sink. The ceiling was mildewed, and festooned with cobwebs.

Pincher padded over to a forty-gallon drum which had been jammed against a closed door. He gripped the rim of the oil drum, rolled it aside, and edged into a dark room. He emerged with several folded canvases under his arm.

He spread one out on the floor. As I studied the large circles and sinuous lines that signified key elements of a Dreamtime journey, Pincher quietly intoned snatches of the songs that spelled out the ancestral story.

"My father used to draw these Dreamings on the ground," Pincher said. "He used to tell me: 'This is yours. Don't part with it. Don't give it to other people. This is yours to carry on, this one.'"

"Can you tell me the story?" I asked.

Pincher pointed to four converging sets of parallel lines. These were the tracks of two Nangala sisters who travelled from a place called Juntawariji (or Ngurlulirrinya: "many seeds"), looking for the edible seeds of a species of wattle (*Acacia tenuissima*) which Warlpiri call *watiyawarnu*.

"Where is Juntawariji?" I asked.

When you ask desert people such questions they gesture unerringly in the direction of the place, but it is hard to work out how far away it is or exactly where one might locate it on a map. However, a key site in Pincher's Dreaming was Paraluyu, which whites know as Mt. Davidson, 160 miles south of Lajamanu as the crow flies. Jampijinpa figured that since the Nangalas journeyed westward toward Paraluyu,

31

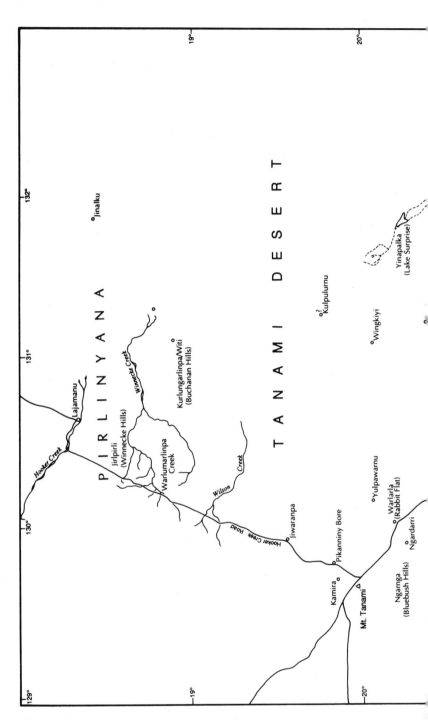

Tanami Desert, Northern Territory, Australia

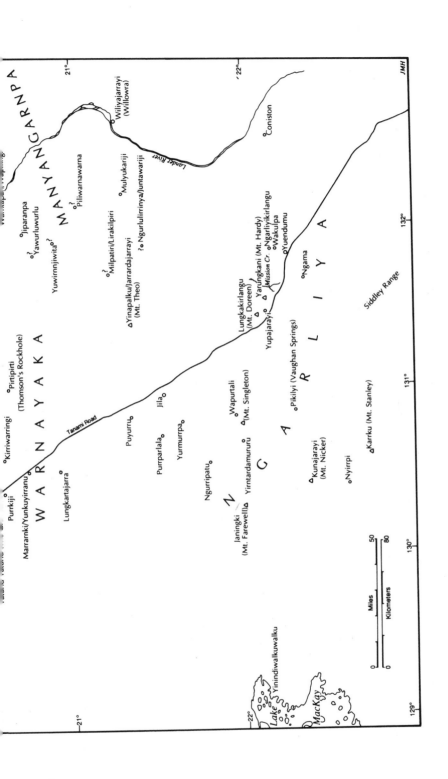

Juntawariji must be in the area of the Lander river.* In any event, the Nangala sisters and their kinspeople (Jampijinpa/Jangala, Nampijinpa/Nangala) walked about in the region of Juntawariji, searching for the reddish edible seed (*ngurlu*) of the *watiyawarnu*. Each day people filled their coolimons with seed and made camp. They ground the seed with stone pestles and cooked dampers in the embers of their fires. But at a place called Kaminajarra ("two postpubescent girls"), the Nangala sisters got separated from their families and drifted farther and farther toward the north-northwest. The Nangalas continued gathering and winnowing *watiyawarnu* seed, leaving mounds of husks wherever they camped. These are visible today as a series of low hills between Paraluyu and Pirtipirti.

Pincher drew my attention to two facing sets of semicircles. These depicted the cupped hands of the Nangala sisters as well as the action of sweeping the seeds into heaps. The small circle between the cupped lines was a heap of grain.

Pincher now unfolded a second canvas, painted in the same colors: red, white, black, and yellow. A cluster of lines and semicircles showed the Nangala sisters sitting down at a place called Walya with their digging sticks and coolimons by their sides. At Walya they made seedcakes and covered them with coals, but when they went to rake the dampers out of their fire they were gone. Around a circle marking the fireplace were the marks that the Nangala sisters made as they scraped back the hot sand searching for their dampers. *Walya* means earth or ground.

Leaving Walya, the sisters journeyed on to Paraluyu, continuing to collect seeds on the way. When they reached Paraluyu, they knelt and began to dig sand from the soakage at the foot of the hill, but two hungry snakes, travelling from Jaluwangu, came upon them and swallowed them . . .

Again Pincher broke into song, his nasal intoning taking up some part of the narrative he may not have been at liberty to relate in detail.

"That is my Dreaming," he said at last. "I track it (*junga mani*). I follow that track on the ground (*Ngaju kana pura yirdi ngajunyangu jungangku*). That Dreaming is my father. *Watiyawarnu* is my father's father's country. I can sing that one. I can dance that one. I can paint

*Jampijinpa's lack of firsthand knowledge of his father's father's country meant that he did not know the names or exact locations of many *watiyawanu* sites. However, Zack Jakamarra knew the area well and in due course gave me additional information on the *watiyawarnu* Dreaming, including the location of Juntawariji east of Mt. Theo (Yinapalku) and north of Yuendumu.

that one because of my father, and my father's father before I was born. That *jukurrpa.* It was there from the beginning (*ngurru warnu*) It was made long ago (*nyurruwiyi warnu*). It is everlasting (*tarnga juku*). We have to hold it, keep it, pass it on from father to father to father."

Pincher folded the canvases, took them back to the storeroom, and dragged the oil drum back across the door.

We went outside. The card players were still sitting around the smoldering fire, but Pincher and I sat apart.

I was pondering the ancestral journeys of the two Nangalas. I was aware that in telling me his *jukurrpa,* his Dreaming, Pincher had told me who he was. Without such a narrative, a person was bereft of any connection between his life and the life beyond himself. He had no background, no bearings. He was alone. But I was beginning to suspect that Pincher had never actually lived in the country of his Dreaming or performed ceremony there. He seemed to know it only from hearsay, and his paintings were as abstract as any map. Where then was home? The distant places of one's Dreaming or the place one actually lived?

When I broached the question, Pincher understandably ignored it. I was demanding consistency where there could be none. Pincher's story was not unusual. Warlpiri are constantly on the move. It is not inevitable that you will spend your entire life in the place where you were born. The Dreamings you inherit are not the only Dreamings you will become familiar with in the course of your life. If you spend most of your life away from the country where you were born, it is possible that you will bequeath to your sons a patrimony you did not so much inherit as acquire. There is no point insisting upon strict continuity over time. Better to avoid mention of the way allegiances shift. Better to forget defunct identities. If there is a discrepancy between the place you hail from and the place you make your home, better not to make an issue of it. In this way the necessary illusion is sustained that laws and names and things given in the Dreaming never change. As it turned out, Pincher's father had also spent much of his life away from the country where he was born. His natal country was on the eastern fringes of Warlpiri country—an area sometimes called Manyangarnpa after the resinous spinifex grass that grows there in abundance. After his initiation, he had set out on a journey which took him southwest into the mulga country of the Ngarliya, then northward via Yurmurrpa and Jila to the central region of the Tanami, known as Warnayaka. There he met a woman whom he wanted to marry, so he gave hairstring, tobacco, hooked boomerangs, and *kur-*

diji and *mirta* shields to the woman's father. Instead of returning with his wife to his own natal country he stayed among her people. But though he traveled and hunted throughout the Warnayaka area, he established his spiritual and ceremonial base at Paraluyu because it lay on the same songline as Juntawariji whence he, like the legendary Nangala sisters before him, had come.

"So you were born in your mother's country?" I asked Pincher.

"Yuwayi."

"Conceived there?" I asked, using the Warlpiri phrase.

Pincher picked up a playing card from the ground, rolled it tightly, and began scraping the greasy dirt from under his fingernails.

I was wondering how to rephrase my question when Pincher announced: "Jupurrlurla, I got to buy *kuyu* (meat)."

I dug in my jeans pocket and gave him a crumpled five dollar bill.

Pincher called one of his daughters over, gave her the money, and dispatched her to the store to buy food.

I got up to go.

"I'll tell you that one," Pincher said, "where I bin born." I sat down, and took out my notebook again.

In the *jukurrpa*, two dogs had emerged from the ground at a place called Maru. The male had a black body and white face. The bitch was black and white spotted. The dogs moved south. At Makararangu, northeast of Jila, the female gave birth to a litter of puppies. Some were spotted like her, others had the black body and white face of the male. Wherever the two dogs traveled, they left the ground seeded with their vital essence or *kuruwarri*. Even rocks and trees along their ancestral track were steeped with this *kuruwarri*.

It happened that Pincher's mother was traveling or hunting along this Dreaming track. She became impregnated, so to speak, by the *pirlirrpa* or "life essence" of the dog Dreaming. Makararangu was the exact site where conception took place.

Pincher likened the *pirlirrpa* to a tiny, invisible homunculus (*kurru-walpa*) which somehow enters into a woman's womb. Conception was a quickening, when the fetus is first felt or the child comes into bodily being (*palka mani* or *palka jarrimi*). Pincher's remarks were consistent with what I had gleaned from my ethnographic reading: that a man's semen is not essential for conception; conception is an expression of the seminal power of the Dreaming. In this way, Aboriginal people stress that all existence springs from the Dreaming, and that every individual is bonded not only to his or her parents but to a particular place. It is not that people are ignorant of the "facts" of physiological

36

paternity, rather that sociological identifications are given precedence over biological ones.

I was keen for Pincher to tell me more about the *pirlirrpa*.

"Does the *pirlirrpa* come from the ground?" I asked.

Pincher placed his hands under his front ribs, at the sides of his abdomen. "It's here," Pincher said, "in this *miyalu*." The spirit was in the kidneys and kidney fat.

Pincher explained that if a shaman stole a person's spirit, the abdomen became shriveled and wasted.

"What happens when a person dies?" I inquired. "Where does the spirit go then?"

Pincher said that the spirit came from the Dreaming and returned to the Dreaming. But when I asked whether the spirit went back to a person's conception site or to a person's father's father's country, he looked perplexed.

I let my gaze drift to the road where Pincher's daughters were approaching with plastic bags of takeout food.

They dumped the plastic bags at their father's feet.

Pincher rummaged in the bags and gave each of the girls a baked potato. He set aside a hamburger and a bottle of Fanta for himself, then passed the bag back to the girls and told them to take the food to their mothers.

A skinny dog with baleful eyes loped over to Pincher's hamburger and sniffed it vigorously. With a snort of irritation, Pincher picked up a stone and flung it at the puppy. It thudded against the dog's rib cage, making it yelp and hobble away.

Pincher said nothing when I walked off. That was the way of it.

It was already May, and the nights were cold. Every morning we would wake to the disconsolate aark of crows and a blustering wind from the southeast.

I stumbled out of the caravan to kindle our fire. Mist clung to the snappy gums and blue mallee along the creek and wild horses were grazing along the edge of the football oval.

I squatted by the fire, squinting through the smoke. Pincher was walking across the oval, the wind whipping up whorls of dust around his feet.

He gave the impression that our camp was the last place he intended to visit, but I was sure he would head towards the big eucalypt, staring at the ground in front of him, and then come on toward the caravan.

When he was in earshot I called out to him: "Morning Jampijinpa!"

He was barefooted and his frayed trousers flapped around his ankles. He sat down by the fire, the souls of his feet hard up against the coals. I asked if he wanted tea.

"It's too cold, this Lajamanu," Pincher said.

I settled the billy down on the fire. It came quickly to the boil, and I threw two teabags into the water. Then I poured Pincher half a mug of tea, knowing he would add cold water to make it lukewarm.

"Here," I said, handing him the tea and a bowl of raw sugar.

He shoveled four heaping spoonfuls into his mug. "*Walya,*" he said.

It was a routine joke between us, the way raw sugar resembled sand, but this morning there was no humor in Pincher's voice.

"Jupurrurla," he said, "I'm really worried. I'm really upset."

My first thought was that I must have said something that had got under his skin.

"Jupurrurla, I got to tell you about that *watiyawarnu* . . ."

I listened uneasily.

"I don't talk about other men's land, Jupurrurla. I just talk about my land, what bin stole. I'm frightened that land bin stole from me. That *watiyawarnu,* that Paraluyu. I got rights for that Paraluyu. No one should push me out. Nobody should steal my land. It's my own family. I'm really upset about this Dreaming of mine, this land . . ."

As Pincher went on in this roundabout, obtuse vein I began to understand for the first time what had prompted him to spend so much time with me since my arrival in Lajamanu. Although he named no names, I knew enough from hearsay to be able to guess at the cause of his grievance. An outstation had been built on his traditional land by a man with considerable political clout in the Lajamanu community. Pincher had grudgingly allowed the outstation project to go ahead even though he regarded this man as having no rights in that part of the Tanami. This had rankled. Pincher felt his patrimony was under threat. And he was disquieted by the thought that he had allowed an interloper to encroach upon land he held in trust from his forefathers.

There wasn't a lot I could do, except listen. As it turned out, Pincher did not expect much more. Often, it is more important to have a chance of airing one's grievances in public than having them redressed. There are so many conflicting interests in a desert community, so many competing points of view, that contentious issues simply cannot be settled to the satisfaction of everyone. Even appeals to the *jukurrpa*—the Dreaming, the Law—don't necessarily reduce the ambiguity. Although the *jukurrpa* is an immutable given, it can be invoked by powerful men in ways which support widely divergent interests. Warlpiri dialectic is like the desert itself. As you walk about in search of scarce resources you have to revise your itinerary continually, depending upon who you are traveling with, the season of the year, the lie of the land. And the desert sands are always shifting in the wind.

Pincher climbed to his feet.

"You going?" I said.

"You come too," Pincher said. "Bring your tape recorder. We got to record this business properly. Then you can take that tape to Yuendumu, anywhere, and people can listen and tell you it's straight, that one."

I fetched my cassette recorder from the caravan and headed off after Pincher toward the northern outskirts of the settlement.

"Where are we going?" I asked.

Pincher pursed his lips and jutted his jaw, indicating the row of aluminum houses ahead. As we crossed the open ground the wind blew grit and dust into our faces.

We ducked under a sagging strand of barbed wire, and Pincher shouted a name at the end house. "Jakamarra!" Then he banged on the side of the house with his fist. "Jakamarra!"

Zachariah Jakamarra is about fifteen years older than Pincher. Pincher called him *jaja* because he was his classifactory mother's mother's brother. Zack was one of a handful of Warlpiri men who had actually grown up in the desert. He knew the landscape like the back of his hand, and was a big man "in the business"—an authority on ceremony and Dreamings. This was why Pincher had brought me to Zack's house: to record his *watiyawarnu* Dreaming in Zack's presence. It amused me that Pincher, who had so often insisted on his own importance, should now so forthrightly acknowledge Zack's greater authority.

He was about to bang on the wall again when Zack Jakamarra shambled out the back door, blinking against the light. He was wearing a pair of dirty trousers, and had the annoyed look of someone who had been rudely roused from sleep.

Pincher quickly explained to Zack what he wanted. I leaned against the wall of the house, away from the wind, fully expecting Zack to tell Pincher to piss off.

But Zack and Pincher sat down and told me to place the cassette recorder in front of them. A dog nuzzled Zack, tail wagging, seeking contact. Zack gently elbowed it away. The dog flopped in the dirt and started licking its penis and groin.

I handed Pincher the microphone and he recounted his *watiyawarnu* story, drawing circles in the dirt as he reeled off key place names. I imagined the line he traced between them as an umbilical cord.

As Pincher talked, Zack sat with his legs crossed, scratching the back of his head. I guessed him to be in his late sixties, though his wiry build and unkempt black hair belied his age. His chest was banded with initiation welts. From time to time he turned his head and spat a dollop of dirty saliva at the same spot in the yard.

I looked toward the airstrip, the windsock jerking in the wind. A group of women were picking up litter along the fence and stuffing it into big orange plastic bags. It was a new government scheme to make Aboriginal people work for their dole.

Zack cleared his throat and spat again. His head was lowered onto his chest. I tried to pick up the thread of Pincher's narrative: the drawn out verbs of movement, the abrupt pauses that marked various places where the travelers stopped and camped.

Then Pincher was through. "I call those places *kirda* (father)," he said, reverting to English. "All those places where the Nangalas traveled."

Zack was working his thumb inside his nostril. He wiped his fingers on the ground.

"Right!" exclaimed Zack. "You got that one?"

"Yuwayi," I said, and switched off the tape.

Zack took a wad of tobacco from behind his ear, bit off a piece and stuffed it behind his lower lip. Then he leaned toward me, his voice hoarse and urgent.

"Jupurrurla," he said, "young people got no *walya*," He scooped up a handful of earth. "They don't know this *walya*. They only got that book, that paper . . ."

I glanced at Pincher.

"We don't use maps," Zack said. "We got the country in our heads. Old people didn't have watches to tell the time; they just watched the sun. But these young people bin move away from their father's father's country. They never walk around their country. They bin sit here. This Lajamanu. But I bin walk around." Zack placed his palm on the ground. "Young people don't know this one, they don't hold it any more . . . this *walya* business. Young people don't interest along culture, they don't look back. They only got paper."

As I closed my notebook, Zachariah Jakamarra spat another dollop of brown saliva onto the ground.

FIVE

He departed with thoughts of home,

He departed with thoughts of home,

He departed towards another place.

—Honey-Ant Men's Song

We were dead beat after driving all day through the desert, and the light was fading as we approached Yuendumu. We turned down a side road, found a clearing, and made camp. After a meal of eggs and hash browns we crawled into our swags by the fire. The mulga looked spectral in the last light. The wind fanned our faces. An insect trilled feebly in the grass. I drifted asleep still feeling the Toyota lurching and jolting over the hard dirt road.

At dawn we broke camp and drove to the *jilimi* on the western edge of the settlement. This was the women's camp—a long, verandah-like structure covered with corrugated iron.

I sat in the Toyota while Francine went to ask if anyone knew where we could find Nola Nungarrayi.

Women straggled out of the *jilimi,* curious to know what was going on. They stood around Francine, questioning her, demanding to know her skin name. Francine tried to explain that we had a taped message from Pincher Jampijinpa and wanted Pincher's mother to hear it.

Francine walked back to the Toyota, followed by the women who clambered noisily through the back door. I was about to ask if she'd found Nola, when I noticed the small, elderly woman standing beside her, wearing a print dress and knotted head kerchief.

Nola spoke no English. She kept calling Francine *jaja,* or granddaughter. As we headed back to the settlement, I figured out why. *Jaja* was the kinship term for maternal grandmother as well as daughter's daughter. Francine was a Napanangka. Accordingly, her mother

41

would be a Nampijinpa. And a Nampijinpa's mother would be a Nungarrayi—Nola's skin grouping.

At Nola's daughter's house, a crowd quickly gathered. We sat on battered mattresses in the yard, Francine beseiged by children with tousled hair and snotty noses. A litter of puppies gamboled on a pile of crumpled blankets. Women picked through their daughters' hair for lice.

When I set the tape going, people seemed uneasy. I wondered if they were bewildered at hearing Pincher's voice captured on tape. One woman referred to Pincher's recorded voice as *yurukurra wangkangjakurra,* a phrase which seemed to have the same connotations as *pirlirrpa-mani,* "to capture a person's likeness on film," implying that an intimate link existed between a person's vocal or auditory image and his life essence or spirit—his *pirlirrpa.*

But people soon grew used to hearing Pincher's voice and began to respond. Men and women cried out in recognition, nodding and laughing. And as Pincher recited the names of sacred sites, they gestured in the direction of these places where they had lived years ago, before Yuendumu and Lajamanu had been dreamed of.

No one was more vocal than Nola's daughter, Wanda. She wanted us to know immediately who was who, and kept jabbing her finger at various people so we would understand that they were directly implicated in this particular Dreaming. Nola seemed oblivious to her daughter's raucous commentary. She looked as though something both profound and commonplace was being affirmed. But instead of speaking, she used her hands and fingers, cryptically signaling to the other old women.

"Yuwayi, yuwayi," people kept saying, confirming details of the narrative.

Nola clapped her hands against the sides of her thighs, as I'd seen Pincher do at Lajamanu. Then she raised her arms, making her open hands quiver, movements you sometimes see in women's dancing, which suggest both the action of "growing up a child" and "growing up the country" through ceremony and song. I watched as the other women swept their hands across the ground, and began tracing marks with their fingers that gave graphic expression to the key events in Pincher's narrative.

It became clear that Pincher's story from the *jukurrpa* evoked more than ancestral travels. To conjure up the *jukurrpa* in sand designs, body paintings, song or story, was also to recall the places you yourself were raised, places you had walked, hunted, and visited in your own lifetime. These old women were listening to something more than myth; they were remembering particular events that had shaped their personal lives, places they were born or married, where a parent died, where they endured a year without rain . . .

Watching Nola, I could not help thinking of what she must have seen and suffered in the course of her life. I knew Pincher had been her first child, born at Warnakirlangu, a rock hole in the desert between Jila and Puyurru. I also knew that Pincher's father died when Pincher was ten, the same year Pincher saw a road for the first time. He and his mother crossed it one day, walking from Paraluyu to Puyurru. It was the old Tanami Track, along which white men traveled to the gold diggings at The Granites. Pincher knew the road could not have been made by Warlpiri, but he had yet to see his first whiteman. As for his mother, she had heard of their brutality and wanted to keep well clear of them. When she remarried, to her late husband's brother, she did not accompany him to the cattle station at Mt. Doreen where he was working, but stayed in the bush.

Toward evening I headed out to the West Camp. Nugget Jangala showed me the way. He wanted me to play the tape to Pincher's "father."

The men's camp (jangkayi) consisted of a couple of corrugated iron humpies and a bough shade. Several old men were sitting near the humpy, out of the wind, shadowy in the failing light.

I shook their calloused hands, using my smattering of Warlpiri to little advantage. The old men wore buttonless shirts, threadbare jackets, torn trousers. Their voices were thin and frail. Most of them, I realized, were blind.

I sat by the remains of a fire, and Nugget introduced me to Old Longreach Jangala, the man who had "grown Pincher up," the man who had taken Pincher to Mt. Doreen and taught him to ride a horse, muster and brand, and track stray cattle in the bush. It was old Jangala, Nugget said, who drove the grader and cut the new road from Yuendumu to The Granites after the war.

One of the old men climbed unsteadily to his feet and shambled off toward the jilimi to fetch a firebrand. Another raked up bits of charred wood and tufts of spinifex to kindle a fire. When his mate returned, he placed the smoldering log in the fireplace. The tinder burst into flame. Feeling the warmth, the blind men shuffled nearer the fire, and Nugget had to shout at old Jangala to prevent him from getting burned.

I played the tape. It had the same effect as the fire. The old men were galvanized into life. Their senses seemed restored. They kept pointing at Pincher's "father," old Jangala. Sometimes they hung their heads as if straining to hear what Pincher was saying. I imagined them borne back to places far from that windswept camp of liminal light, to another country. I remembered W. B. Yeats's poignant lines from "Sailing to Byzantium":

> An aged man is but a paltry thing
> A tattered coat upon a stick, unless
> Soul clap its hands and sing, and louder sing
> For every tatter in its mortal dress . . .

When the tape was finished, Nugget urged me to get old Jangala to record something. But the old man could hardly hold the microphone in his hand.

"He bin too old now," Nugget said. Apparently, old Jangala's dearest wish was that he be taken back to Puyurru where he could live out his last days in his own country.

"He bin look back to his own country now," Nugget said. "Not this Yuendumu. This one 'nother country."

I was moved by the old man's equanimity in the face of death. I had the impression that if a man met death in his own country he had nothing to fear.

"What did people do in the old days?" I asked Nugget. "What happened if a person got too old to walk, or could no longer fend for himself?"

"Sometimes we bin lose 'im," Nugget said.

"You mean you left the old ones in the desert to die?"

Nugget explained how a bough shade would be made, and food and water left for the person too old or infirm to keep up with the group. A day or so later, someone would be sent back to see if the person was dead. The body was then placed in a tree, away from wild animals, and later the bones might be taken to a sacred site.

"So a person would go back to his proper country?"

"Yuwayi," Nugget said.

That night, my thoughts kept going back to something which had happened months before. A couple of weeks after arriving in Alice

Springs, Francine and I had driven out to Glen Helen Gorge, planning to have dinner at the Lodge and camp overnight in the desert.

The gorge had been one of the great gathering places of the Western Arrernte. There was permanent water fringed by bulrushes and river gums, where the Finke River had cut through the quartzite escarpment of the Western Macdonnell Range. Seeing the eroded walls of the escarpment for the first time I was reminded of Matisse's great bronze bas-reliefs.

We drove to the end of the sealed road. A dirt track led out into the spinifex desert and there were bluish hills like enormous lizards basking on the horizon.

A woman seemed to materialize out of the desert air.

She was distraught. Her breath reeked of booze. She stammered something about her car being stolen, and implored us to give her a lift to Alice Springs. Her name was Maisie. We explained we'd just come from Alice. We were going to camp the night in the desert. We would gladly give her a lift home in the morning.

She clung to us, insisting we help her, and kept chopping and changing her story in a desperate bid for our sympathy. Her brother and some other men had commandeered her car. They had gone north to Papunya. She hadn't wanted to go into the desert, so they ditched her at Glen Helen. She hated the desert. It was full of snakes and centipedes. What was she to do? She had no money. Her car had been stolen.

In the end, we suggested she camp with us. This immediately prompted Maisie to give thought to other needs. Could Francine give her some sandals? What about the pair Francine was wearing, could she have them? No?—well, could we drive her to the store?

I explained that there was no store at Glen Helen, only a hotel.

As it turned out, Maisie wanted to buy some grog. Or rather, she wanted us to buy grog for her. I explained that the Lodge had no off license. "No worries," Maisie said, "we can have a beer in the pub."

We took a table on the terrace, overlooking the river and the gorge. Maisie swigged her VB Bitter.

"This my home, Michael," she whimpered hoarsely. "This my home."

Her lachrymose tone irritated me. And I was beginning to realize that our plan to dine at the Lodge would have to be abandoned.

"Look," Maisie said, pointing downriver. The great cliffs were biscuit-colored in the late afternoon light, and tears welled up in her eyes as Maisie singled out the forked ghost gum at the foot of the bluff which was her conception site. Another site, further along the riverbank, was where her father and mother dug white ocher for ceremonies.

"Uncle," she said, clutching my arm, "this my place, really dear one."

Maisie was ready for another round of beer. But Francine insisted we get moving. We would have to make camp before dark.

As we left the Lodge a tourist bus was pulling in. It looked like a wedding party, and Maisie was all for joining it.

We drove back onto the highway, then headed out into the desert, stopping near a desert oak well away from the road.

Maisie had grown more maudlin. As we unpacked the Toyota and sorted out some bedding for her, she bemoaned the fact that we were so far from the Lodge. "It's too dark here, Uncle," she wailed. "We got to go back."

She then declared that the very desert oak beneath which we were spreading our swags was the place where her mother had died twenty years before. Maisie had been a small child at the time. She had fallen asleep in her mother's arms. When she woke in the morning, flies were buzzing around her mother's mouth and eyes. A couple of white tourists found her. They took her to South Australia and looked after her for several years. Then she left them and made her way back to Alice Springs. She heard her father was living at Jay Creek. "He stared at me," Maisie said. "When I came back he just stared at me. Everyone said they didn't know me, they didn't know who I was."

The following year her father was killed in a car crash near Serpentine Gorge.

Maisie was blubbering in the darkness, remembering her dead parents. The tree was where her mother was "sleeping." The place was filled with bad memories.

It was the last straw. Francine and I said we would take her home.

"Hang on!" Maisie cried. She grubbed around in the sand under the desert oak and turned up the grinding stone her mother had once used. I had no idea whether she was conning us or not. Somehow it didn't seem to matter.

Maisie then found the stone pestle that belonged with the mortar. She showed us how it fitted the worn groove in the mortar perfectly. "I'm going to take this home with me," she said.

It was after midnight when we dropped Maisie off at Jay Creek. The dogs came out in a pack, barking at our vehicle. Maisie dragged us into a fetid room where a crowd of people were watching *The Three Amigos* on television. No one took the slightest notice of us. We walked out into the night with dogs snapping and barking at our ankles.

We were five miles from Jay Creek before we realized that Maisie had left her mother's grinding stones in the vehicle.

I sat up late, scribbling in my notebook, struck by the irony that I should feel so free in the very landscape where people like Maisie had been alienated, that I should come into my own in a place where she had lost her way. "Home is where you feel free to be yourself, without apology or doubt," I wrote. But for Maisie, the desert oppressed her with the shades of the dead. Her people had been scattered, and she along with them. The place where she had been conceived and born was now a tourist spot, where foreigners swam, and shouted, and snapped their cameras. Grog was not at the root of Maisie's confusion. It followed it. It parodied it. When she got blind drunk, lost her footing and fell, it was as if she were involved in some grotesque reenactment of her early life, and we were her audience. It was as though she exercised a perverse freedom, making of her own body an image of her broken world.

Next morning I gathered hunks of mulga root and other firewood for the old men in the West Camp.

I was dumping it from the roof rack of the Toyota when a beat-up Falcon drove up in a cloud of dust. As it lurched to a standstill, Pincher Martin Jampijinpa got out.

He'd come down from Lajamanu with Japaljarri on the spur of the moment. Had I played the tape to his mother and old Jangala?

"Yesterday," I said.

I climbed down from the Toyota and piled the wood nearer to the fire.

"Where's Napanangka?" Pincher asked.

"She's over at your sister's place, talking to your mother."

We sat around the fire. One of the old men laboriously unwound a dirty bandage from around his ankle. Scabrous dogs lay in the dirt, gnawing at their hindquarters.

I was baffled by the way Pincher scarcely spoke to his "father." Thinking that he was perhaps waiting for me to start up a conversation, I decided to satisfy my curiosity as to why people avoided using the names of the dead.

"What does *kumunjayi* mean?" I said.

"It means you can't call the name," Pincher said.

"Why not?"

"It makes you think of that person."

"But why shouldn't you think of people who have passed away?"

"They might be somewhere else," Pincher said.

I took this to mean that the shades of the recently dead are likely to linger among the living, unwilling to leave them—a projection, possibly, of the grief of the bereaved, who cannot bear to be separated from their loved one. A prohibition on speaking the name of the dead assists the process of separation. The idiosyncratic personality must be swept away or forgotten before the *social* personality, associated with the Dreaming, can be brought back into circulation. Names are lost, but then recovered. Even today, most Warlpiri individuals bear a grandparent's name, thus creating an identification of alternate generations.

But what of the spirit? Where did it go when a person passed away?

Pincher translated my question for the old men, who discussed it earnestly while Pincher recounted what had happened when his father's sister died at Yuendumu some years ago.

Her *pirlirrpa* had gone up into the sky, becoming a small raincloud. The cloud moved northward, taking two days to cross the desert and reach Lajamanu.

At Lajamanu, Pincher's brother had a dream in which his father's sister spoke to him. "That Nangala spirit told him: 'Don't worry, Billy, I'm not finished. Your father's sister is here with you. I'm not dead. I'm still your boss.'"

In due course, Billy's wife gave birth to a baby girl who took the first name of Billy's father's sister.

"They were lonely there," Pincher said, meaning that the family at Lajamanu pined for their kinsmen who had remained at Yuendumu, far to the south. "When that Nangala came, we were really happy. We were happy when that little girl was born, because the spirit was there, same as my father."

"You mean your father's spirit also came north?"

"Yuwayi," said Pincher.

One of the old men clutched my arm. "If I go 'nother country, 'nother land, well, I worry somebody might kill me, might sing me. In our own country, our own place, our father's fathers look after us. Sometimes that *manparrpa* bin come, wake you up. You sit down for a while. It tells you what to do. If you are sick, it tells you how to get

48

better. Sometimes it tells you when someone is going to die. When you die, that *manparrpa* goes back to your father's father's country."

Pincher explained that *pirlirrpa* was a generic name for spirit. The spirits of the dead were known as *manparrpa*. But I was more interested to know how the word *jukurrpa* applied to both dreams and the Dreaming.

Pincher was happy to elaborate. "People can see into the Dreaming when they dream. The *pirlirrpa* goes out of you, here . . ." He pulled up his shirt and touched his navel. "My brother looked in his dream and saw the *manparrpa,* the spirit of our father's sister. That Nangala then came north as that cloud."

I was stirred by these insights into spiritual migration. They suggested some kind of homing impulse, the yearning of a dispersed people to be "rooted in one dear perpetual place." I had the impression that dreams articulated this longing for reunion, and thought of Robert Tonkinson's compelling account of Western Desert Aborigines, settled far from their ancestral lands, who sustain spiritual contact with sacred places by making journeys to and from those places in dream-spirit form.

I glanced up. An old man was inching his way across the ground toward us. It was old Towser, who had fetched the firebrand last night. He lowered himself onto the ground. His feet were gnarled and cracked. His hand trembled.

I asked Pincher to tell him what we were talking about.

At the mention of the word *pirlirrpa,* old Towser tapped his forefinger against his abdomen.

"Where does the spirit go when a person dies?" I asked.

"*Wapirra,*" he said, and pointed skyward.

Wapirra was a generic term for father. It was the word the Uniting Church used to refer to God the father.

"Not the ground?" I asked.

Old Towser patted his skinny hand on the ground and shook his head.

"These days, people don't always take the trouble to track the spirit," Pincher explained.

The old men made no comment. There was nothing to say. For some, the center had not held. Home had become everywhere and nowhere, abstract and ethereal, like the sky.

SIX

I don't really know what happened.

If one wished to be solemn, it could

be said that I had found my landscape,

my real home.

—*Ingmar Bergman*

Deserts have been all things to all men. Some see them as hostile and inhospitable, as places of loss and punishment. For others, deserts are where one becomes fully aware of one's human finitude, "shamed into pettiness," as T. E. Lawrence put it, "by the innumerable silences of stars." Edmond Jabes observes that "in the desert the sense of the infinite is unconditional and therefore truest. In the desert you're left utterly to yourself." The leitmotif runs through the writings of many mystics, for whom the harshness of the desert is a precondition for self-realization. "I succumbed to the desert as soon as I saw it," writes Antoine de Saint-Exupéry in *Terre des Hommes*. "For the first time since I was born it seemed to me that my life was my own and that I was responsible for it." Saint-Exupéry goes on to compare his experience of the desert with the experience of falling in love—the same image Bergman chooses in describing his attachment to the island of Faro.

Deserts both free and fill the mind. Recalling the time he was forced down in the mineral wilderness of the Sahara, Saint-Exupéry wrote, "I possessed nothing in the world . . . yet I discovered myself filled with dreams." W. H. Auden observed that in a desert you are likely to be "visited by desperate longings for home and company." Perhaps this is why Saint-Exupéry, in the solitude of the Sahara, dreamed of his childhood home with such hallucinatory vividness.

The first time I traveled through the Tanami desert I was overwhelmed by its emptiness and silence. Instead of leaving it at that, my subconscious set to work to inscribe the tabula rasa with its own idiosyncratic graffiti.

Beyond Yuendumu you cross a vast spinifex plain studded with termite mounds. In due course I would learn that this was a landscape of the rain Dreaming—a natural enough connection for anyone with an intimate knowledge of the desert, because termites in their flying stage swarm immediately after the first summer rains. But when I saw the termite hills they reminded me of piles of rusty slag. Or Paleolithic figurines with pendulous breasts, gravid bellies, tiny heads. One minute I would be seeing Giacometti figures welded into a dark conglomerate, the next I would be recalling Monet's haystacks.

Each night my dreams took me deep into my past. I was flooded by memories of Sierra Leone and of Kuranko friends. These things which had marked me and made me who I am were like the ancestral journeys of the Dreaming which had marked the desert landscape and continued to leave their imprint upon the living. I wondered if any person is ever free to begin anew, to walk out into the world as if for the first time. But during those initiatory weeks in the desert, camping each night under the myriad stars, I began to feel that the residue and detritus of my past was being swept away. As I spaded the spinifex from the hard, brick-red earth to make a camp, or lit a fire of mulga in the gathering dusk, I felt renewed. If home is where a person is at peace with himself, where he can honestly say there is nowhere else he would rather be, then the desert had become my home.

It wasn't only the landscape which had this effect on me; it was the people. I felt at home among the Warlpiri, sitting with them, being with them. It was only when you moved out of the desert and attempted to *do* things with them that everything went haywire. Warlpiri are pragmatists who give as much as they get. And the *habitus* of nomadic existence dies hard. People tend to make the most of a resource when and where it is available, spending money freely, driving vehicles into the ground, gorging themselves on food, and—if they are drinkers—binge-drinking grog. Outsiders like us were a new resource. People were always asking us to drive them somewhere, to hunt, collect firewood, or visit kin—particularly those with whom we had ties of adoptive kinship. That we would provide food for whoever spent time with us went without saying. Yet there were no hard feelings if we failed to meet these demands, or ran out of money and supplies. The nomadic spirit prevailed. Even small children learned that sharing required forthright demands, not passive expectation. If a resource ran out you did not waste time protesting; you simply moved on, or you gave where once you took. Since it was impossible for large numbers of people to settle for long in any one place, you did not bargain on constancy. Outside your immediate family, social ties were forged and allowed to fall into abeyance as the exigencies of desert life changed. Much of the year you were moving far afield in small groups, only occasionally encountering your countrymen. Their presence was like the presence of the Dreaming itself: sensed but often unseen.

We were heading back to Lajamanu, and had decided to break our journey at Jila, some ninety miles northwest of Yuendumu.

Francine ran the Toyota off the track and we got out to stretch our legs. The spinifex was flecked by the setting sun. Flocks of birds flew up like flung grain before settling back into the grass. The vanes of the water bore creaked in the wind.

Pincher, Nugget, and another man called Pepper Jupurrurla wandered around, inspecting the ground. This happened wherever we traveled. People would scan the landscape for bush tucker and examine the road for familiar footprints or tire tracks, deducing from scant signs what had happened in the country since they last passed through. While I would be lost in thought, Warlpiri would always seemed to be focused on the world immediately at hand. I was constantly being reminded of how hard it is for intellectuals to desist from seeking general laws and abstract patterns, how rarely they notice the singular details of things—individual trees instead of undifferentiated bush.

I followed Nugget, who pointed out the spoor of a brown snake in the dirt. Then we peered into the four empty houses of the outstation, the dead hearths on the tamped earth, chips of wood where someone had rough-adzed a boomerang. Nugget told me who it had been.

I walked back to the Toyota and untied the bedrolls and swags from the roof rack and threw them down. Pincher took the spade and began brushing a campsite. The women heaped the spinifex into a windbreak. Then Pepper and I headed off toward a dead tree to gather firewood. When we got back, the swags were laid out in a line and fires lit between them.

Nugget, Pincher, and Pepper Jupurrurla camped to my right. On my left, Francine was engaging Nola in a conversation, informed more by goodwill than understanding. Finally, Wanda rendered a strident translation of what her mother was saying. Nola was worried that we had built our fire too close to the windbreak; the grass might catch fire as we slept. Wanda then returned to her task of cooking the goanna she had caught, holding it by the tail and flipping it over in the coals. The goanna flinched and stiffened as the heat scorched its flesh.

Nola appeared to be both elated and saddened by Jila. This was her own country, of the rat kangaroo Dreaming, belonging to Japaljarri and Jungarrayi, Napaljarri and Nungarrayi.

She kept repeating the word, *wiyarrpa*, referring to the dear departed as much as to the place in which the living and the dead were now reunited.

It made me think back to the events of the afternoon. Every place we passed had called out some response from the people with whom we were traveling. No longer was the landscape filled with the noise of my own past. I was beginning to see it through Warlpiri eyes.

Ten miles out of Yuendumu we had crossed the first of many dry creek beds. Pepper explained that this was his Dreaming. The *wampana* (hare wallaby) had traveled this way in the *jukurrpa*. It came from a place called Winparaku (Blanche Tower) in the south, accompanied by a snake called Yarrapiri. They traveled on toward the north, eventually reaching Darwin and the sea . . .

Nugget interrupted Pepper to say that we were now crossing a rain Dreaming track. But the shadowy tors and jumbled boulders held other meanings for Nola. Here at Yupajarayi, she gave birth to one of her daughters. Not far away, beneath a wall of red rock, a brother died. "She can't go there, she can't camp there," Wanda shouted from the back of the Toyota.

It was a foretaste of what was to happen twenty miles further on. Francine and I had hoped to make camp in a creekbed where we had stopped to boil a billy when we first drove north. But as Francine braked the Toyota and began to turn up the creekbed, Nugget cried out. I glanced back to where he and Pepper were sitting in the back, looks of disapproval on their faces.

"What's wrong?" I asked.

"No room here!" Nugget exclaimed. "Too many dead fellas here. We got no room."

I glanced at Pincher. He pursed his lips and stuck out his jaw, pointing us back onto the road. "Lots of people bin pass away here. Too many *pirlirrpa* here. We can't camp here, we got to go to Jila."

That night I fell asleep listening to Nugget and Pincher intoning verses from the rain Dreaming. They sat facing their fire, clacking their boomerangs as they sang.

When I woke at first light, they seemed not to have moved. Blankets were drawn up over their hunched shoulders. Then Nugget stretched out a skinny arm and began to scratch at the mosquito bites on his shin. Further away, Pepper was shoving a log into the embers of his fire. His hair was tousled. He seemed absorbed by the flickering flames.

I shook the dew from the canvas cover of my swag. The desert wind was cold, the sky reddening in the east, and birds breaking into song.

My revery was broken by Wanda's gruff voice as she shared shreds of cold goanna meat among her kids. Nola sat apart, murmuring something to herself.

Wanda explained to Francine that her mother had dreamed of one of her aunts who had died at Jila many years ago. In the dream her aunt had been in another country, singing songs of the *mala* (rat kangaroo) Dreaming. "She is homesick for her own place," Wanda said.

I told Wanda that I had also had a dream. I had dreamed of my daughter who lived in Canberra.

Wanda looked gravely at me. "That means she is thinking of you. She worry for you. She upset you've gone away."

We boiled a billy, made tea, ate a breakfast of dried bread and baked beans, and broke camp.

Francine took the wheel. Nugget and I sat beside her. The Toyota stank of sweat, ash, goanna meat, orange peel, and tobacco.

The road to Puyurru was seldom used. "This grass is too long," Pincher exclaimed, as saplings and seedheads scraped the underside of the Toyota. "It's got to be burned off. You got to look after the country." Burning was a way of "cleaning" the country, similar to sweeping and dusting the floor of a house.

At Puyurru we stopped to look around. As usual, the men stalked about, eyes glued to the ground, picking up the spoor of animals, deducing what had happened there. Nugget was in his element. This was his place. He showed me the silted up depression where water could be found. He pointed out old campsites.

Suddenly, he walked quickly from where we were standing and headed for a group of gnarled dogwoods. I followed him as he zigzagged through the scrub.

Then he knelt and began grubbing about in the sand. A few seconds later he grunted with satisfaction, and held up a rusty knife blade. He had left it there a long time ago. The handle had been eaten away by termites.

Nugget sat down under a dogwood, and picked at the rust with his thumbnail. The brim of his soiled red Stetson was pulled down over his eyes, his face in shadow.

I sat down beside him.

"What is the Dreaming here?" I asked.

"*Ngapa* (rain)," Nugget said. "That rain bin come up from Kala-pinpa, bin travel north, past that place I bin show you yesterday, right up here, this Puyurru."

Nugget named the key sites along the songline, tracing it north as far as Kulpulurnu. As he spoke he drew circles in the sand with his forefinger, linking them with a firmly drawn line.

Kulpulurnu was where all the rain tracks converged. Nugget had been conceived there. Though he hadn't visited the place for many years, he was confident he could find his way back there, just as he had found his old hunting knife.

He drew his hand across the stubble of his chin and smiled. "Maybe we can go there sometime, Jupurrurla, in your Toyota."

We wandered back to the Toyota where the others were waiting. Francine relied on Nugget to find the track. The vehicle bumped and lurched over the rough ground, bashing through scrub and porcupine grass, guided by his hand.

Nola shared Nugget's memory of the land. Every now and then she would ask Francine to stop, and wander a few yards into the spinifex to gather bush tomatoes or bush raisins. Wanda and the kids blundered after her, yelling for Francine to bring plastic bags which they could fill with bush tucker. Nola appeared rejuvenated. She dragged Francine after her, regaling her with stories of how she walked through this country, sometimes traveling as far north as Laja-manu. Once she stumbled and fell, but picked herself up laughing, and went on pointing out places on the horizon where she had walked and hunted.

Wanda, who grudgingly translated some of her mother's reminis-cences, seemed to get more and more morose. She kept telling Francine about a place where "Japaljarri passed away, where Japaljarri turned into a tree."

Hours later we stopped near the place Wanda had been talking about.

I was shocked to see that Nola was in tears. The men said nothing. But Wanda jumped out of the vehicle and led Francine and I across sparsely grassed ridges of red sand to a desert walnut tree. One branch of the tree had been snapped off in a desert tornado. It lay on the ground, surrounded by withered foliage. This tree, Wanda explained, was Nola's father.

Nola was walking about with her face streaked with tears.

"She's crying!" Wanda exclaimed, as though this might amuse us.

Japaljarri was indeed Nola's father. One summer he had gone north to meet up with other countrymen and perform ritual at Kunalarunyu. When the ritual was finished he set out for home. But the dancing had tired him. He fell asleep where the tree now stands, and died there in the morning.

"So he was your grandfather?" I said.

"He true bloke," Wanda assured me. "He bin pass away here, turn into this tree." She pointed with her lips at the fallen branch. "He goin' to lose his other arm now, my grandfather, poor bugger."

Nola was still crying, wandering away into the spinifex and inspecting the ground for traces of the past.

Pincher came up behind me. "Her father's *pirlirrpa* is here," he said, "his *kuruwarri*."

I observed that a lot of seedlings were springing up in the sandy ground around the tree, but it seemed to mean nothing to Pincher. He told me that his mother's brother used to get drunk and come to this place. "He used to sit under the tree and cry too, like my mother is crying. Crying for their father."

"What would happen if someone cut that tree down?" I asked.

"If you cut down a tree where the *pirlirrpa* is resting, then the spirit will go to someone who has the same skin name and same *kuruwarri* and fight with that person's *pirlirrpa* until he dies."

Nugget joined us. His forehead puckered as he listened to what Pincher was saying. "If you spoil a sacred site," he said, "you destroy its owners. When you take away the *pirlirrpa* of the place, you take away the *pirlirrpa* of the people who call that place 'father.'"

Wanda made further conversation impossible. She was raucously ordering her mother to get back into the Toyota.

As we drove away, Nola gazed out the window, lost in thought, indifferent to Wanda's kids clambering all over her. The present over-riding the past. Like Wanda's voice as she earbashed me with place names, repeating the story of Japaljarri's demise. I wished she would shut up. I wished she would respect the avoidance relationship which supposedly existed between us, since a Nampijinpa is "mother-in-law" to a Jupurrurla. Unhappily, I was not a Warlpiri and Wanda had waived the rule.

I turned to Pincher and asked him how old he was when his mother's father passed away.

Wanda answered for him. Pincher had been a little boy at the time. And "that Nangala" (Nancy Munn) had been living at Yuendumu. I concluded that Japaljarri had died about 1957.

Pincher's mouth was hanging half open. He had not shared for several days. I could not get over the wildly different personalities of Pincher, Wanda, and their mother. They looked utterly unrelated too. The notion that a person's character owes as much to his conception Dreaming as to his parents seemed very plausible. Perhaps the pattern of traditional social life, whereby people had to split up into small foraging groups for much of the year, also fostered an extraordinary degree of independence and individuality. I got to wondering what Japaljarri had been like. Did his daughter, Nola, resemble him in any way? It was difficult to imagine the man whose spirit now infused a desert walnut tree as a real person. Both his life and death had been assimilated into the Dreaming.

We reached Lajamanu late that night and dropped everyone off at their respective camps. I had not washed or shaved for a week. My hands were grazed and grimed with ash. I could not rest. I wanted to try to piece together some of the insights I had gleaned during the course of our trip.

I had learned that for the Warlpiri, as for other Aboriginal people, the world was originally lifeless and featureless. It had been given form, instilled with life, and charged with meaning by totemic ancestors. This happened "a long time ago" (*nyurruwiyi*), Nugget had told me. "We never put that one; it's just before." The *walyajarra* (autochthonous beings), so called because "their body is in the ground," possessed extraordinary powers that Nugget compared with the powers of a *ngangkari* or shaman. Typically, they emerged from the earth and set out on epic journeys across the land, leaving marks and traces wherever they walked, camped, fought, performed ceremony, or laid down the law. A heap of stones, a strange design on a rockface, a sacred song, a site name, or even a tree were all *yirdi*—signs of the Dreaming.

After journeying far and wide, the totemic heroes grew weary and yearned for home, much as mortals walking in great circles across the desert in search of water and game long for their base camp. As the exhausted heroes sank back into the earth, their bodies were often transformed into rocks, or trees, or sacred objects. But the Dreaming is not something which occurred once only. Though ordinarily out of reach, it remains eternally present, with the potential of being made visible again. It is somewhat like the difference between the public and secret names for sacred sites, or the difference between the way you perceive the landscape before and after initiation, or the difference between a person asleep and awake. The outward or superficial form may belie the inner reality. In increase rites, and in song and dance, the Dreaming is "drawn out" (*wilypi-manu*), as Nugget put it, and its power tapped. The Dreaming may also enter human consciousness of its own accord, through dreams, or reenter the world of bodily existence through conception. Nugget told me of a man called Wagon Joe Jungarrayi who had been conceived at the rain Dreaming site of Pirti-pirti. In the Dreaming, a certain Jangala speared his brother there in a fight to abduct one of his wives. Today, a pile of boulders is the petrified body of Jangala set atop the bodies of the two Nungarrayi wives. According to Nugget, Wagon Joe's crooked arm and pockmarked skin were scars from that primordial spear fight, physical manifestations of the *kuruwarri* of that place.

In his masterful ethnography of the Pintupi, Fred Myers describes the Dreaming as "the ground of being." The same can be said of the Warlpiri. Lifetime and Dreamtime are coalesced. Biography and myth are fused. It is reminiscent of the intimate connection in European thought between biography and history.

We owe the word "history" to Herodotus for whom *historie* was a kind of tracking down. History is the story of the traces and tracks of human lives over time. History is the story of Everyman writ large. Hannah Arendt puts it this way: "That every individual life between birth and death can eventually be told as a story with beginning and end is the prepolitical and prehistorical condition of history, the great story without beginning and end."

As with history so too with myth. The Dreamtime, like a person's lifetime, involves a journey. "We follow the Dreaming," Nugget observed, comparing it to the way one follows a person or a spoor across country. But though particular lives begin and end, their vital essence remains in the ground, seeded along the tracks they left, constant in the names they received, reborn through the songs, and dances, and designs each person inherits and hands on.

I closed my notebook and went outside. The sky was cloudless and filled with stars. The dark side of the moon was smudged with craters, like dirty ice.

Already the local rock band was beginning to tune up. I walked away toward the edge of the settlement, followed by the jangle of electric guitars, the thudding of drums, and amplified voices singing . . .

> Will the circle be unbroken
> by and by, oh, by and by
> and a better life be waiting
> in the sky, oh, in the sky?

SEVEN

It is suicide to be abroad. But what is it

to be at home, . . . what is it to be at home?

—*Samuel Beckett*

At Lajamanu there had been a death. We heard the women keening in the darkness and at daybreak people were gathering on the south side of the football oval. Men walked across the open ground, singly or in small groups, carrying spears, woomeras, and fighting boomerangs. The women carried digging sticks. They sat apart, in closed circles, under the shade trees.

I scarcely knew the man who had died. I had visited his camp once to talk about The Granites. The old man was suffering from diabetes and was blind. His son had helped him into a sitting position. The old man had clutched at his blanket, and his eyes rolled up under the lids as he struggled to answer my questions.

All morning the women's doleful voices were borne to us on the wind. And in the afternoon groups of women, their foreheads, cheeks, upper arms, and breasts caked with wood ash and kaolin, moved through the settlement trailing wilted branches of eucalypt. They were close kinswomen, sweeping away the footprints of the dead man, erasing every trace of his presence.

Jedda, a classificatory mother of the dead man, came by to see Francine. She had gashed her scalp open with a sharp stone. She held her hand gingerly against the bloodstained scarf around her head. "Sorry business," she explained in a tone both rueful and proud. Jedda later told Francine that a person who failed to show grief by inflicting such wounds upon herself was hard-hearted "like a black gidgee tree." According to ethnographies I had read, death is often said to be the result of sorcery. To lacerate oneself allays any suspicion that one was implicated. But in the case of old Jungarrayi, there had been no inquest. He was old and infirm; people had expected him to die.

I joined Nugget and Pincher under the men's bough-shade on the other side of the oval. Nugget was staring into space, tugging his grubby windbreaker close against his chest. "Poor bugger," he muttered.

I looked over to where the women were moving around the perimeter of the oval, sweeping the ground with leaves.

"Clean 'im," Nugget said tersely. The identity of the dead man was already being annulled. His clothes would be burned, his footprints swept away, his name not spoken for several years.

"All the Jungarrayi and Japaljarri got to go to that sorry camp now," Pincher said. These were the bereaved kin. In the old days they would have abandoned their camp to the shades. Nowadays people moved out of their house, but in due course allowed others to occupy it. But the memory of a death was hard to expunge; it haunted those who survived in the same way that it tainted the place where the dead person had lived.

But life went on. On the oval every afternoon the young men assembled for their practice game. They were getting ready for the football competitions at the Barunga festival in a month's time. As for the older men, they were preoccupied by talk of the American entrepreneurs who were flying in to Lajamanu to see some "tribal corroboree." If everything worked out, groups of local men and women would be signed up to travel to the United States for a concert tour.

A patch of scrub was cleared by the council's front-end loader, and a *parnpa,* or ceremonial ground, marked out. During the day, the men came and went, discussing the forthcoming *purlapa:* the public ceremony when a group of men would enact part of their Dreaming.

Pincher informed me that he was to be a principal performer. But he would have to make a trip to Tennant Creek to get red ocher and then drive south to Tanami to collect a soft grass which grew there. He would be away for several days.

I spent the days in the company of the older men. We sat in the shade of snappy gums around the edge of the dancing ground. Most of the men I knew by name, though had never had a chance to talk to them at length. Now they were only too willing to discuss "*purlapa* business" with me. They brought their boomerangs to the *parnpa.*

61

They stashed their emu feathers, chunks of red ocher, hanks of hair string, and other ritual paraphernalia in the forks of trees. They talked about country and ceremony.

Nugget took it upon himself to instruct me. Pointing at Archie, his brother, he said, "That one Kulpulurnu," meaning that Archie, like himself, hailed from that place. He then pointed to each man in turn, naming their fathers' countries, their *ngurrara wardingki,* the places where they originated. It was a telling reminder of the way skin groupings are mapped onto the landscape and social relationships conceptualized in geographical terms. It was also reminiscent of how seldom we in the West now identify ourselves and others in terms of provenance and kinship, asking "Where are you from?" or "Who are your people?" Time has become a more powerful metaphor than space, especially when one considers the way invidious distinctions between *us* and *them* are customarily promulgated in the West. So many books about Aborigines begin with the observation that Aboriginal life in Australia dates back 40,000 years, as if, in contrast with the progressive culture of Europe, Aboriginal culture has not changed much during this time. Placing ourselves and the Other in different times we thus deny coevalness.

Archie described his life in the desert when he was growing up. Kulpulurnu was his *ngurrara,* the main camp. He passed one hand over the other in a circular motion to describe how his family used to walk in concentric circles (*waru wapajalpalu*) through the desert, always returning in summer to the permanent water of the main camp. When whites came to The Granites to dig for gold, Archie went to work for them. He was the first Aboriginal to drive a truck at the mine. But every summer he walked back to Kulpulurnu, a journey of about 200 miles, to check that no strangers were in his country, and see that no trees had been felled or sacred places violated.

As Archie talked, his hunting dog, Jampijinpa, nuzzled his armpit. Like Archie, the dog's head and thighs bore a lifetime of scars.

I kept glancing at Zack Jakamarra, curious to know what he might have to say. But Jakamarra was dead to the world, stretched out on the ground with his parka hood pulled up over his head.

"Too much *pama* at Top Springs," Nugget muttered. *Pama* was the Warlpiri word for delicacies such as wild honey and witchetty grub. Nowadays it also means grog. Zack had been at Top Springs, 170 miles north of Lajamanu, on one of his benders.

Pepper Jupurrurla also looked the worse for wear. His eye was bunged up and his breathing labored. He was making a coolimon, hacking away at the stringy beanwood with a wood rasp. Every few minutes he stopped to catch his breath and rub his palm over the rough surface. Though we had traveled and camped together I did not feel comfortable with Pepper. He brooded. He was taciturn. I could not fathom what was weighing on his mind.

He picked up a scrap of sandpaper and resumed work on the coolimon.

Japangardi and some of the others were engrossed in a game of cards. Japangardi was a thickset, coarse-featured man who seldom spoke. He dealt from a dog-eared deck and sneered as the other players tossed crumpled two dollar bills onto the ground.

I opened my notebook, and asked Archie if he minded my writing down what he told me. He grinned. "You got to write things down, Jupurrurla," he said, "but we got everything here, in our head." He tapped his forefinger against his head to make the point. "I don't need that writing, I hold it all in here. That Kulpulurnu, my father's country. It was there from the beginning. It goes on forever. It is like the grass, Jupurrurla. You burn it, but it grows up again, over and over."

Archie's cynical allusion to literacy reminded me of what Zack had told me about young people knowing nothing of their country, knowing only what they read in books.

Zack was still out like a light.

Nugget seemed to read my mind. He tossed his head back, pursing his lips in Zack's direction. "Snoring, poor bugger," he said, "probably thinkin' about his country."

I asked Archie and Nugget to name the principal sites along the rain track for which they were "bosses."

"We gotta tell you all those *ngami warlalja* (coolimon ones)," Archie said, "all those *jukurrpa warlalja.*"

Archie marked the key sites in the dirt, and drew a line between them. Then he indicated how a second rain track, belonging to Jaka-marra-Jupurrurla / Nakamarra-Napurrurla, split off from the main one and ran to a place called Wingkiyi. Still other tracks converged on Kulpulurnu from the west. I recognized enough of the site names to realize that Archie's sand diagram was an objectification of how he *thought* of their interrelationships: the tracks would actually meander and dogleg in linking all the places he had named.

I asked about the hand-over points, the sites at which Archie and Nugget relinquished control of their songline.

Archie ran his forefinger along the line he had traced in the sand, from Puyurru in the south, to Jinalku, north of Kulpulurnu—a distance of more than 200 miles.

"We call that one father (*kirdana*)," Archie said, "We run that one. But south of Puyurru, that different country now, we don't know that one."

After more talk it became clear that another Dreaming was involved: an emu track that ran parallel to the rain track for some of its length. Archie described emu and rain as "level, like that," and held his forefingers side by side to describe them.

I happened to know that some of the places Archie had named were also associated with a hare wallaby track. What then was Archie's relationship with this Dreaming?

"*Jintangkalu yanunu*," Archie said. "We all came together."

By this remark Archie meant that in the Dreaming these ancestors accompanied one another on their travels.

"*Jintangka juku*," Nugget added. "Still all one. One way, one mob."

"So they are all countrymen?" I asked.

"Yuwayi," Nugget agreed, "all *walya warlalja*, all belong to the same land."

"Is everyone in Lajamanu *warlalja*, close family?" I asked.

The question sparked a boisterous debate. Even the card players pitched in.

Morrie Japanangka stuck several bits of stick in the sand, forming a rough rectangle. This defined the Warnayaka area, he declared. He named the places he had pegged out, referring to them as "the four corners of Warnayaka." Within this area everyone was, allegedly, *warlalja*.

Archie stared somberly at Japanangka's diagram "That's the white-fella way," he said irritably, "fixing boundaries!"

I felt chastened. I too had contemplated making a box of the word *warlalja*, assuming that it designated some determinate and bounded grouping.

As the discussion went on, I began to see why boundaries could not be fixed. The Warlpiri social universe was made up of skeins of relationships, not just songlines. A Dreaming defined a person's descent. It was immutable and given. But during the course of a lifetime, a man made contacts with others outside his own home area. Networks of ties developed which were different for each person, reflecting the contingencies of where he traveled, lived, worked, married, and learned ceremony. It went without saying that alliances shifted, things changed.

Sharing ceremony was central. From one's father, one learned the totemic rituals associated with one's own Dreaming. But one also acquired knowledge of other Dreamings and other rituals from men elsewhere with whom one formed alliances and shared resources.

Pepper Jupurrurla waved his rasp in the air to get my attention. With labored breath, he explained that his home place was Pawala. It was where one of the hare wallaby tracks finished up. Pawala was a Jupurrurla-Jakamarra site. But within a thirty-mile radius there was Paraluyu, associated with the watiyawarnu Dreaming (Jangala-Jampijinpa), and a two snake Dreaming (Japaljarri-Jungarrayi), as well as the Mamangirri area associated with Japanangka-Japangardi. So Pepper considered men of all eight subsections as countrymen. "*Walya warlalja* are people who belong to the same place, to the same country," he said. "We all one camp (*ngurrara jinta*), we all one mob, we all chuck in together."

Japanangka was now in complete agreement. It was on the strength of such ties, he said, that marriages were often made. "When you are close in the business," he observed, "you talk together and arrange for your children to marry."

"We call those ones *jurdalja*," Nugget said helpfully.

In anthropological parlance, *jurdalja* would be called affines: people related through marriage.

Zack was now awake and keen to tell me how he was related to Nugget. A generation ago, his classificatory fathers—Mupuka Jupurrurla and Kurrurumanpa Jupurrurla—gave Nugget's father—Murrukuru Jampijinpa—a Napangardi wife who hailed from Yawurluwurlu, north of Mt. Theo. Another Napangardi was given to Archie's father. She was from Mt. Theo. In reciprocation, Murrukuru gave Kurrurumanpa a Napanangka wife from Kulpulurnu, and to Zack's real father, Wijimi, he gave another Napanangka from the same place. "Bin *jurdalja*," Zack said, "swapping nieces (sister's daughters). Square back. Made it fair."

Such sister's daughter exchanges cemented alliances between powerful men. But they were spoken of as alliances between *places,* as Nugget explained:

A *jurdalja* relationship existed between Puyurru and Yurmurrpa. A Jangala from Puyurru might give his sister's daughter (a Napaljarri) in marriage to a Jakamarra at Yurmurrpa. Reciprocally, Jakamarra would give his sister's daughter (a Nungarrayi) in marriage to Jangala. Jangala and Jakamarra were thus *jurdalja*. Or, more exactly, Puyurru and Yurmurrpa were *jurdalja*. Affinal relationships, like all others, were grounded in the need for mutual help in hard times. And this was still true, even though people had settled in Lajamanu, far from their traditional country. Country was, so to speak, good to think, even if you didn't actually live in it any more.

Something Nugget said brought home to me this intimate connection between person and place. "We call our sister's daughter *miyalu warnu*," he said, "because she comes out of our sister." He touched his abdomen as he spoke. It suggested to me the natural link between the several senses of the word *miyalu*: sacred site, seat of the soul, and stomach. These were all places where life is held and nourished. Just as ceremony at a sacred site sustains the desert species on which one's livelihood depends, so marriages guarantee the continuation of human life. But the exchange of women also had political implications.

"We can't harm those ones," Nugget said, referring to in-laws, "because we married with them. And they can't harm us. We got the right to hunt in their country, because we grow up their kids. And they got the right to hunt in ours."

That night, writing up my hastily scribbled notes, I saw that my idea of home would have to be approached in two ways. Home was a central *place* to which you or your thoughts constantly return. But home was also a group of *people* without whom your life would cease to have meaning. I had to remind myself not to get carried away by the poetic resonances of Warlpiri metaphors of country and ignore the field of kinship and affinity—the sites of individual lives—that give those metaphors their vitality and value.

Next morning was cold and windy. After breakfast I headed across the oval toward the smudges of smoke that indicated that the men were already at the *parnpa*.

Suddenly, I was aware of someone coming up behind me. I heard the wheezing of Pepper's bad lungs. Then I saw his shadow, and the shadow of his spears on the ground.

Startled, I wheeled around.

He was shirtless, wearing a pair of shorts, his body smeared with red ocher. He was carrying several spears in one hand; in the other he clutched two fighting boomerangs and a shield.

He stood in front of me, breathing heavily. His eyes were bloodshot and his breath reeked of grog.

66

His sentences were fractured, hard-bitten. Snatches of Warlpiri and English. Hoicking at intervals, he spat gobbets of saliva in the dirt.

I had to calm myself before I could listen properly to what he was trying to say. It seemed he had been cuckolded. A young woman had been promised in marriage to him. She had got involved with a young man, one of Lajamanu's best football players. But today Pepper was going to set things straight. The other men would back him up. They'd see that justice was done. None of this whitefella law. Aboriginal Law would prevail. The young man would have to stand his ground, out in the open (*karrimi yarlungka*), and Pepper would spear him. That was the penalty for stealing another man's wife. Pepper's wounded pride would be healed by the injury he would inflict.

Lamely, I asked if there was anything I could do to help.

A feeble smile played across Pepper's face. It was the first time I had known him to smile.

He pressed his shield against my chest. "Nothing, Jupurrurla," he said. "You don't have to do anything. I just want to tell you, so you know. That's all."

We walked on to the *parnpa* together.

Japangardi, Nugget, and Archie were playing cards. Pepper plonked himself down and demanded to be dealt a hand.

I sat on the scuffed ground near Pincher Jampijinpa, who had returned from Tanami with his grass and red ocher. He was using a hammer to pound it on a stone. Other men were busy nearby. Morrie Japanangka was rubbing red acryllic paint onto his spear-thrower. Tommy Jangala was reshaping the edge of his boomerang with Pepper's rasp. And Zack Jakamarra was disentangling a ball of black hairstring.

Pepper played and lost several games of cards. He grumbled constantly, hoiked and spat. Finally he threw in his hand, climbed to his feet, took up his weapons, and began to pace up and down the *parnpa*.

He gestured belligerently toward the settlement, railing against the man who had cuckolded him. "They all like that!" he bellowed. "All them young blokes! They don't know nothing!" With all his bluff and bluster it was difficult to make out a half of what Pepper was saying. But the general drift of it was that the young men did not know their heritage, did not know who was boss, and did not know the Law.

That he was talking in stilted English suggested that Pepper's complaint was partly for my hearing. But it was also clear that he was trying to drum up support from the other men.

They remained unmoved. The card game went on. Pincher pounded away at his ocher. Zack teased out the hairstring between his thumb and forefinger and rolled his spindle against the side of his thigh.

With his words falling on deaf ears, Pepper stalked off in the direction of the Napangardi camp, about fifty yards away. Brandishing his boomerangs, he began haranguing the women.

Lena Napangardi was quickly on her feet, hurling the abuse back, telling Pepper he was a drunken old man and should be locked up.

The unstoppable Pepper strode back to the *parnpa,* spoiling for a fight.

"Sit down, old man!" Pincher shouted.

Zack assured me that Pepper was just sounding off. "It's just piss and wind," he said, "just talk."

"I bin talk!" Pepper railed. "After *purlapa,* they goin' to bring 'im!"

I caught Nugget's eye. Nugget smirked. "Too much grog," he mouthed, and went on with his card game.

It was about as much sympathy as Pepper was going to find. Before long he was picking up his spears and blundering away across the oval.

"He sleep it off now," Nugget said, as if Pepper had done his dash and got his grievance off his chest.

At first I felt sorry for Pepper. I felt he had made a fool of himself and would not show his face in public for a long time. But this wasn't so. Pepper, who seldom got drunk, had had good reason to have recourse to booze. Years of disparagement and pressure from white managers and administrators had made men and women of his generation abashed and self-conscious about many traditional practices. Grog often served as a way of breaking down inhibitions about expressing one's feelings in traditionally appropriate ways. In fact, Pepper had saved face by venting his humiliation in front of his peers. He had reminded them of the Law, shown that he was man enough to fight for what was rightfully his. By challenging the other men to stand up and be counted, he had shown *them* to be wanting. If Aboriginal Law was no longer to be upheld, then it wasn't Pepper's fault. The others had elected to give up on it, not him. Pepper's departure left me wondering about the men's commitment to ceremony. After all, ceremony, like the Law, stemmed from the Dreaming. Had it too been sapped of its original significance, gutted of meaning? Was it something you did only when a group of rich Americans and the promise of a tour to the United States made it worth your while?

I stayed on at the *parnpa* after nightfall. The men sat clumped around flickering fires, their skin gleaming like anthracite. As they began to sing, their eyes blazed with intensity and their voices merged in a nasal intoning that made the hair on the back of my neck stand up on end. Each man held his boomerangs in front of his face, clapping them together in rhythmic accompaniment to his singing. From time to time the men's voices trailed off, and they brought their boomerangs together in a wooden vibrato as if to shake free the spirit of the song and dispatch it into the night. This was how you learned the songs, Pincher said. You learned them by sitting with the men and listening. "You learned them from the boomerangs."

Whenever the men stopped singing, Pincher helped me get the drift of the song. Ironically, it was the story of a vengeance raid. In the Dreaming a certain Jampijinpa had abducted some women from another country. The aggrieved husbands tracked Jampijinpa across the desert. They ambushed him at a rock hole where he gone to drink, and killed him with their spears. It was going to be the first time in memory the story was acted out. It was an episode from a fire Dreaming. Two Lajamanu women had recently recovered it in their dreams. Lorna Nakamarra had seen ghosts in her dream, among them the ghost of her dead husband. He had told her the story, revealed to her the painted designs, given her the song.

The Americans flew in next day. I was sitting with the men at the *parnpa*. We watched as the aircraft came in from the north, buffeted by the southeasterly, then landed and taxied along the red dirt airstrip.

The dancers were out of sight of the *parnpa*, sitting behind windbreaks of eucalypt branches while their *kurdungurlu*, or ritual managers, busied themselves with the task of painting them up. Blood-red ocher, mixed with animal fat, had to be smeared over the face, body and limbs of the dancers. Down had to be applied to the greased skin, emu feathers fixed to bonnets of hairstring, and weapons prepared.

Pincher was already unrecognizable. I sat back while Pepper gummed tufts of down on Pincher's face and bound the hairstring bonnet to his head. He was utterly wrapped in his work.

"I bin learn this at University Yapa kirlangu," he said cryptically. It was an analogy Warlpiri men often drew—between Aboriginal initiation and European university education. But there seemed to me a world of difference between initiation, which impressed understanding upon a neophyte through hazing and pain, and Western education with its preference for abstract knowledge over lived experience.

Pepper wanted me to understand everything properly. The principal dancers were the *kirda*, he explained, the bosses or owners of the Dreaming. But the *kirda* depended upon the knowledge and skill of ritual helpers, called *kurdungurlu*. *Kurdungurlu* were like policemen, Pepper said. They saw that the *kirda* did everything straight and proper.

Kurdungurlu were a person's close uterine kin. The logic of how Pincher and Pepper were related went like this: Pepper's mother was a Napaljarri. Pincher's mother was a Nungarrayi. Napaljarri-Nungarrayi are patrilineally linked. As children of these women, Pepper Jupurrurla and Pincher Jampijinpa were bound together as *kurdungurlu*. "We drink the breast milk from those Napaljarri-Nungarrayi places," Pepper said. "We drink from the mother, we drink from the land. *Kurdungurlu* are children of their mother's land."

Pincher had to have his say, despite the ocher and fluff over his mouth. He explained how he was *kurdungurlu* for Pepper. *Kurdungurlu* often gave each other their sisters' children in marriage. It was a way of affirming the bond between them.

I could not help but wonder whether Pepper's promised wife, who had caused him such distress, was Pincher's sister's daughter. But these idle thoughts were swept away in the flurry of activity around me. Word had reached us that the Americans were on their way.

Not wanting to make a nuisance of myself I walked back to the dancing ground and sat down with the men.

The women were also assembling now. They too had been practicing for ten days. They stood close together at the edge of the *parnpa,* wearing red cotton skirts and white headbands, their breasts and upper arms decorated with designs from the fire Dreaming.

Two local councillors brought the Americans to the *parnpa* in Toyotas. The councillors wore laundered shirts and pressed trousers. They had slicked and combed their hair. The visitors carried video cameras and wore dark glasses. They were dressed in safari shirts, twill trousers, embossed cowboy boots, and Akubra hats. They seemed a bit nonplussed, and stood together in the shade of a big eucalypt, trying to look benignly upon the scene in front of them.

Zack muttered irreverently about the councillors not wanting to get their clothes dirty by sitting on the ground with us. I felt anomalous. I edged closer to Zack, wanting to lose myself in the tight-packed group of seated men. I cast my eyes over to where Francine was sitting among the women, and thought how much at ease she seemed, how much at home.

The two local councillors began to throw their weight around, shouting to the dancers in the scrub to get ready, ordering their sidekicks to drive the Toyotas away from the oval so they wouldn't spoil the picture.

Around me the men started singing. The guttural chanting and metrical clapping of hands and boomerangs drew the dancers from the bush.

Dance, like most things in Warlpiri life, impresses upon both outsider and performer that Being is earthbound, and that the earth empowers.

Jampijinpa was the first to appear. His back rigid, his arms flung straight out from his sides, he moved through the scrub with a powerful, accented stamping. Dust whorled around his ankles. Bunches of eucalypt leaves, tied to his upper arms and calves, shucked and shuffled as his bare feet thudded down on the earth. His chest was thrust forward, his arms laid back, and his head swiveled and jerked in half-circles as he moved.

Then the other men appeared carrying spears and boomerangs, their feet thudding on the hard-packed ground, their painted bodies gleaming with sweat. They fanned out through the scrub, enacting the Dreamtime pursuit of the errant Jampijinpa.

The women had now joined their voices to the voices of the men, and the far-fetched din of the fire Dreaming filled the air, urgent and inexorable.

Every few minutes the singing petered out and the dancers quivered their thighs and shed down from their bodies. Then they straightened up, relaxed, adjusted the bindings on their legs and arms, before the massed chanting called them back to the dance.

Gradually they began to close in on the hapless Jampinjinpa. At first oblivious to the ambush, he moved through the bush, swiveling his head, sustaining the same rhythmic tread as his trackers. But as he bent to drink at a rock hole, he seemed to sense his plight. His eyes jerked from side to side in desperation. He lifted his boomerangs, ready to parry blows. But as the droning continued, and with it the measured stamp of feet and the churning dust, his pursuers were upon him, feigning spear thrusts to his body, chopping at his head with their boomerangs.

The entire drama lasted no more than ten minutes.

The dancers retired into the scrub. The women got to their feet and prepared their part of the *purlapa*.

The video cameras rolled. The chanting went on. Then it was all over.

Pincher was the first to return to the *parnpa*. Panting and sweating, he collapsed into a sitting position on the ground, his arms at his sides. As one of the Americans pointed a video camera at his face, Pincher gasped, "My name . . . is Pincher Jampinjinpa. My Dreaming is . . . *watiyawarnu* . . . but this dance, today, is . . ."

He might have been a stone or tree for all the effect it had on the man with the video camera, who did not take his eye from the viewfinder. The camera recorded the scene: Pincher sputtering through down and grass fiber, trying to impress his identity and name on the man behind the viewfinder. But the man did not see Pincher. He saw only an Aboriginal decked out in ritual paraphernalia.

When it was time for the visitors to say their piece, they formed a straight line in front of the exhausted dancers.

One of the women in the party spoke first.

"Hi," she said nervously. "I'm Tamsin Meyerhoff of Tamsin Meyerhoff and Associates Incorporated in New York. I must say it's been a truly valuable and heartwarming experience coming here today. We in America have lost our culture. But you've still got yours. That's the wonderful thing. That you people are holding on to your culture, passing it on to your children, keeping it alive . . ."

The irony was that, as Tamsin Meyerhoff was talking what Zack would later refer to as "hard English," the young men of Lajamanu had begun their football practice out on the oval behind her. One player had kicked a goal and was racing down the oval with a clenched fist raised high.

Tamsin stepped back to allow one of her colleagues to speak. All five of them took turns to say something, telling us of various ethnic festivals that were scheduled to take place in New York in the coming year, of the interest Americans were taking in Aboriginal art, the importance of traditional culture in the modern world. And in one way or another they all pretended to derogate their own culture as a way of extolling the Warlpiri one. The implication seemed to be that "culture" was, by definition, premodern and "traditional"—something one clung to for sentimental reasons. Hence the romantic condescension. The myth of the noble savage. The hackneyed theme of Western man's fall into barbaric materialism.

That evening, after the visitors had flown out, I strolled back toward the caravan with Zack. Francine was sitting by the fire with a group of women. They were still in their red skirts, the painted designs still showing on their arms and breasts. Their skins glowed, steeped in the redness of the setting sun.

Zack walked on toward his camp. I sat on the step of the caravan. The women were grilling Francine about what it was like in America, how long it took to fly there. Francine was explaining that it took a night and a day; you slept and ate your meals on the plane.

"We don't want to sleep up there in that plane," I heard Jedda say. "We got to get up earlybird so we can get there in a day."

"The trip takes longer than a day," Francine said.

"Then we got to get the plane to stop somewhere on the way so we can sleep there. Then we can go on."

The women were drawing circles on the ground: America, Australia, Darwin, Sydney, New York. Their excitement was tempered by trepidation as they charted the new totemic geography of the world they might be plunged into.

As I got up and went into the caravan, Napaljarri was saying to Francine: "I gotta go bush and make myself strong and healthy. I gotta eat bush tucker. Bush turkey, kangaroo. Not tea and sugar. When we eat whitefella food that makes us weak. If we go to that America we got to be strong."

EIGHT

Man's real life is not a house, but

the Road, and . . . life itself is a journey

to be walked on foot.

—Bruce Chatwin

This is Ringer's story. This is the story I piece together as we drive north to Katherine.

Francine has taken the wheel. The Toyota judders over the corrugated road. Dust billows up behind us. I scribble notes as best I can: snatches of conversation, the names of plants and places. Ringer is watching the road ahead, looking for the telltale trace of a washout or pothole. Nora and the other women are in the back, noisily distributing the soft drinks and chicken wings we bought for them and their kids at Lajamanu.

A week ago it rained. Sandhill wattles and desert broom are in flower. Among the blue mallee scrub and snappy gums there are scarlet slashes of harlequin mistletoe and holly grevillea. Along the roadside the dark red earth is smudged with the pinks of mulla mulla, the soft yellows of wild daisies and billybuttons. With Ringer's help, I jot down the Warlpiri names, though he is much more interested in pointing out the location of Catfish waterhole and the old Number 6 Bore. He hunted kangaroo here when he was a young man.

The scrub gives way to a blighted landscape of dead trees and laterite. The only green foliage is poisonous to cattle. We have reached Wave Hill Station.

"Bugger 'im up this country!" Ringer says. He remembers when this cattle-trampled place was covered with grass and scrub. He worked here once as a stockboy. The war had just ended. He was in his teens.

The Aboriginal stockmen lived in makeshift humpies of spinifex and torn canvas, shored up with branches and scrap iron. There were no shade trees. Firewood had to be fetched from miles away. A dry creek bed served as a latrine. The men washed themselves in a horse trough. In summer, when the windmill tank ran dry, they had to draw their drinking water from the same trough.

Once a year, the Station bosses issued each stockman a swag cover and blanket. Every few months they were given a pair of trousers, a shirt and hat, boots, razors, and a pipe. Every week: two or three plugs of cheap tobacco. Three times a day, seven days a week: a slice of dry bread, a piece of cooked offal or bone, and a dipper of tea. Dry rations for a week consisted of two to three pounds of flour, half a pound of sugar, and a handful of tea. Sometimes the flour was infested with weevils. Sometimes you got lucky: the homestead supplies went bad, and you were given a jar of rancid jam, a tin of moldy treacle, a packet of stale Quaker oats.

Ringer is in his early sixties, laconic, tough-minded, self-effacing. He was born and raised in the desert. His father was killed in an intertribal fight when he was a small boy. He wears a sweat-stained Stetson that has seen better days. He cradles one arm in the other. The veins on his right arm stand out; his hand is swollen. Four days ago, when I was sitting under a bough-shade with Ringer and some other men, Ringer suddenly lost consciousness and toppled over. The men moved as one, helping him sit up, holding him steady. Everyone laid his hands on Ringer's body or head. For a terrible moment, Ringer's life had gone out of him. When he came to, we helped him walk to the clinic. The sister examined him, but couldn't diagnose what was wrong. She said Ringer should go to Katherine Hospital for tests. I told her that Francine and I were taking a group of women to the Barunga festival in a few days' time; Katherine was on our way; we could easily take Ringer along.

At Kalkaringi we stop at the store for cold drinks. There is a pay phone outside, and on the spur of the moment I decide to call home.

It isn't easy talking to my mother and father, describing what I am doing, the Toyota crammed with Aboriginal women, bedding, and billy cans, the red dust everywhere, peanut hulls, chicken bones, chewed tobacco. I listen as my parents take turns to relay news of my brother and sisters. My mother describes the weather in Auckland, but I find it hard to stretch my imagination and take in what she is saying. My attention drifts to the backbone of distant hills, river terraces like broken biscuit, corkwood and gidgee marking the line of some creek.

I quickly use up my coins and have to end the call in a hurry. I feel frustrated and angry at myself. I vow to make amends by writing my parents a letter as soon as I get to Barunga.

Ringer is sitting under a bloodwood tree, drinking from a bottle of diet Coke. I ask him if he wants to walk with me to the road sign we passed on our way into the township. I am curious to know what it says.

We pick our way across the stony ground, past the parked cattle trucks, toward the yellow sign.

I read aloud: *Pioneer Grave. The Northern Territory's Man From Snowy River.* When Ringer makes no comment, I ask him about the Wave Hill stockmen's strike in 1966. Was he part of it?

Ringer quit working at Wave Hill some years before the strike. "I bin shoot through, longa whatsaname, Montejinni Station," he says. "I bin make little bit trouble at Wave Hill. They bin push me out, you know."

But Ringer recalls the strike all right, and the events that led up to it.

Until 1952, Aboriginal stockmen were paid no wages. After 1952 they received a derisory $6 a week. Underpaid, living in conditions unfit for dogs, the stockmen decided they had had enough. In the winter of 1966, 200 men, women, and children picked up their swags, billy cans, and meager belongings, and walked ten miles to Wattie Creek where they camped. A few months later, they petitioned the Governor-General of Australia for help in getting back 500 acres of their traditional land so they could run their own cattle station.

"Whitefellas didn't own that land," Ringer tells me as we approach the "Historic Marker." "Aboriginal people are the proper bosses. Whitefellas only brought in cattle, and horses, and drilled bores."

The Aboriginals' land claim was dismissed, despite the fact that it had been their hard labor—mustering, branding, droving, fencing, fixing bore pumps—which had helped the pastoral industry boom and made the cattle barons rich. Equal pay for equal work did come to Aboriginal stockmen—in the 1970s—but with grim repercussions. Rather than pay Aboriginal workers the same money that whites earned, station owners stopped hiring Aboriginal stockmen and advertised in eastern cities for white jackeroos. The Aboriginal stockmen lost more than their livelihood. The cattle stations were their traditional land, where they hunted and performed ceremony. Cattle and horses had been their life. Pushed off the land, they drifted to the fringes of towns like Alice and Katherine. There was no work. They sat around. They received welfare handouts. They drank.

Ringer and I inspect the memorial: a wedge of concrete and a stainless steel plaque. Ringer waits while I copy the inscription into my notebook.

"You got 'im?" Ringer asks. He speaks of everything I write down as something I have got or caught.

I wish I could convey to him the irony of the words I have just read:

In Memory of
Owen Stephen Cummins
Born Bargo, Bogong High Plains, Victoria. 13th September,
1874.
Died Wave Hill Station, N.T. 15th August, 1953.
The Territory's Own Man From Snowy River
Respected as a horseman down Kosciusko
way and admired as a stockman, drover
and horse breeder during more than 50
years in the saddle in the Territory.
ETQ WAS HIS BRAND
HORSES WERE HIS LIFE
REST IN PEACE

We drive on to Wattie Creek, the settlement a few miles north of Kalkaringi. We are looking for the house of Ringer's son, Gary.

Gary and his wife have a newborn baby. Swaddled in a blanket, the infant lies asleep in a coolimon made from a piece of roofing iron. Nora sits by the sleeping child and tells Francine about her other grandchildren.

I stroll over to where Ringer is sitting with his brother-in-law, Jakamarra. It was this same Jakamarra who initiated him, Ringer tells me. This is one of the reasons he regards Wattie Creek as his second home.

I ask old Jakamarra if he too worked at Wave Hill.

"We bin work there one time, that Wave Hill," he says.

Ringer and old Jakamarra recall old times, how they started work before sunup and finished after dark. It was rough, but they were young. They stuck together. There is no self-pity in their anecdotes, no bitterness. They do not speak of the black tax Aboriginals have always had to pay in the country whites call lucky, their land despoiled, their kids dying of disease and hunger. There is no rancor when they speak of how they were laid off the stations in the 1970s. Only pride in what they have kept alive all these years, nostalgia for what they made of the hard times, how they bore the brunt of white ignorance and endured as a people, and still endure.

Jakamarra climbs to his feet. He winces as he straightens up. Many years ago he was breaking in a horse. The horse threw him and crushed his ankle. He received no first aid. His ankle mended. But now that he is old it is seizing up. He walks with a limp.

"Bloody good horseman, this here Ringer," Jakamarra says as we walk around the side of the house. "Best horseman at Wave Hill, you know."

"That so?"

Ringer smiles. "Pretty good," he says.

We come to a tin shed. On the wall of the shed someone has scrawled in crayon: DAVID DANIELS ONE AND ONLY OK.

Jakamarra tugs at the tin door. The door scrapes an arc in the red dirt and we step into a dark room that smells of rotten wood and wet earth.

As my eyes get used to the gloom I notice four painted posts stuck in the ground. These are "tjuringa," Ringer says, sacred objects. They are not Warlpiri. They are Kartangarurru. If anyone damaged or stole these objects he would be killed. On a wooden shelf against the back wall is a moldering saddle and a bunch of spears. Old Jakamarra brings the flat of his hand down on the saddle, slapping off the dust. He grips the pommel with one hand and gestures at the painted posts with the other. "Now I bin show 'em you," he says. "I bin show 'em you these tjuringa."

I imagine Jakamarra to be saying that his saddle is as much a relic as the painted posts.

We return to the yard where Nora is standing by the fire, holding her grandchild against her breast. I tell Francine we should be going. It's 450 miles to Katherine and we need to get there before nightfall.

The road is a strip of bitumen through the bush. The desert is already well behind us. This is cattle country now.

Ringer points out the cuttings of old roads, abandoned stock camps, droving routes, the sites of bores. He describes how he walked the length and breadth of this country long before he rode across it on horseback.

There is a question I have been wanting to ask Ringer ever since we left Kalkaringi.

"What made you leave Wave Hill?"

Ringer relates what happened:

They were at the main camp. It was dinner time. Ringer was sitting outside his humpy with a pannikin of tea and a hunk of bread and dripping. When the station manager rode up, Ringer took no notice. Even when the manager's shadow gashed the ground in front of him, Ringer did not bother to look up.

The manager moved to one side and kicked Ringer hard in the sole of his boot.

"On your feet, mate!"

Ringer flinched, but still did not look up.

"Come on you lazy bugger, get up!"

"Tucker time now, boss," Ringer said, "I go back to work after dinner."

The manager swung his rifle up and flicked Ringer's hat away into the dirt.

"None of your cheek, you black bastard! Tucker time's over. You saddle up now!"

Ringer placed his pannikin on the ground, stood up, and took three paces to retrieve his hat. He stuck it back on his head. Then he walked over to his humpy. He pulled a spear from among the ribs of wattle that supported the roof. Then he strode back to where the manager was standing.

The manager saw Ringer coming and snapped back the safety catch of his rifle.

Ringer kept coming.

Ten yards from where the manager was standing, Ringer lifted his spear. The manager shouted that he would shoot. Ringer did not hear the abuse. He tensed the sinews of his arm and gripped the shaft of the spear. Five yards from the manager, he rammed the spear hard to within inches of the whiteman's chest.

"Chuck it down!" Ringer ordered.

The manager let the rifle slip from his hand into the bulldust.

Ringer finishes his story:

"Had to cut out now," he says, with no hint of sarcasm or humor. "Go north, longa Victoria River Downs, work there a little bit . . ."

I look out at dusty roads leading off into the wilderness, ghost gums clinging to outcrops of red rock, dry creek beds, windmills, cattle standing in paddocks of churned up earth.

Ringer worked on almost all of these stations. Sometimes it was for a season, sometimes two, but always he moved on.

We do not talk now. We stare at the changing landscape.

My train of thought is interrupted by the women calling out the name of the creek we are crossing. They too recognize this road, know all the stations along it. Each has her own story to tell of working in white homesteads as a kitchenmaid or cook, waiting at tables, fetching and carrying for the missus, minding her kids.

It is dark when we see the lights of Katherine above the bush. Everyone is hungry. I drive nervously along the road into town, blinded by the headlights of oncoming cars.

At the first fast-food shop, I clumsily turn the Toyota across the road and ram the concrete curb. Some young blokes on the footpath step back, startled. They gawk in astonishment, then shout out that I should use the fucking parking lot.

I park the Toyota and climb out, limbs cramped and sore from the hours behind the wheel. Nora, Jedda, and Pearl hurry into the shop to order the inevitable parcels of fish and chips, sausages, chicken wings, and diet drinks. The kids crowd around a video game, watching cosmic sparks fly.

I catch a glimpse of myself in the plate glass window: gaunt face, the stubble of a five-day beard, hair matted with dirt and yellowed by woodsmoke. I examine my hands in the neon light of the shop: the skin grimy and calloused, the fingernails broken. The shock of seeing myself in the shop window gives way to a sense that I am a stranger in this place, disoriented by the arctic lighting, the freezers stocked with food, the video game lurid and sizzling in the corner, the signs informing me that Coke is the real thing and Pepsi the right one, and the measured tone with which the newsreader on the counter TV gives details of some calamity on the other side of the world. I walk back to the parking lot to find Ringer.

When the women arrive with the takeout, we sit bunched together on the asphalt lot, picking at the greasy food with our fingers. Locals pass up and down the street. I feel perversely happy.

An hour later, at Katherine Hospital, Ringer looks anything but happy. He sits cross-legged on the hospital bed as if he is sitting under a bough-shade in the desert. He is garbed in a green gown. His arms and legs resemble burned sticks. He is clutching his two boomerangs, wondering where to stash them. I help him slip them under the mattress where he can easily reach them.

Nora fills a pitcher of water and places it on the bedside table. Jedda says something to her in Warlpiri, her voice hoarse and hushed. The kids skate about on the polished linoleum, their faces smeared with mucus and lollipop.

It makes me shudder to see Ringer looking so forlorn. I grasp his hand, assuring him everything will be OK, that we will be back on Saturday to pick him up. "That's all right, Jupurrurla," he says. "You can go now."

Driving through the night toward Barunga, we keep running into smoke from bush fires. Filaments of ash waft through the windows as we crawl through the smoke.

At the turn off to Barunga there are battered cars parked on the roadside. Our headlights move over knots of young men swigging beer from cans.

Nora is alarmed. "We don't want no grog. We don't want to camp with drunken fellas."

Driving into the settlement Nora and Jedda fall silent. They peer into the bush, where campfires flicker and the dark shapes of people move to and fro. "We gotta find that Lajamanu mob, Napanangka," Jedda says to Francine. "We gotta find that Warlpiri camp."

We locate the Lajamanu mob, camped along the creek near a sports field. Heaps of firewood have been dumped every few yards on the grassy domain. There is an ablution block too, with water gushing from a broken faucet.

We unload our swags, spread our groundsheets, light fires, brew tea. The kids disappear into the long grass beside the creek.

Nora and Pearl and Jedda sit on their swags with enamel mugs of tea, looking glum and wary. A rock band is playing. Francine suggests we go over and see what's going on.

We cross the road and make our way among the wigwams of white hippies. As we approach the sound stage the noise is deafening.

It is like walking into a painting by Bruegel. Aboriginals of all ages mill around a hotdog stand. Young men wearing land rights T-shirts and red sweatbands clutch cans of beer and cast lascivious looks after groups of giggling girls. A man supports himself unsteadily with one arm behind the sound stage, then vomits. Another man pisses against the trunk of a tree. Mangy dogs sniff around the fast food stalls. The ground is a trampled pulp of plastic bags and orange peel. There are VB beer cans everywhere.

On stage the rock band is belting out an anthem about oppression and black pride. Didgeridoos, clapping sticks, electric guitars. Hoarse declamations about stolen land and the need to stand up for one's rights. A black girl in a white tasseled dress shimmies sensually and flashes her white teeth, lip-synching the words of the song. A young man rips his shirt off and clambers up on stage to join her. She dances in a daze, as though he were invisible.

We push through the crowd. There is the pungent odor of unwashed bodies and stale beer. Jedda and Pearl shriek as they recognize kinfolk and friends from far-flung settlements. People have come by bus and car from all over the Top End, and as far away as Alice Springs and Yuendumu. Everyone is smashed. A young woman stumbles up to Jedda and thrusts her baby into Jedda's arms before plunging back into the crowd. "Do you know her!" Francine shouts above the din. "That Warlpiri mob from Alice Springs," Jedda shouts back. "This my granddaughter!"

Exhausted from the long day's journey and battered by the music we wend our way back to our camp, Jedda holding her granddaughter against her shoulder.

We crawl into our swags. Across the creek, the bush echoes with drunken catcalls. Someone hurls abuse at someone else in the darkness. We hear the explosion of glass as a car windshield is bashed in. "No good here," Jedda mutters from under her blankets. "Might be too much drinking tonight, too much fighting." The band thumps away. I lie on my back, looking up at the stars. My last thoughts before falling asleep are of Ringer, sitting bolt upright on his bed in the Katherine Hospital, his boomerangs under the mattress.

By the time we leave Barunga, everyone is fed up. Nora is disgusted that the Lajamanu football team went on a binge and were too hung over to play their game. Pearl mumbles about the drunken fights that kept her awake at night.

We drive back to Katherine through the smoke of smoldering bush fires.

Ringer is waiting outside the hospital, sitting under a tree with his old Stetson pulled down over his eyes. His arm is in a sling, and he has a bottle of pills in his hand.

It is too late in the day to hit the road, so we decide to camp overnight in Katherine and push on to Lajamanu in the morning. Nora says we can camp at the trucking depot, just south of the railway tracks. This is where they usually go when they are in Katherine.

But the depot is surrounded by a high fence and the gate padlocked. "*Kardiya* [whites] bin lock 'im up," Nora says.

I suggest we try the public camping ground; there are signs out along the highway—white caravans against blue backgrounds—indicating how to get there.

No one demurs, and ten minutes later we are driving through the brick entrance gates onto what could be a golf course. The grass is kept green by a sprinkler system, and there are young eucalypt trees everywhere, tied to white stakes. I pay a fee at the office and drive on toward the phalanges of tents and tourist caravans.

It is like driving through the streets of some middle-class neighborhood. The campers have replicated their suburban lots. Mums and dads sit on folding chairs at folding tables, reading newspapers or peeling spuds. You can smell barbecued sausages and coleslaw.

We park well away from the crowd. Everyone gets out of the Toyota and stands around. After a while Pearl and Jedda sit down on the grass and start a game of cards. The kids wander over to the fence and crawl through into the ploughed paddock beyond. Ringer and Nora make no move to unroll their swags or light a fire. Though no one says anything, I know it is a mistake to have come here.

When I announce we are moving on, the relief is immediate. "No firewood at that place," Nora says. "Too many *kardiya,*" Pearl adds, touching a common chord. "Too many *kardiya,*" everyone choruses, laughing awkwardly, as we head down the river road to Morrow's Farm.

Nora and Ringer know Morrow's Farm from way back. The Morrows have always allowed Warlpiri people to camp at their farm. The Morrows are missionaries, Ringer explains, though Mr. Morrow was widowed several years ago. "He bin lose missus belong 'im," is the way Ringer puts it.

We stop at the house and introduce ourselves, then drive down a rutted track past groves of mango trees, fields of carnations, and greenhouses, to the river.

We clear the ground, light fires, and spread out our swags in a line. The kids race off into the bush. The women keep repeating how good it is to be here, away from the drunken revelry at Barunga, away from the camping ground which has already been mythologized as "that *kardiya* place."

I wander upstream on my own, following a path along the riverbank. There are groves of native palms, tresses of green weed in the current. I walk as far as the weir and sit on the gnarled bole of a paperbark gum from where I watch black grebes diving into the pool and a solitary white heron stalking the shallows.

Unbroken
the weir water
runs through my mind,
smoothing
like a hand
over rucked sheets
or as the wind
might comb
long grass

Something Ringer said comes to mind. When I asked him what it was like in the hospital he said he did not like being closed in. He did not like walls. They made it hard for him to see or hear or smell what was going on around him. He missed a fire in the open, a windbreak, the bush. I was reminded of something Pincher Jampijinpa once told me in Lajamanu: "A house is just like a big jail."

In the West we have a habit of thinking of home as a house. Walls make us feel secure. Individual rooms give us a sense of privacy. We tend to believe that living in a house is synonymous with being civilized. We have an ingrained prejudice against nomads and drifters. With proprietal pride we will defend the privacy of our homes but fail to grasp that nomadic people feel just as strongly about the places they hold dear, the landscapes they call home. Perhaps this bias has its origins in the Neolithic when human beings first learned to domesticate animals and cultivate grain. Those who remained beyond the pale of human settlement were seen as threatening and barbaric.

This was the drift of what whites told me about Aboriginals when I first came to Central Australia. Backpackers, barbers, bus drivers, and barflies all presumed to lecture me on how Aboriginals couldn't handle liquor and couldn't handle responsibility. It was because of their traditional hunting and gathering way of life that they were such no-hopers. They were naturally disposed toward a catch-as-catch-can existence, greedily taking advantage of whatever resources came to hand but laying up nothing for lean times, setting no store by the future. Whites are dismayed at the seeming indifference of Aboriginals to possessions. I was told how an Aboriginal will buy a brand-new Toyota with mining royalties, then wreck the vehicle in a matter of weeks. Houses were also allowed to go to rack and ruin. I was told that Aboriginals couldn't hold down jobs or stick at anything for long. Sooner or later they "go walkabout" and leave you in the lurch. The fact that Aboriginals visit kindred and sacred places or attend funerals was never mentioned. "Walkabout" is invariably described as a wholly irrational or instinctual urge that seizes every Aboriginal from time to time. Recently, I watched an international tennis tournament on TV during which a woman commentator observed that Evonne Goolagong, who won the Wimbledon Women's Single title in 1971, sometimes "went walkabout." By this she meant that Evonne Goolagong's concentration sometimes wavered.

We live in built-up environments. Our habitual patterns of movement in the everyday world are constrained by the parameters of houses, buildings, rooms, and thoroughfares. Ours is a *habitus* of walls and enclosures, of well-marked exits and entrances, paths and roads. This material *habitus* determines a particular sensibility which sees boundaries as a precondition of meaning. The constructed world— nailed, bolted, screwed, and cemented into place—predisposes us to make sense of experience by cutting it up and framing it with concepts and categories. For us, security is a function of the substantiality of the ideas and places we construct. Existentially and discursively we are less at home with indeterminate images and open horizons.

For the householder, life without walls is practically inconceivable. Belongings, family members, one's very thoughts, have to be held and housed. "Good Homes Build Character," is the slogan of the Better Homes in America Movement. A broken home means a broken life. This is undoubtedly why many Westerners regard nomadism as the epitome of primitiveness. Nomads are made out to be negations of ourselves. We cultivate; they plunder. When whites first encountered the Athapaskan Indians in northern British Columbia they felt contempt, suspicion, and fear at the Indians "forthright manner, indifference to material goods, and lack of permanent dwellings." Early European descriptions of Eskimos compared their "uncertaine abodes" to dens and "holes like to a Foxe or Conny berry," so calling into question the people's "capacitie to culture." Emile Durkheim, in *The Elementary Forms of the Religious Life,* called Australian Aboriginal religion "the most primitive and simple religion which it is possible to find." Aboriginal worldviews are "rudimentary," he wrote, because "the house and even the hut are still unknown" among them.

This is the voice of the propertied middle classes, of the realtor. This is the image of home as a private, domestic, comfortable abode. A place of retreat. A metaphor for intimacy and inwardness.

But in Europe this notion of home is no more than 300 years old. Its origin is inextricably tied to the rise of the bourgeoisie in the seventeenth century. Before that time, as John Berger notes, home connoted a place, a village, a group of kin, a state of being.

The term *home* (Old Norse *Heimr,* High German *heim,* Greek *komi,* meaning "village") has, since a long time, been taken over by two kinds of moralists, both dear to those who wield power. The notion of *home* became the keystone for a code of domestic morality, safeguarding the property (which included the women) of the family. Simultaneously the notion of *homeland* supplied the first article of faith for patriotism, persuading men to die in wars which often served no other interest except that of a minority of their ruling class. Both usages have hidden the original meaning.

The modern imagination is profoundly conditioned by the habits of household life. Gaston Bachelard speaks of the house as our "first universe," and recounts how it shelters our daydreaming, cradles our thoughts and memories, and provides us with a sense of stability. Throughout our lives, the house in which we are born remains "physically inscribed in us." In an essay called *My House,* Primo Levi speaks in a similar vein of the house in which he lived almost all his life: "I live in my house as I live inside my skin."

The Eurocentric bias to see all human existence from the perspective of the sedentary cultivator or householder finds expression in the work of Martin Heidegger, who observed that the German verbs *bauen,* to build, *buan,* to dwell, and *bin/bist*—words for be—are cognate; hence, human existence is a matter of building, of being housed. "To be a human being," he writes, "means to dwell . . . to preserve and care for, specifically to till the soil, to cultivate the vine." Marx, Jung, and Freud also employ house as a root metaphor. Marx describes economic infrastructures as the foundations (*grundlage*) on which are raised the edifice (*überbau*) of a social structure. Jung compares the human psyche to a house: the cellar is the unconscious, the attic the imagination. Freud extends the metaphor. The unconscious, he remarks, can be likened to an anteroom adjoining "a sort of reception room, in which consciousness resides." On the threshold between these two rooms stands a doorkeeper, who censors out unacceptable stimuli. Architectonic metaphors of construction also pervade the sociology of knowledge, structuralism and post-structuralism.

Among the books I took with me to Lajamanu was Germaine Greer's compelling memoir, *Daddy, We Hardly Knew You.* There is a passage in this book that arrested me. Speaking of the lure of academe and of the orderly world of books, Germaine Greer writes: "In any library in the world, I am at home, unselfconscious, still and absorbed."

Nothing could have been more foreign to how I felt in the field. For the most part I thrived on the boisterous and makeshift life I was obliged to lead among the Warlpiri. I liked the way men circled around a point when I questioned them. They moved about in their discourse as they moved about in the desert, never going in a straight line, always alive to the landmarks around them, changes in the weather, movements of game, scarce reservoirs of water.

In the West we tend to establish routines, determine boundaries, draw up timetables, fetishize our fixed addresses. Rules of perspective draw the eye back to one fixed point of view. We strive for watertight arguments, truths that hold good for everyone, for all time. We print our thoughts in indelible ink and bind the pages in a book.

I got to thinking of the phrases we commonly use to dismiss an argument we do not agree with: Does not come to the point. Wanders off the subject. Goes off on a tangent. Goes around and around in circles. Loses the thread. Chops and changes. Fails to follow an idea through . . .

I thought of the eternal conflict of interests between townsman and itinerant. The uneasy glances of whites as Nora, Pearl, Jedda, and their kids wandered barefoot and ill-kempt through a Katherine shopping mall. I kept thinking of gypsies camped on the edges of European towns where they were not welcome. The stereotype of the vagabond as a liar and a thief. Errant and irreverant. Beholden to no one. Laws unto themselves.

But isn't this the language we use of anyone who goes beyond the pale, who challenges the established order of things? And isn't it also true that banishment and forced migration are the very condition of modernity, a condition Peter Berger calls the homeless mind?

"The house is past," writes Theodor Adorno, reflecting on the post-war world. In an obvious allusion to Heidegger, he writes, "Dwelling, in the proper sense, is now impossible." Today, one is fated "not to be at home in one's home."

I walk back upstream to where the kids are swimming. I strip and plunge into the warm, amber water, and swim with them. I roll over on my back and let myself drift. Above me, clouds like anonymous continents fray and thin at their edges, dispersing into the cobalt spaces of the sky.

NINE

There's too much poverty below us.

Every leaf defines its limits.

All roots have their histories.

—Derek Walcott

The boulders glowed like cyclopean firestones in the fading light. To the south there seemed nothing but the drab green of spinifex desert.

I followed Zack's hand signals, turning the Toyota onto the rutted track that led along the fence. Every few yards there were signs: ABORIGINAL SACRED SITE. KEEP OUT.

"This our country," Zack said. "We boss here."

It had taken a long time. Zack Jakamarra is a hard man to pin down. The few times I did succeed in getting him talking, he had responded perfunctorily to my questions then stood up and walked away. I had all but given up on him when, one morning, he turned up at the caravan to see me.

Zack suffered from sandy blight. He kept wiping his eyes with the sleeve of his parka. He seemed irritated. He complained about having no firewood.

I suggested we go bush and collect some.

I let Zack decide which track to take.

"Keep going," he said, chopping at the air with the edge of his hand.

We ended up off the beaten track, and walked around for half an hour wrenching branches from dead trees.

Zack was keen to know what people had been telling me about The Granites.

"A lot of things," I said, but admitted I was at a loss to understand all the ways people traced connections to the area.

We sat down, and Zack reviewed the different Dreamings at The Granites, tracing circles and songlines in the red dirt, recalling key place names. Though well-versed in the ceremony associated with these Dreamings, Zack had to confess that there was a limit to what he knew.

"Maybe Pincher Jampijinpa knows that one," he said caustically. "Maybe Pincher Jampinjinpa can tell you about that one."

I tried to steer the conversation away from the ambiguities of The Granites. I asked Zack where he was born.

He turned his head, jutting his jaw, and named a place far to the south. Ngurripatu was an important two-kangaroo Dreaming site.

"Your father's father's country?" I asked.

"Yuwayi."

But Zack's father had died when Zack was still "in the coolimon." His mother married one of her late husband's brothers, and Zack moved north with her to the Lander River area. Zack was "grown up" there (*wiri manuju*) by his second father, an important man "in the business." "When you young," Zack said, "you travel 'round, learn business. Where my father died, where my father's brothers lived, I bin go there. They bin grow 'im up me. Make me a man."

Of his father's Dreaming, Zack did not know as much as he would like. But he knew the section of the songline that ran through the country where he was born.

"From Warlangurlu to Ngurripatu," Zack said. "I hold that one. I boss for that one. After Ngurripatu, we hand it over now. Another mob run 'im south. Different country now . . . don't know that one . . ."

I thought Zack had told me all he was going to tell me. I got up and began throwing the firewood onto the roof rack of the Toyota. But then he surprised me by saying we should go to The Granites.

"You and me," he said. "Just you and me."

I stopped the Toyota at the gate and reversed into the mulga. Zack got out and inspected the gate. It was padlocked. He was all for opening the gate "Yapa way" by unbolting it at the hinges, but I shouted to him that it wasn't worth the trouble.

We climbed through the fence. Zack was astonishingly nimble for a man in his late sixties. Or was it that returning here had reinvigorated him? All day, traveling the long road from Lajamanu, Zack had entertained me with accounts of what it had been like at The Granites when he worked there in the late 1930s. I was curious to know what

Zack thought of it now, what memories would be jogged loose, what he would have to say about the immense mounds of detritus half a mile from us, the laborious ore trucks in low gear toiling up the spiral road from the pit, the devastated landscape.

"Is this where you used to camp?" I asked.

"Yuwayi," Zack said.

The closer I came to Purrkiji, the more overawed I was. Huge boulders, heaped as if by hand, pitted by rain, burnished by wind, scorched by the sun. In the Dreaming, this was the main camp of the possum men. To the south, a low hill marked the single women's camp. The single men's camps were slightly to the north.

Zack pointed out two rust-red boulders on top of the hill. This was where, in the Dreaming, the two mulga men had climbed and looked homeward.

I had heard the story many times but now, confronted by the place where those long-ago events had unfolded, I wanted to stop and let it all sink in. But Zack was hurrying on, following a camel track across the grass stubble.

I trailed him around the boulders to a grass-fringed, sandy depression at the foot of a massive slab of granite. "Proper Purrkiji," Zack said. This was where people used to dig for water. The soakage was formed in the Dreaming when the two mulga men uprooted spiderbushes here.

Zack led me into a defile where some smooth spiderbush (*yirdimardi*) was growing. It was in flower. This was the tree which the two mulga men, traveling from Manjamanja ("mulga-mulga") in the east, had sought so avidly. Its shiny black fruit had been too bitter to eat, but they had learned to cook the tuber-like roots in the embers of their fires.

A flock of diamond finches fluttered suddenly above us, their crimson wings catching the light.

"*Jiyiki*," Zack said. He told me that you could always rely on diamond finches to lead you to water in the desert.

I followed him around the rock face to a waterhole, deep in the shadows beneath a fissured boulder. In the Dreaming, a snake had come up from the south. It had camped near here, eyeing the possum women in their *jilimi* from a safe distance. It then came to this place and plunged downward, surfacing at the soakage on the other side of the hill. One of the possum men fought and killed it there.

Zack climbed down into the shadows, and beckoned me to follow.

"Proper Purrkiji water, this one," he said, scooping up a handful and slaking his thirst. I drank too. The water was cool and tasted of the rock.

There was some wild tobacco growing in the wet sand. Zack picked it gleefully and stuffed it inside his parka. "Proper cheeky one!" he said. In the past wild tobacco was exchanged for spears, boomerangs, and grinding-stones. But it had also caused as many wars as women.

The sun was getting low in the sky. I suggested to Zack that we think of making camp. We walked back to the Toyota and fetched our swags and supplies.

An eerie silence had fallen. The crackling of our fire did nothing to dispel it.

Zack drew a billy of water from the rock hole. I opened cans of bully beef and baked beans. When I cut my finger on a jagged edge of the tin, Zack reprimanded me. Then he fell silent, sitting hunched in his parka, staring out across the plain. For some reason, he had stuck a stalk of aromatic grass (*jujuminyiminyi*) through the pierced septum of his nose.

I handed Zack a plate of food. As we ate, he spoke a little about the place where we were camped. Warlpiri used to live here. It was where they used to initiate young men. They had made Nugget a man here.

But there was no trace of anyone now on the wind-blown ground, or among the half-buried boulders . . .

The moon, in its last quarter, was a sliver in the darkening sky. But the stars made up for the light the moon failed to give, blanching the spinifex and throwing ominous shadows across the ground. I could feel the body heat of the gargantuan boulders behind me.

I was remembering a remark Zack had made earlier in the day when he was talking about the gold lust that had brought white men into this wilderness. "Gold is the whitefella's Dreaming," Zack had said.

It is a story as old as humankind, because it is the story of Everyman. Sometimes it is cast as the story of a journey into a wild and distant place in search of riches, knowledge, or enlightenment. A questing hero leaves home and hazards his life on discovering some magical property which will restore a lost reputation or fortune, grant immortality or great power, or bring the boon of civilization to his people. But whatever the goal, be it spiritual illumination, scientific knowledge, or material wealth, the existential theme is always the same. We are told that everyone must sooner or later leave the secure confines of his homeplace and strike out into the world, make his own way, assume control of his own destiny. Only when one has proven oneself able to withstand the vicissitudes of the world can one return home and create a world. It is the theme that underlies rites of initiation in which a neophyte must take leave of his kith and kin, go into the bush and die to his childhood in order to be reborn a full adult. And the same theme finds expression in the structure of scientific inquiry in which one ventures a hypothesis and then tests it out against the rigors of the real world. Perhaps the allure of anthropology is the way it merges initiatory experience and experimental method in the same project. The changes wrought in the ethnographer living in another culture are as significant as the changes he or she observes in those with whom he or she lives.

Sitting in the semi-darkness, looking into the flickering flames of our fire, my thoughts kept returning to the parallelism between the ethnographer's pursuit of knowledge and the prospector's search for gold. Gold is both a material thing and a metaphor. Good as gold. Worth its weight in gold. The golden mean. In Central Australia, Aboriginals are not surprised that whites so often find mineral wealth at sacred sites. Nowadays, they sometimes speak of such sites as "gold," reminding us that there are many equivalent metaphors for what one holds dear, for what one values most.

Suddenly, Zack got up without a word and walked off into the darkness. I supposed that he was going to have a piss.

I crawled into my swag and lay on my back. The stars were like hoar frost in the cold spaces of the sky.

When I was a boy, I was entranced by books and films about the search for treasure in exotic places. *King Solomon's Mines. The Treasure of the Sierra Madre.* The narratives were allegorical. It was not the prospect of gold that captivated me, but the imperative sense of that arduous journey away from home without which no one ever proves his worth or comes into his own.

One book appealed to me more than all the others, possibly because it chronicled events that took place in my part of the world. In *Lasseter's Last Ride* (1931), Ion Idriess recounts the story of an expedition into the Central Australian desert in 1930 in search of a gold reef that a man called Harold Bell Lasseter had stumbled upon more than thirty years before. According to Lasseter, he had gotten lost in the desert in 1897, while traveling to Western Australia. One horse dead, the other dying, his food supplies running out, he stumbled upon a gold reef that ran for seven miles across the desert. After being rescued by an Afghan camel driver and recovering his health, Lasseter and a mate went back into the desert to find the reef. After four months of great hardship they located it 300 miles west of Alice Springs. But they were less lucky in their search for backers to finance a mining company. Lasseter's companion died. Lasseter went abroad.

The expedition that set out in 1930 would also fail to find the reef. The six white men who threw in their lot with the enigmatic Lasseter were defeated by the desert and increasing doubts in the veracity of Lasseter's story. In the end, Lasseter was left to press on alone. His companions never saw him alive again. Exactly what befell him may never be known. The diaries found with his body contain notes that are often at odds with accounts subsequently given by the Aboriginal people with whom Lasseter lived his last days. Whether Lasseter's reef exists is still an open question. But it is Lasseter's story which is important, not the whereabouts of the gold. When Billy Marshall-Stoneking was researching his book on Lasseter he spoke to Aboriginal people who knew Lasseter and buried him when he died. For them, Lasseter's story participated in the Dreaming. As Shorty Lungkarta, an elderly Pintupi man, put it, "That Lasseter, that's a whitefella dreaming."

That night I was awakened by voices in the darkness. I propped myself up on my elbow and listened. My heart raced. Zack was gone. The fire was only a heap of embers. I listened again, peering into the darkness.

"Jakamarra," I called.

He seemed to materialize out of the rocks.

"Was that you?" I asked.

"*Kurdaitcha*," Zack said. He sat down and poked a piece of wood into the embers.

"Where?" I asked.

"Can't seem 'im," Zack said. The *kurdaitcha* wore feather shoes and left no prints.

I asked him to tell me more. They were *milalpa*, Zack said. They were the real custodians of the place. Zack had heard them talking in the darkness. They wanted to know who we were and what we were doing there. Zack had gone out to greet them, telling them who his father was, and his father's father, explaining how he was linked to The Granites. He had also explained my presence. But Zack was troubled. He felt that we should not have come alone. You should always come to a sacred site with your *kurdungurlu.* You should really approach the site naked, so that the *milalpa* can identify you properly.

"And if you don't?" I asked.

"*Kurdaitcha* can sing you, make you sick, make bad things happen to you."

"Do you want to leave?"

"No. This my place. Me belong Purrkiji."

We talked for a while about the *milalpa,* who reminded me of the *djinn* (*nyenne*) among the Kuranko. Here too was a shadowy, parallel society of bush spirits who, according to Zack, could be glimpsed at times or heard whistling and talking, who had skin names like ordinary human beings, who married, and walked around looking for water, digging yams, hunting kangaroos, but left no tracks or traces of their hearths. What I found most arresting about Zack's description of the *milalpa* was that they had obviously been unaffected by contact with whites—an abiding image of a half-remembered social world that Zack, in his lifetime, had seen so transformed.

I asked Zack what life had been like in the old days, and pressed him to tell me about his upbringing.

When his father, Wijimi, died, Zack was "grown up" by two classificatory "fathers." Mupuka hailed from Yuwirnnjiwita, near Piliwarna-warna. Zack spoke of his authority in terms of the politics of marriage. "Mupuka bin grabbing wives from every place," Zack said. "Every-time a brother died, Mupuka took up the wife." Zack's other "father" was Kurrurumanpa, whose home country was centered on Pawala. Kurrurumanpa had no children of his own. Both Mupuka and Kurrur-manpa were kinsmen of the traditional owners of The Granites. They were *ngurrara jinta,* "one camp," or *walalja,* "countrymen," Zack said. But the traditional owners for The Granites (*Yaturlu Yaturlu*), were all killed in bloody skirmishes with whites. Since Mupuka "knew the business" for The Granites he took over the place, "looking after it" and running its rituals—just as he'd looked after Zack when his father passed away. When Mupuka died, Kurrurumanpa took over custody of the site. It was through these men that Zack acquired his knowledge of the possum Dreaming from Wapilingki ("Coolibah") in the east, and the bush currant (*yawakiyi*) Dreaming closely associated with it. He also knew many other Dreamings throughout the Tanami that belonged to the paired subsections of Jakamarra/Jupurrurla—Nakamarra/Napurrurla. But Zack did not claim to be *kirda* for The Granites. "I bin grown up there," he said. "I know that one. I can run that one. But that place is really for Jupurrurla. Nobody else. We hold that one. We look after it like you whitefellas look after your house and garden."

As Zack went on to name the places where his "fathers" had passed away, I realized that what informed his sense of belonging to the land was the fact that his forebears were buried there, and there was nowhere that was not permeated by the memory of their absence.

The dawn broke windless and cold. The silence penetrated to the core of my being, a silence unlike any silence I had ever known, a silence unlike the hiatus between sound and sound, because it was unyielding and unflagging. It possessed that place, dispersing my sense of who I was.

I got the fire going. Zack went to the rock hole and filled our billy can. We made tea and watched the sun rising over the plain.

Zack's eyes were bad. He wiped his sleeve across his face.

"Lot of people bin pass away here," Zack said.

Pincher Jampijinpa had told me a story his father had told him about whites killing many Warlpiri people at The Granites. I asked Zack if this was true.

"Take girls," Zack said, "shoot 'im man, grab 'im woman again, take her away now, shoot that man. That's all."

Zack explained that when white miners first came to the Tanami, Warlpiri men often sent their wives to sleep with them as a way of getting flour, tea, and tobacco. "Might be a blanket, might be sugar, might be anything." Frequently, whites simply abducted Warlpiri women, telling their husbands they had too many wives. There was often bloodshed when Warlpiri men sought to reclaim their women.

One of the bloodiest incidents took place at Walangala rock hole. It involved a Warlpiri woman who had been working for a white cook at The Granites mine, washing his clothes, sharing his bed. The woman's husband, Kutji Jungarrayi, wanted his wife back. There were only four other whites living at The Granites. One day, three of them went off prospecting while the fourth set out for Alice Springs to buy provisions. That same day, Jungarrayi sent his *kurdungurlu* to the cook and demanded that his wife be sent back to him. The cook refused. Jungarrayi took his spears, fighting boomerangs, and a knife. He tried to spear the cook, but his spear flew wide of its mark. Jungarrayi then overpowered the hapless cook and slit open his belly. Later, with the help of other men, Jungarrayi buried the cook in a shallow grave.

When the miners returned and discovered the dead body they took off for the police post at Ti-Tree, 250 miles to the west. A police expedition was mounted. They came on camel and horseback.

The night before the police arrived at The Granites a Warlpiri man had a dream of mayhem and gunfire. For many people it was a bad omen, and they sought refuge in a cave called Jukukarinjiwarnu. Others remained camped in the open. The police surrounded these people as they slept. As the dawn came up they opened fire, killing many. Then they went in pursuit of the others. Among those killed were many men who were "really Purrkiji," ceremonial custodians of the sacred sites. "Too many," Zack said ruefully. "Might be a million they shot."

What stunned me about Zack's account was his insistence that Warlpiri had been "cheeky" (aggressive) and "silly" (ignorant). Those people were "myalls," Zack said. Bush people who did not understand white ways.

But what of the savagery of the police reprisals? Could this really be compared with vengeance raids in the pre-European past?

Zack wasn't sure. Certainly, in the old days, if an Aboriginal man abducted the wife of another man, there would be a vengeance raid to get her back. But, yes, Zack agreed, though it was all right for Jungarrayi to kill the cook who stole his wife, it was wrong that so many innocent people should be murdered in retaliation. "They shouldn't shoot that big mob now," Zack said. "They belonged to that land."

"Were any of your family killed?" I asked.

"Not there," Zack said. "Other places. Early days. Before we." He recounted what happened at a place called Yulpawarnu, some twenty-five miles from The Granites. A group of Warlpiri came upon the camp of some white stockmen. The whites weren't there, so the Warlpiri took their tent and some tobacco and flour. It was evening when the stockmen returned to their camp and found their supplies gone. They waited until morning, saddled their horses, and tracked the Warlpiri eastward. "Clear country, no mulga," Zack said. The stockmen came upon some Warlpiri girls who directed them to Kakarawarnu where the main group was camped. By the time the whites arrived at the camp, the thieves had fled. The whites told people they could keep the flour and tobacco, but they demanded that their tent be returned to them. Zack's uncle, Warana Jukurrpa Japanangka, was there. Japanangka's answer to the belligerent demands of the whites was to hurl his boomerangs at their horses. The whites opened fire, killing Japanangka and two other men. "Finish now, no humbug," Zack said, concluding that his uncle had been "too cheeky" and should not have accosted the whites.

We rolled our swags, packed our cooking gear, and trudged back to the Toyota. Off in the distance two camels crossed the plain.

The mine was a complex of modular offices and living quarters with eucalypts planted around them. Here and there were rusted relics from the old days. The skeletal chassis and cab of a truck. Bits of machinery.

We drove around for a while until we found the main office. Zack went in ahead of me. He was nervous, but wanted to tell the mine manager who he was and explain our business at The Granites.

The office was air-conditioned. In his bare feet, frayed bell-bottoms, and grubby windbreaker, Zack looked as incongruous as I felt. It was hard to guess what the mining manager made of us, but he took pains to show us the greatest courtesy. Zack's manner was an odd mixture of bravado and deference. He forthrightly announced that he was a traditional owner for The Granites, then stood cap in hand, so to speak, waiting for the mine manager to respond.

The manager asked Zack if he remembered Gordon Chapman, the son of Colin Chapman who headed the company that owned The Granites' leases in the 1930s when Zack worked there. Apparently, Gordon Chapman was dying of cancer in Darwin.

Zack seemed not to understand. He was looking increasingly nervous. He shifted his feet, then declared, "Right. We going now!"

We walked out into dazzling sunlight and climbed into the Toyota. Zack directed me down the road to where the old stamper battery stood. This was where they used to work, shoveling ore into the mortar box. This is where old Jakamarra got his army greatcoat caught in the machinery one night and was crushed to death.

"That battery working all night, all day. We bin working, no money, poor bugger, no anything! Working all day, just for tucker and tobacco! I bin chew tobacco, drink tea, that's all. Little bit of clothes, short trousers, only singlets, that's all. No blankets! Just this bag, big bag, we got to have a lot of big bags, oh really big ones, flour bags, big one, you know, like a 100 bags of flour. That one we bin use 'im. Working no money, poor bugger."

"How many whites were at The Granites when you were working there?"

"You know how many *kardiya* we bin have 'im? Old Chapman. And

Gordon Chapman. That's his son. And Paddy Chapman. That's his son too. Chapman is boss for everybody."

Colin Chapman in 1943 reached this conclusion, after fifty years employing Aboriginals: "I must admit that they still puzzle me in many ways & all old hands will tell you the same story, they are much like grown up children with advanced Socialist tendencies . . ." I was intrigued to know what Zack remembered of him.

"Right, I tell you!" Zack said enthusiastically. "Old Chapman, he bin finish right along Alice Springs, poor bugger. He big bloke. He never work, that old fella. He wait for his sons gunna work all day. And yapa! Big mob yapa. Yapa people bin working hard, too many people, working for nothing, only tucker. And no blankets!"

Nowadays, a lot of well-meaning whites lament the way Aboriginals were ill-treated and exploited. But like other men of his generation, Zack did not see himself as a victim. He spoke of how they used to outwit the whites, stealing amalgam from the battery plates, filching food from the store. It was not so terrible that their nomadic life came to an end. The desert was "hungry country." They took advantage of what whites had to offer, but kept their own counsel, working at The Granites for a while, then heading off to Tanami or Mt. Doreen, or out into the desert to hunt native cat, possum, and goanna. But always coming and going, Zack insisted, in their own good time. Riling the whites by going "walkabout."

"Start work six o'clock. Work all day, shoveling dirt. But I might walk away from there! Too much hard job! 'Right, well, I'm going now!' I can't let you know that, Old Chapman, Paddy Chapman, that *kardiya.* No, we just walk away. We never tell 'im, 'Well I'm going now.' We never say it that way. We just walk off the job. 'Come on, we go!' Might be two of my mates. Working at that job. 'Right, keep a little tucker!' Go on now, walk around somewhere. Walk rouuuuuund . . ."

Zack had a habit of dragging out a syllable to signify the passage of time as people circled out into the desert.

"Then we bin go back. *Kardiya* say, 'Let 'im come! Billy can! Bring 'im down. Fill 'im up, *mangari.* Making damper now. Sit down there nowwwww . . .'"

In the 1930s and 1940s The Granites was a harsh place for the Warlpiri. Water was often polluted, and people suffered from dysentery, skin diseases, venereal disease, trachoma, scurvy, TB, pneumonia, and malnutrition. But in Zack's view there was no escaping the fact that life was tough wherever you lived.

His attitude reminded me of something I had read in David Grossman's account of Jewish and Palestinian people in the Occupied Territories. In his book *The Yellow Wind,* Grossman mentions a Palestinian family who, after twenty-four years in a West Bank refugee camp, were resettled in their traditional village of Wadi Alfuqin. Paradoxically, these people confessed to missing the camp where they had endured the degrading years of exile. "I miss the people who were there," said one woman. "I miss my house. What, aren't they people, the ones there? Weren't we close to them? That's what I miss." As David Grossman notes, "A person can miss even a hard, bad place, if there were beautiful moments there, and if he has a memory of a single instance of grace . . ." And he goes on to say that even neutral, dead places become dear to us. Indeed, one might say that home is not always somewhere cut off from the world. Sometimes it is a place *in* the world where one triumphs over adversity. Certainly, Zack considered his home to be the place his father hailed from and the places his second father grew him up. But The Granites was where he had met hardship head on, had been tested, and had endured. This, then, was also home.

It was late in the afternoon when we saw the plume of smoke rising in the distance. "Maybe someone broken down," Zack observed.

As I slowed to stop, Zack recognized Oscar Japaljarri's shambling figure coming toward us along the road. His yellow Ford sedan was parked at an angle. The smoke we had seen was from his campfire in the spinifex.

Zack greeted Japaljarri while I went over to the car to see if there was anything I could do to help. A flat tire. Dead battery. Blocked fuel line.

Oscar's son was sitting by the fire, mending the punctured tube with melted plastic from a ballpoint pen.

I returned to the Toyota and drove it front on to the Ford. I connected my jumper cables to the terminals of Japaljarri's battery.

"Might be no petrol," Oscar said as he got into the car and fiddled with the ignition wires.

Oscar's son primed the carburetor with petrol from a jerrican.

"OK?" I called.

The engine wheezed and whirred but wouldn't start.

"Let's go Jupurrurla," Zack said, "It's cold."

"We can't leave these blokes out here."

"Let 'im come."

I unclipped the jumper cables and glanced inside the car we were about to abandon. No hood. The interior stripped to the metal. No dashboard. No ignition key. I liked the graffiti someone had scratched on the mudguard: *You scratcha my car I don't give a damn.*

In the West we compare people to machines. On the back of a packet of Kellogg's Special K I once bought at the Lajamanu store: "The human body can be likened to a piece of fine machinery. If you feel that you're too busy to eat breakfast, you're leaving your body 'machine' without fuel for anything up to eighteen hours." An article I tore out of a *Cosmopolitan* in a dentist's waiting room in Alice Springs gave tips on "How to recharge a stale relationship": "If your car develops a loud knock, for example, you take it to the mechanic before it stops dead in peak-hour traffic. Why, then, do we allow love relationships to end up at the dump without even attempting a repair?"

Such analogies would seem absurd to the Warlpiri, for whom "A Toyota's just tin and iron, not a person."

In the West we are expected to devote the same care to the upkeep of ourselves as to our vehicles. Rather than celebrate the changes time wreaks on us, we do everything we can to camouflage them. We admire unblemished complexions, we embrace myths of the ageless body. For Warlpiri, however, the scarring effects of life are part of one's very identity. The sorry cuts on Zack's thighs, the welts on his chest, the deep lines on his face, the burn marks on his body. To be marked by life, to be different, is not seen as a problem. Difference is not shunned as deviance. If anything, it is a sign of the self-reliance a person must have to survive in the desert. You have to look after others, to be sure, but you have to fend for yourself too, keeping a weather eye open for whatever resources are available, cultivating people to whom you can turn in hard times. Idiosyncracies are grist for the social mill. Nicknames spring from them. They tell the same story as scars. Even the quirky names whites gave to people at The Granites—Mosquito, Billy Bunter, Five Bob, Michelin, Cheeky, Popeye, Peter Pan, Misery, Tatters, Lamey, Baggy, Short Shirt, Big Eyes, Milky Way, Gloomy, Snifter, Boomerang, George A Bad Character, Greta Garbo, Mrs. Bullswool, Mae West, Cleopatra—are vivid reminders of how singular people were. Though the miners saw them as figures of fun and made them the butt of sick jokes, these names outlast the slurs, reminding us of the forthrightness and ebullience of people who under the sternest conditions saw themselves as bosses for themselves.

It came through in the story Zack told me as we drove north in the gathering dusk. In the late 1940s the government moved Warlpiri away from The Granites and resettled them in a new community at

Yuendumu. Zack did not stay for long. He "pinched" another man's wife and was ordered to leave the settlement.

"I bin little bit naughty boy! So they bin push me out, you know, welfare people. Ha ha ha ha! I was a young fella. They had big argument there now, for me. All my fathers and uncles bin tell me to get out. 'Come on, pick up your swag, you troublemaker, on your way!' I bin go for good."

Zack worked on cattle stations for five years, moving as far east as the Queensland border.

"Long way from home," I said.

"Yuwayi," Zack said. "But I was still happy. I never sing for my people, for my family."

TEN

My country is the place where I can

cut a spear or make a spear-thrower

without asking anyone.

—*A Western Desert man*

=

It was to be our last trip into the desert that year. The plan was to go to Paraluyu with Pincher. Nugget was to accompany us. But the morning we were packing to leave, Zack turned up at the caravan and wanted to know where we were going. He unshouldered his swag and dumped it on the ground. His shirt tail was hanging out and his sleeves flapped around his thin arms. He'd just got back from a bender at Top Springs.

When I explained we were going to Paraluyu to see Pincher's country, Zack declared that he was coming with us.

As Zack stooped to pick up his swag, a dilapidated panel van drove up in a cloud of dust. Zack's son was at the wheel. Zack walked over to the van, dragged open the side door, and rummaged inside. A week ago, he'd left some pieces of dogwood in the van. He'd been going to make boomerangs out of them, but they'd disappeared. He promptly accused his son of using the logs for firewood.

"You *warungka!* " his son bawled. "Get in, you drunken loony!"

Like a scolded child, Zack climbed awkwardly into the van.

"You coming or not?" I asked.

"Wait, Jupurrurla. I gotta get an axe."

Half an hour later we were on our way. Francine and Pincher sat in front. Zack and Nugget sat behind me, calling my attention to important landmarks. I kept glancing back at them in the rearview mirror, Nugget in his red Stetson, Zack with a baseball cap jammed down over his mop of hair.

Our first stop was Pikanniny Bore, an outstation 120 miles to the south. A few old men and women lived there. After spending most of their lives away from their traditional country, they had come home.

As we climbed out of the Toyota a mob of pariah dogs surrounded us, snapping at our heels. Pincher picked up a stone and hurled it at the nearest dog. It hobbled away toward the water bore, whimpering.

The women were playing cards. They sat huddled against a wind-break of torn plastic tarpaulins, sheets of iron, and eucalypt branches. They were tossing blankets and articles of clothing in a heap in front of them as bets.

Francine went to sit with the women. I followed Pincher, Zack, and Nugget over to join the old men. They stood in bare feet on the pocked ground. They wore knitted caps. Their jackets were full of burn holes.

The old men were only too happy to corroborate details of Dreaming tracks we had crossed on our way south. We spoke of the fire Dreaming in the vicinity of Warlumarlinpa Creek, where the rocks were blackened from the fire which swept through there in the Dreaming; of the rain Dreaming at Jiwaranpa, where the limestone outcrops in the red dirt were "*kumpakumpa*"—the Warlpiri word for the foam that collects on the surface of floodwater; and farther south, where we had disturbed flocks of lime-green budgerigars along the road— the country of the budgerigar Dreaming. In the desert, every species, every person, and every landform has its proper place in the scheme of things. In this sense, the Dreaming is practically synonymous with the original meaning of the word ecology, whose root, *oikos,* means house and, by extension, habitat and home.

I walked back to the Toyota and got some flour, canned food, and tea.

The women quit their game of cards and began preparing damper from the flour.

Everyone moved toward the fire. An elderly woman climbed to her feet and tottered over to join us. Her skin was wizened and ashen. She took Francine's hand, held it against her face, and said something in Warlpiri which I could not pick up. Black kites were wheeling overhead. The wind blew smoke into our faces.

As the women raked hot coals over the dampers, the dogs crowded around us. I counted seventeen of them. Two fell to fighting, snarling, and writhing in the dirt until one rolled onto its back in submission. The victor stood over it, baring his fangs, resting his front paws on the pink and scabrous belly of the loser.

We opened cans of baked beans and corned beef. The women

emptied the cold beef and beans into a billy can, then stirred in the contents of a packet of cornflakes.

The dogs nuzzled my shoulder and sniffed at the air. I watched as old Japaljarri fed a spoonful of food to his dog, then dipped the spoon into the billy can and took another spoonful for himself.

It was dusk when we reached Paraluyu. The bone-like trunks of ghost gums were spectral in the blue light. I made out slashes of red grevillea in the darkening landscape, and the occasional tall silhouette of a desert poplar.

The journey had been long and fraught with tension. We had stopped about twenty-five miles south of the Tanami turnoff so Zack could point out Ngardarri hill to me on the horizon. The conical hill was said to be the bound hair of a Dreaming hero. But Pincher had been adamant that the hill was more to the southwest. And so it would be if you were looking at it from further east. Both men were right; it was simply a matter of where you took your bearings. But the disagreement did not end there. It turned out that Pincher was having difficulty actually seeing the hill at all. He was myopic. Zack was silent for the next fifty miles. Pincher sat beside me with his Mauser rifle between his knees.

Not far from The Granites I spotted a big gray kangaroo in the scrub. As soon as I drew Pincher's attention to it, he bade me to stop the Toyota and back up. To my surprise the roo did not move.

Pincher leveled his rifle and squinted down the sights. He squeezed the trigger but the rifle did not fire. He fiddled with the action and aimed again. The shot went wide of its mark, and the kangaroo bounded nonchalantly away into the desert. This was Zack's moment.

"Maybe you bin aim too far west, Jampijinpa," he said.

I cleared away the spinifex with a trenching spade and we unrolled our swags on the hard earth. The low hill of Paraluyu was black against the dark blue sky. Not a breath of wind. The landscape still.

That first night Zack, and Pincher, and Nugget slept badly. They saw lights on the horizon and heard voices in the darkness. They went out and spoke to the *milalpa,* explaining who they were and why they were camped there.

At dawn we woke to the steadfast silence. The moon in the western sky was like eggshell.

As the sun came up, flecking the seedheads of the spinifex and making the ground glow, Pincher began intoning the opening phrases of a song from the rain Dreaming.

> At daybreak
> the sun rising behind a long dark cloud
> and butcherbirds singing . . .

He was interrupted by Zack hoiking and coughing loudly as he clumsily ripped up a cardboard carton to kindle the fire.

Nugget sat bleary-eyed on his swag, flicking his fingers as he always did when he was thinking of what he wanted to say.

We boiled a billy and sat together, dunking ginger biscuits in mugs of hot tea.

After breakfast I spread a map out on the ground, anchoring the corners with stones. I wanted to pinpoint some of the places Zack had told me about. But Zack said a map was no good. We had to walk over the country to know it properly. So we set off for Paraluyu, half a mile away, from where we would be able to identify key places on the horizon.

On maps, Paraluyu goes by the name of Mt. Davidson. Davidson was the first white man to journey through this country, and he gave the hill his father's name. The landscape I gazed upon was no different from the landscape Allan Davidson surveyed in 1900, except that what I saw was strongly affected by what Zack told me, while Davidson's view was shaped by his interest in finding gold and precious stones. Where he examined "promising runs" in the quartzite, and dollied or panned samples in his camp at the end of each day, I followed Zack's finger as he drew Dreaming tracks in the red dirt and recited litanies of names. When we lifted our eyes from the ground and scanned the horizon, we saw the dark tors or blue smudges of places along the rain Dreaming track which ended at Kulpulurnu, more than two day's journey to the north. Where Davidson described a "lonely looking hill of some prominence" or a "flat tableland," Zack spelled out details which made the landscape replete with meaning. Yet it was ironic that where Davidson reported a "suspicion of smoke" to the northeast during the afternoon, I looked out into a landscape long deserted except in the memory of a few old men.

Pincher was keen for me to see with my own eyes some of the places he had told me about in Lajamanu months ago. And so, with his help, I identified the low hills on the SSE horizon as the heaps of *watiyawarnu* seed which the two Nangala sisters winnowed and left in their wake as they traveled toward Paraluyu in the Dreaming.

But Pincher had not been to Paraluyu for a long time, and had to rely on Zack to augment his uncertain knowledge of the place.

Zack didn't need to be asked. He urged Francine and me to follow him.

We were the only ones wearing shoes. In bare feet, Pincher and Nugget had trouble walking over the broken stones. As they lagged behind, Zack led us over a low saddle and down to the floodout area where people used to camp. He examined the ground for traces of the past. A grinding stone. A familiar tree.

"All this area up here bin my track," Zack said. "I bin walk 'round here. That young mob from Lajamanu, they don't know what's going on here."

We walked back to the other side of the hill where witchetty bushes and saltbush marked the line of a dried-up watercourse. The two ravenous snakes had gouged this runnel in the Dreaming as they crept up from different directions on the unsuspecting Nangala sisters.

Zack pointed out two piles of rubble on the nearby slope. This was the petrified excreta, left by the two snakes after they had eaten the Nangalas.

Pincher and Nugget came up behind us and stared down at the sandy depression in the dried watercourse. This was the soakage, where people used to dig for water.

"That's the real Paraluyu," Pincher said somberly. "That's the two Nangalas, where they were, *wiyarrpajarra.*"

"Right!" said Zack, "we got to move along and look that country more!"

That afternoon we drove to a quarry where men used to make stone knives and spearheads. I sat in the stippled shade of a whitewash gum and watched Zack and Nugget wander around, looking for stones to knap. Pincher drifted off on his own, taking his rifle. He wanted to shoot bush turkey for supper.

The ground was littered with shattered flint. Zack tried to strike some flakes from a core stone, but quickly grew disgusted at his lack of skill and tossed the stone into the rubble. Nugget sat apart, nonplussed in his red Stetson, twirling his fingers.

I picked up a stone I thought might be jasper. There were white blemishes in its terra cotta surfaces. Nugget said these were *kuruwarri* from the hare wallaby Dreaming. This was a hare wallaby place.

"Big mob, Jakamarra/Jupurrurla, bin traveling everywhere," Nugget said. He jerked his chin and pursed his lips in the direction of Pawala to the northwest, a low-lying area of claypans and dense mulga where the hare wallaby tracks all converged.

Zack clattered across the stones. He was impatient to move on. He wanted to cut some dogwood to make boomerangs.

When Pincher returned, we got back into the Toyota and headed out into the spinifex, looking for dogwoods. Many were too gnarled or knotholed for Zack's purposes, but finally we found a stand of trees whose trunks had the right diameter and curvature.

Zack axed off the top of one, then cut a little way into either side of the trunk at its base. After adzing off the bark, Zack used Pincher's axe as a wedge, hammering it down the middle of the amputated trunk until it split cleanly in two. From these pieces, already roughly shaped, he would fashion a pair of fighting boomerangs.

Pincher took back his axe and began chopping at another tree. He wanted to make a hooked boomerang, sometimes called a "Number 7" because it is shaped like a seven. To get the obtuse angle, Pincher had to cut a section of the trunk where it became the main root. It was hard work clearing the earth from the bole of the tree, grubbing around the root so an axe could be brought down on it. When we got back to our camp that evening, Pincher would tell Francine that he was pissed off that I had helped Zack and not him. "I got no helper, Napanangka!"

But this wasn't the cause of the gloom that descended on him that night. Nor was the cause his failure to shoot a bush turkey for our supper. It was the impact of his return to Paraluyu after so many years away, of realizing that for all his talk of taking his family there to live and carving coolimons or painting Dreamtime canvases for the tourist trade, he would in fact never make the move.

And Zack did not help matters, ribbing Pincher for being afraid of the *milalpa*.

That night we sat around a mulga fire as Nugget and Zack recalled the names of the men who grew them up, the names of places out in the darkness where they had passed away. Zack said they were "sleeping." "I bin sorry about that," he said, "I can't call those names." They had gone back into the Dreaming. In another generation the names of the men who raised Nugget and Zack to manhood would be forgotten too.

Then Nugget started talking about a woman called Talkinjiya.

At first I was at a loss to know who on earth he was referring to.

Then he said her *kardiya* name was Missa Pinka, and I realized this was Olive Pink, the anthropologist who lived at Thomson's Rockhole in the 1930s and campaigned to protect Warlpiri from the depredations of whites. Thomson's Rockhole was some fifteen miles to the south. Its Warlpiri name was Pirtipirti. This was Nugget's father's father's country.

"Missa Pinka bin grow 'im up me," Nugget explained. In fact she "grew up a whole mob of *yapa*," giving them clothes, flour, corned beef, sugar, and tea. She lost her husband in the First World War, Nugget said. He was a sea captain. Missa Pinka didn't like other whites. Only *yapa*. She was always giving white miners a piece of her mind. She lived at Jila for a while before she came to Pirtipirti. Then she went back to Alice Springs. Warlpiri people wept when she died.

I encouraged Nugget to tell me more, but he simply repeated what he had already told me. "That's all," he said.

In fact, Olive Pink never married. And Captain Harold Southern was not a sea captain. He was a "special friend," who was killed at Pope's Hill on the Gallipoli peninsular in 1915. Olive Pink kept his portrait above her bed for many years, and once confided to a friend that her reason for living had died at Gallipoli. She wanted the portrait buried with her when she died.

Some day, someone will do justice to Olive Pink's story and trace out the poignant connection between the dreams shattered at Anzac Cove and the Dreamings wiped out at Coniston: the world Olive Pink lost in 1915 and the world of the Aboriginal which she fought to preserve. Anyone who does research in Central Australia comes up against her legacy. Her indignant and self-righteous voice can still unsettle the Australian conscience. There are bundles of her letters in archival files, ironically tied up with red tape, in which she rails against assimilationist policies, and demands citizenship and land rights for Aboriginals. And there are letters from various government departments, answering her charges, objecting to her cantankerous manner, observing that she is "temperamentally unfitted" to work in the outback among Aboriginals. She died in poverty in Alice Springs at the age of ninety-one, disillusioned with academic anthropology.

It was partly Nugget's memories of Olive Pink that made us all decide that we would go to Thomson's Rockhole. It would mean bush-bashing our way across country for fifteen miles, but Zack and Nugget were confident they could find the place even though they had not been there for forty years.

There were two ways we could go. We could take the Toyota along the same route that people traveled in the old days, or we could try to find the old Tanami track from the Lander to The Granites, then follow it east to Thomson's Rockhole. Pincher was convinced we should try to find the old road rather than plunge off into the unknown. But for Nugget, the country between Paraluyu and Pirtipirti was by no means unknown. However, after much wrangling, he deferred to Pincher. Zack didn't seem to care one way or another.

As soon as we left the stony track near Jupurrurlawarnu we were in unfamiliar country. The Toyota jolted and lurched over the spinifex. Acacia bushes disappeared under the bull-bars, branches scraping and whipping along the metal underside of the vehicle. The grass was waist high. It glistened in the sun like bleached hair. Francine sat beside me, and Pincher sat beside her waving his hand to direct me away from thickets of mulga or impenetrable scrub. Nugget and Zack sat in the back, bumped and jerked about as we zigzagged laboriously through the oceanic grasslands. They tried to pick up landmarks. But the barren ridges of blackened stone we bypassed or the occasional desert walnut or large corkwood that stood out on the horizon never gave any reliable indication of where we might be.

We drove for hours, expecting each swath of scrub on the endlessly succeeding horizons to mark the old track.

And then we found it. Pincher picked it up and shouted for me to stop. To my eyes there was no evidence of any road, only eucalypt saplings, red dirt, and clumps of spinifex. But when I got out of the Toyota and looked more closely, it was possible to make out the shadowy and parallel tracks, worn long ago by wheels on the annealed earth.

"Tragedy Track," I muttered to Francine. This was the track Michael Terry blazed in the early 1930s with his Morris trucks, through a landscape which F. E. Baume described as a "tragedy of desolation—380 miles of heat and flies, dust and spinifex." Along this track scores of white men had come, hoping to strike it rich at The Granites.

Since the track was all but obliterated by saltbush and spinifex, I asked Zack and Nugget which way we should go. Despite all our meandering they had kept an unerring sense of how far we had traveled and how far we had deviated from our initial bearing. In order to figure out how to reach Thomson's Rockhole from where we were, they seemed to backtrack in their imagination and take a new bearing from Paraluyu, our base camp. We now set an eastern course.

Negotiating the scrub became more and more arduous. In the end we headed for a stony ridge, hoping to get some inkling of our location from the higher ground. But this meant bashing our way through dense stands of mulga, and it was only a matter of minutes before the first mulga stake ripped through one of our steel-belted radials. After jacking the Toyota and replacing the front offside wheel, we pressed on. Minutes later I caught the whiff of stale air escaping from another punctured tire. Again the same back-breaking process of lifting the front of the vehicle with a kangaroo jack and changing a tire.

We had three spares. We used them all. With the fourth puncture we were faced with the time-consuming task of patching tubes and bringing them up to full pressure with a small foot pump.

Francine and I were sunburned. Our hands were cut and bruised. Zack and Nugget said they were buggered and didn't have the strength left to work the pump. And Pincher was beginning to panic.

I changed the tire and with Zack's help axed a path through the worst of the mulga. We sank to the ground, exhausted. For a while I was too tired even to drink from the plastic bottle Francine brought me.

No one spoke. The blood was pounding in my temples. I watched ants scurrying across the gritty red dirt.

A hot wind brushed the spinifex. I heard the momentary trill and lisp of a bird. The landscape seemed to claim me.

This was the landscape the explorer Giles described in 1876 as "the centre of silence and solitude . . . despair and desolation." These were the horizons that Michael Terry said "you could see till the seeing made eyes hurt." This was where white men had suffered "desert sickness" and "desert nerve strain," and come to see Aboriginal people as the very embodiment of the cruel, treacherous, and unstable character of the desert itself.

I was drifting into a kind of reverie when Zack startled me, pointing skyward. A jet plane was crossing the sky, 35,000 feet above us. Sunlight glinted on a wing. The drone of its engines was barely audible.

"Going to Europe," Zack said. "Singapore."

Then, it was as though some weight shifted inside me. I felt an all-encompassing calm. A window flung open onto a field of light. I had not the slightest desire to be on my way to Europe, or to be anywhere else. I had come to the place I had always wanted to come.

At that moment, sitting there with Zack and Nugget, Pincher and Francine, I think I knew what it means to be at home in the world. It is to experience a complete consonance between one's own body and the body of the earth. Between self and other. It little matters whether the other is a landscape, a loved one, a house, or an action. Things flow. There seems to be no resistance between oneself and the world. The *relationship* is all.

> I was nowhere else;
> the wind filled me only
> with the noise of myself.
>
> There was nothing to be likened
> to anything . . .

ELEVEN

And the end of all our exploring

Will be to arrive where we started

And know the place for the first time.

—T. S. Eliot

══

We had come full circle. At Lajamanu I sat with Zack, Nugget, Pincher, and some of the other men for the last time. The men talked in hoarse whispers about things they had never until that moment mentioned in my presence. I had to come back, they said, so they could show me everything properly.

I told them I would be back in a year's time.

Undoubtedly that is what all the *kardiya* say.

Nugget and I got up to go. Nugget was accompanying us as far as Yuendumu.

"See you, Jupurrurla," Zack said.

I was going to miss being called Jupurrurla.

It was dusk when we dropped Nugget off at the West Camp at Yuendumu. A no-nonsense leave-taking like all the others. No standing around, postponing the moment of departure. No pretense that your absence is going to bring the world to a standstill. You simply pick up your swag and go.

We took the so-called "ghost road" out of the settlement to the place we usually made our camp. Our headlights picked out the bodies of derelict cars among the mulga. It wasn't difficult to imagine ghosts there, or to experience ourselves as ghosts. After months of living with Warlpiri, run ragged by a social round that did not let up from daybreak to dark, or traveling hundreds of miles without a moment free to collect your thoughts, you begin to hear voices or imagine things moving in the darkness. Steeped in the silence of the desert, you miss the frenetic activity of the settlement. It is like the haunting afterimage of some object that you have stared at for a long time.

"We are *lawa* now," Francine said. "We were *palka,* now we are *lawa.*"

Palka means embodied in present time (*jalanguju palkalku*). *Lawa* means just the opposite. The words well apply to the perpetual coming and going in Warlpiri life. Anything that has "body" is *palka*—a rock hole or river with water in it, the trunk of a tree, a person whose belly is full, country where game is plentiful, a person who is present. But if a rock hole is dry, a stomach empty, tracks erased, or a person faints, falls asleep, or goes away, then there is *lawa,* nothing. *Palka* is that which is existent, the wherewithal of life, including people and possessions. By contrast, *lawa* connotes the loss of the persons and things that sustain one's life. However, just as people disperse, then gradually come together again (*pina yani*), so ceremony can bring the ancestral order back into being, fleshing it out in the painting, song, and mimetic dance of the living. Thus, giving birth to a child, singing up the country, or dancing the Dreaming into life, are all modes of "bringing into being" (*palka jarrimi*). And the passage from absence to presence is like the passage from night to day . . .

The sky was the color of charred earth. The stars like mica. I watched a satellite moving swiftly and steadily toward the northern horizon. The night wind buffeted our fire.

> At Lajamanu
> for two nights running
> I was woken before first light
> by the hooves of wild horses on the road
>
> But at Yuendumu
> it was the shadow of bullocks
> past siring
> in the blue hour
> before the wind gets up
> that made me forget what I had dreamed . . .

Next day we drove to Alice, arriving in late afternoon when the shadows were like graphite on the red earth. On the horizon, the Western Macdonnells lay like a collapsed column of eroded vertebra in the light of the setting sun.

Soon we passed the first of many road signs:

It made me wonder where, indeed, was home. Driving through the outskirts of Alice and seeing suburban streets for the first time in many months, I imagined families sitting around tables, eating dinner, watching TV . . . "the place where they live with others of their kind, the place they call home." This was the world I had wanted to get away from. Now it felt good to be coming back to it.

We rented a cabin at the Wintersun Caravan Park where we had stayed at the beginning of the year. The familiar surroundings brought back memories of how daunting our journey had seemed when we first embarked upon it. Now I saw that our anxieties had been trivial and chimerical. I felt purged. I felt I had reached bedrock. But for several days I felt awkward and out of place in the environment to which I had returned. I could not get used to sleeping in a bed, so each night I unrolled my swag and slept on the floor. It felt strange to sit perched on chairs around a table.

On our first day back, I walked into town for lunch, but could not face the prospect of eating indoors. So I bought a salad sandwich at a lunchbar and sat on the grass near the municipal offices, in sight of groups of Aboriginals also sitting there. Afterward I strolled through the main street. Australian folk Muzak was coming from loudspeakers mounted on lampposts. *Click go the Shears* and *The Wild Colonial Boy* in grating, nasalized accents. I wandered past a tourist shop. An old Arrernte man with swollen face and bandaged hand was tottering about among the racks of T-shirts talking loudly to himself about "olden times, my culture." White shoppers pretended to be oblivious to him. It is astonishing how whites stare past blacks, as though they did not really exist. Tourists want Dreamtime artifacts but no contact with the people who make them. Culture has become synonymous with coffee table books, red beads, and decorated boards, a far cry from the ongoing practical activity of the lived world.

Living with Warlpiri people had restored to me a sense of proportion. Many of the trappings of contemporary life—TV, newspapers, running water, furniture, books—had become superfluous. Mere home comforts.

But the bloke I met that afternoon had another story to tell.

I was sitting on the concrete step outside our cabin, eating a slice of rock melon, when Barry Horn invited himself over for a yarn.

"G'day mate," he said. "How's it going?"

He was wearing jandals and black athletic shorts. LOVE was tattooed on the backs of the fingers of one hand, HATE on the fingers of the other.

"You new to the Alice?" he asked.

"Sort of," I said.

He suggested we sink a couple of tinnies. He had a couple of cold ones back in his cabin.

He came back and sat on his haunches. He rubbed his hand over his bare chest.

"Barry," he said, stretching out his hand.

We shook hands. "Michael," I said.

"Well, Mike," he said, raising his styrofoam beer-bottle holder, "here's to it!"

He came from Perth. He described himself as fed up, fucked, and far from home. He was a plumber by trade. He'd been in the Territory for eight months, installing ablution blocks and water pipes in remote Aboriginal communities. He described these places as "the pits."

"Fuckin' flies everywhere! And rubbish, mate! I've never seen so much fuckin' rubbish in my life."

What got under Barry's skin was the way people managed to destroy the expensive plumbing within days of its installation. Kids dismembering the cisterns, flushing stones down the lavatories.

Barry kept shifting his pack of Marlboros around on the concrete. His hand kept straying back to his chest and belly. He insisted he wasn't prejudiced against the Aboriginals he'd met in the bush. They weren't like the "river rats" who sat in the Todd and blew their dole checks on grog. "But what can you do? You give them a decent house and they wreck it. They don't respect anything you do for them."

"Maybe they'd prefer you did other things for them, things they decided they wanted," I said.

Barry didn't seem to hear. He had a girlfriend, he said, called Elly. "She's dark," he confessed.

Apparently Elly had cancer. She had only about ten months to live. Barry and Elly liked to go partying. Perhaps me and my wife would like to go out on the town with them one night. "Elly's living it up," Barry said. "She's making the most of the time she's got left."

I did not know what to say to Barry. It was the same impasse I seemed to reach every day. I would get into a conversation with someone in a shop or downtown office, it would fall out that I worked for an Aboriginal organization, and I would be immediately earbashed with stereotypes about Aboriginals no different from those in circulation a hundred years ago. I would be told in no uncertain terms that Aboriginals were the most primitive people in the world. Living remnants of the stone age, their culture unchanged for 40,000 years. They had no sense of ownership of land. They were congenitally incapable of settling down or living in a house. They were always going walkabout.

Every evening I would go for long walks around Tyuretye, trying to work out how I might get across to such people something of the understanding which Warlpiri people had imparted to me. I wanted whatever I wrote to be accessible to people such as Barry who were mystified rather than malicious in their attitude to Aboriginals. But what did I have to say?

I sat for hours among the rocks. The hot wind flicked over the blank pages of my notebook. Sugar ants scurried over the creamy bark and rust-colored knotholes of a river gum. I watched as a small gray bird skimmed over the landscape, its shadow tugged fitfully after it.

I had the impression that the red rocks tumbled around me had once been stacked as in a drystone wall. It had crumbled, and a few mulga bushes had found purchase among the ruins.

Then, it was as though the landscape gave me back the measure of who I was.

> I put pen to paper
> as though placing my palm
> on the red rock

I found myself returning to the time Francine and I got lost trying to find our way to Thomson's Rockhole with Zack, Nugget, and Pincher, when everything had been so simple and clear.

In the desert, I had become convinced that it is not in the nature of human consciousness to enter the world of nature. The truth of nature does not participate in the truth of human consciousness. The fallacy of cosmology is to assume that images given in our experience of the human world may equally well describe the essence of the world beyond us—the unthought, unnameable darkness of inner or outer space.

Heidegger remarked, "Man alone exists. Rocks are, but they do not exist." Yet we strive to discern the essence of who we are in the essence of things we are not. Scientific theories of big bangs and anthropomorphic thinking that endows the sun, moon, and stars with consciousness and will are both attempts to deal with the same anxiety. We respond to the trauma of the unresponsiveness of matter by imputing to it human meanings it cannot by its very nature possess. Thus we contrive to make the world work in obedience to our designs.

But what of the possibility of my consciousness entering into the world of other human beings? On what grounds can I presume a knowledge of the world as the Warlpiri know it? What possible pretext can anthropology have?

Unlike astrophysics, anthropology does not call for a knowing subject to confront a world of unknown objects. The paradox of how Being can enter Nothingness, of how thought can encompass the unthought, or mind make sense of matter, does not arise. Anthropology begins with unity, not difference.

All human beings share the same evolutionary history. We are social animals before we are anything else. A common phylogenetic heritage exists for us all. And from this is born the possibility of our humanity.

When New Guinea Highlanders first saw white men they were stunned and terrified. People supposed that the whites were the dead returned to life. Some thought they were mythical demiurges or avenging spirits. But then they noticed that in their bodily habits and corporeal being the strangers were no different from themselves. They saw that the white men ate, drank, urinated, defecated, and had sex with women. One man spied on the strangers when they were washing in a stream. Seeing them naked, he concluded "they were just the same as all us men." Another man was convinced the strangers were human when he saw them defecate. "Their skin might be different, but their shit smells bad like ours."

From what people like Zack and Nugget told me, something similar happened when Warlpiri first encountered whites. Assuming the strangers to be persons like themselves, Warlpiri men expected mutual recognition through reciprocity and exchange. That dealings went tragically awry was not because the principle of reciprocity was different for whites and blacks, but because whites refused to recognize this common ground. In the summer of 1909–10, Lionel Gee traveled to Tanami where he was to be warden and magistrate. A number of Aboriginals had gathered at the gold workings there. Gee regarded them as "like most savages . . . suspicious, hostile, and treacherous." But the adjectives were probably truer of the whites than the blacks. Gee describes how a group of six white prospectors, returning to Tanami from a trip to the south, met five Aboriginal men and a boy who camped overnight with them. It was a cold night, and the whites gave food and blankets to the blacks. One of the Aboriginal men then showed that he was "anxious to help in any little way he could," collecting and carrying firewood for the prospectors. Gee seemed not to realize that such reciprocity was of the essence. It was not merely, as he suggested, a clever camouflage for hostile intentions. Violence toward whites followed broken promises and infringements of the law—as when whites reneged on deals they had struck with Warlpiri men who "lent" their women in return for flour, tea, and tobacco, or when whites failed to acknowledge Aboriginal rights by not asking permission to travel, camp, cut trees, draw water, or hunt on their land. In their efforts to get something for nothing it was whites who were hostile.

The course of European history is so steeped in the habits of denying humanity and basic human rights to non-European peoples that it is necessary to remind oneself that what we have contrived through rhetoric belies our origins. In shared bodily needs, in patterns of attachment and loss, in the imperatives of reciprocity, in the *habitus* of the planet, we are involved in a common heritage.

On these prediscursive grounds rests the possibility of recognizing the Other as self, and oneself in the Other. To speak of any person as a bounded and distinct entity, possessing a unique essence, is as illusory as speaking of a distinct and autonomous society. It is for this reason that it may be wise to abandon our attempts to identify a person as an entity or essence, and give ontological priority to the *experience of being a person*. Such a shift would accord full recognition to the fact that every human being has life only in relation to others—something the Warlpiri accomplish in their notion of the Dreaming.

We may also approach the primordial setting of our relation with the world ontogenetically.

No human being comes to a knowledge of himself or herself except through others. From the outset of our lives we are in intersubjectivity. Ego and alter ego are mutually entailed. Identity is a byproduct of modes of *inter*relationships. The particular person, like the particular event, is an illusion. There are, observes Theodor Adorno, only "moments of the whole." Or, as William James put it, a person "has as many social selves as there are individuals who recognize him and carry an image of him in their mind. To wound any of these his images is to wound him." It is in the gaze, touch, smell, taste, and hearing of the mother that a child first becomes aware of his or her own presence. Without the sustaining interplay of self and another, one is as nothing.

The question as to how one can think oneself into the mind or experience of another is absurd, since our existence is primordially grounded in being-with-others. "Prior to the process of becoming aware," writes Maurice Merleau-Ponty, "the social exists obscurely and as a summons."

> We must therefore rediscover, after the natural world, the social world, not as an object or sum of objects, but as a permanent field or dimension of existence: I may well turn away from it, but not cease to be situated relative to it. Our relationship to the social is, like our relationship to the world, deeper than any express perception or any judgement . . . We must return to the social with which we are in contact by the mere fact of existing, and which we carry about inseparably with us before any objectification . . . The social is already there when we come to know or judge it.

The social not only defines the field of anthropology; it is the ground of its very possibility.

Yet, ironically, anthropology has often constituted its project as an exploration of difference, as if one approached the other from somewhere outside his or her space and time. If difference *were* of the essence, how could a knowledge of the other be possible? What common ground would there be between the anthropologist and his object? Many anthropologists claim that crossing cultural divides is merely a matter of method and logistics—learning another language, using techniques of disinterested observation, gathering data. Getting knowledge of the other is thus likened to gaining an empirical knowledge of objects in natural science. It is assumed that disinterested observation and accurate recording will reveal underlying principles and governing laws.

But knowledge of others is primarily, not secondarily, a matter of sociality. The possibility of anthropology is born when the other recognizes my humanity, and on the strength of this recognition incorporates me into his world, giving me food and shelter, bestowing upon me a name, placing upon me the same obligations he places upon his own kinsmen and neighbors. I am literally incorporated into his world, and it is on the basis of this incorporation and my reciprocal response to it that I begin to gain a knowledge of that world. Anthropology should never forget that its project unfolds within the universal constraints of hospitality.

To speak of common ground is not, however, to imply total identification. In another society I may be thrown and disconcerted by new experiences, and my linguistic and social ineptitude may convince my hosts that my humanity is childlike and underdeveloped. There are times when I am utterly immersed in the world of the other, but there are times when I withdraw and seek to reconnect myself with the world with which I have momentarily lost touch. In fieldwork there is never absolute fusion or unanimity; neither is there absolute estrangement. I live a tension between that which I share and that which I do not. My being-with the other implies no more than the recognition, the provisional faith, that we have enough in common to coexist.

Ultimately, I may reach a point where cross-cultural differences are no less remarkable and problematic than the differences that exist within any one culture. Four hundred years ago, Montaigne stumbled onto the key to anthropology when he wrote about the diversity of the experiences that make up a person's life. This diversity, he suggested, was no greater than the diversity that exists between different people. " 'If I speake diversly of my selfe, it is because I looke diversly upon my selfe.' We are not 'parcels of one Warehouse,' but 'framed of flaps and patches and of so shapelesse and divese a contexture, that every peece and every moment playeth his part. And there is as much difference found betweene us and our selves, as there is betweene our selves and other.' "

This is why there is always some shadowy part of myself from which I can begin to reach an understanding of experiences which are fore-grounded in the world of the other. As Jadran Mimica puts it, "every other is the *possibility* of oneself." This is why comparison in anthropology always involves finding somewhere in one's own world from where one may put oneself in the place of another.

But what of the experience of home? Was there any common ground that made cross-cultural comparison possible and justified a universally viable view?

In the course of my research I had collected an astonishing number of definitions of home from different people, different cultures, and different periods of history. Here are some of them:

Among the Maori, home is the land whereon one's forefathers lived, fought, and were buried. *Noku te whenua, o oku tupuna* (Mine is the land, the land of my ancestors).

Among the Tallensi of northern Ghana, place and person come together in the figure of an ancestor. A man's father's original home (*daboog*) must always be maintained, even if this means that one must migrate from fertile land where one has established one's own settlement and rebuild the ancestral home on barren soil.

In their great dictionary, the brothers Grimm define home (*heimat*) as "the land, or simply the region where one is born or has permanent residence" (das land oder auch nur der landstrich, in dem man geboren ist oder bleibenden aufenthalt hat).

Home, for the conductor Bruno Walter, was the world of classical music, not his native Austria.

"All really inhabited space bears the essence of the notion of home," wrote Gaston Bachelard.

"Home is an intimate place," observes Yi-Fu Tuan.

Among the Kuranko, the quintessential human space is the house, which is metaphorically the body of a person. Its thatched roof is likened to hair, its door to a mouth, its wall surfaces to skin, and houses and humans are formed of the same earth. The house *is* family, and family *is* home.

Robert Frost: "Home is the place where when you go there they have to take you in."

Home is England, my grandmother used to say, never having gotten over the fact that she left it to live in New Zealand.

"The world is an exile," wrote Thomas à Kempis, "home is with God."

According to Pure Land Buddhism, home is at the heart of our own being, when stripped of the delusions of the ego.

Home is a room of one's own, Virginia Woolf might have said.

David Lean once remarked that he felt most at home behind a camera.

Home is where you start from, wrote T. S. Eliot.

You *can* go home again, said the poster in a New York city bar, advertising Israel as a place to which to immigrate.

Many writers note that the relation of place and space is primordially given in the *social* relationship between self and other. "The first environment an infant explores is his parent," says Yi-Fu Tuan. "If we define place broadly as a focus of value, of nurture and support, then the mother is the child's primary place." This suggests that one's incipient sense of space lies in the to and fro movement between attachment and loss, separation and reunion, distance and nearness, and that one's relationship to a house or to landscape is informed by the primordial structures of one's relationship with the parent's body. Thus, Gaston Bachelard defined the phenomenology of space—topo-analysis—as "the systematic psychological study of the sites of our intimate lives."

Another way of approaching the psychology of home is to see it in terms of an intimate relationship between a part of the world a person calls "self" and a part of the world he or she sees as "other." Sometimes, people speak of this relationship metaphorically as a bond between themselves and a landscape, or a house. Sometimes it is expressed as an affinity toward others of one's kind: one's close kin, or someone dear to one's heart. It is the sense of being perfectly understood by someone else, so that the person you are to yourself and the person you are to the other is, for a moment, one and the same.

Anjelica Huston once said of Jack Nicholson: "He's at home with himself, and when you're with him, you feel as if you've come home."

What it is to build a "a nest in the heart of another" is also captured by Hannah Jelkes, talking about her beloved grandfather in Tennessee Williams's *The Night of the Iguana*: "We make a home for each other, my grandfather and I. Do you know what I mean by a home? I don't mean a regular home. I mean I don't mean what other people mean when they speak of a home, because I don't regard a home as a . . . well, as a place, a building . . . a house . . . of woods, bricks, stone. I think of a home as being a thing that two people have between them in which each can . . . well, nest—rest—live in, emotionally speaking . . ."

The more I reflected on these diverse conceptions, and worked through my fieldnotes, the more ambiguous and elusive the idea of home became. Home is a double-barreled word. It conveys a notion of all that is already given—the sedimented lives of those who have gone before— but it also conveys a notion of what is chosen—the open horizons of a person's own life. For Warlpiri, home is where one hails from (*wardingki*), but it also suggests the places one has camped, sojourned, and lived during the course of one's own lifetime. Francine and I had seen this poignantly on our trip to Jila and Ngurripatu. When we set out from Lajamanu, Jedda could hardly contain her excitement at the prospect of seeing the country of her *warringiyi* (father's father) for the first time in perhaps twenty years. But Jedda was just as elated when we returned to Lajamanu. We were back in the place (*ngurra*) where she actually lived. Lajamanu was where she had married and raised her children. Lajamanu was the place she had made her own.

Home is always lived as a relationship, a tension. Sometimes it is between the place one starts out from and the places one puts down roots. Sometimes it is between the experience of a place when one is young and the experience of the same place when one is old. Home, like any word we use to cover a particular field of experience, always begets its own negation. Home may evoke security in one context and seem confining in another. Our consciousness shifts continually between home and the world, as in those Gestalt images where figure becomes ground and ground becomes figure.

For more than twenty years, my anthropological work has been informed by a single existential question: how do people transform givenness into choice so that the world into which they are thrown becomes a world they can call their own. It is a corollary of Marx's concern for fetishization—the process whereby the world we make becomes transformed into a seemingly frozen, alien, divine, and determining world of things. My bias has always been to describe how, in different societies, people work—in reality and through illusion, alone and in concert with others—to shape the course of their own lives. This existential project is, I believe, a universal human imperative.

It was this view that now led me to eschew thinking of home as an entity or essence that could be *defined,* and to focus instead on *describing* the lived relationship suggested by the phrase "being-at-home-in-the-world."

We often say that we feel at home in the world when what we do has some effect and what we say carries some weight. We feel equal to the world. We have the whole wide world in our hands, though without any sense that we govern or possess it. There is a balance between knowing that we are shaped by a world which seems largely outside our grasp, and knowing that we, nevertheless, in some small measure, shape it. This balance we might call grace. It is very rare.

Much of the time, it is all weighted one way. Either we seek world-mastery, acting as if we were gods, or we find the world too much for us and seek asylum, blaming the world for our woes. But between the megalomania of the tyrant and the reclusiveness of the mad, there must be some middle ground. Some balance must be possible between the world into which we are thrown without our asking and the world we imagine we might bring into being by dint of what we say and do. In this sense, at-homeness suggests an elusive balance which people try to strike between being acted upon and acting, between acquiescing in the given and choosing their own fate. And this existential struggle always entails political questions of equity and justice. Something Ringer once said captures this view: "Getting land back, we feel like we got more freedom. We feel we own the land now, instead of having a boss telling us what to do. I reckon when you're on the land you feel free, 'specially after the way we bin treated, you know." All too often, people nowadays feel the world is beyond their control. It appears alien and indifferent. All balance between self and world is lost. We feel thrown. The ground gives way under our feet. We lose our footing and fall. Since we do not feel at home in the world we come to think of home as a place of retreat. We take refuge in the imagination, do drugs or drink, endow our workplace with undue significance, take comfort in house and home, repair to remote corners of the earth where we can get away from it all. In the sanctuary of the small we seem to recapture something of the meaning and power we felt once in relationship to the world.

It is this same disequilibrium that tribal people experience when they enter our global village. Drunkenness is often both a symptom and metaphor for this condition. The drunk person is "crazy." He has lost his balance trying to walk between two worlds.

In his monumental work, *Songs of Central Australia*, T. G. H. Strehlow speaks of the Arrernte (Aranda) notion of *pmara kutata*: "the everlasting home and eternal mother of totemic ancestors and of mortal men." Strehlow observes that love of home and longing for home are ubiquitous motifs in Arrernte myth as well as prevailing sentiments among Arrernte people.

This love of home is always tinged with grief, because one's homeplace is also the place to which the spirits of the dead return. Since the coming of the European this grief has been even greater. Everywhere, the intimate bond between person and place is under threat.

As late as the nineteen twenties a group of Unmatjera natives pleaded with the owner of a newly-established station in the Northern Territory not to erect any buildings on the actual site of the central *ragia pmara kutata* of their group territory. The sacred soak was situated in a belt of limestone which ran through the whole of the newly-leased station property; and wells with good water at shallow depths could have been dug at many other places in this belt. But the new owner had been warned by white neighbours not to stand any "nonsense from these niggers." Their pleas and protests only increased the lessee's determination to teach them a lesson. The station was set down on the *pmara kutata,* the trees were cut down for yard posts, the soak was filled in, and the stones around it were scattered. A new well was then dug some little distance away to supply water for the station and the cattle. The owner was surprised that even after these "firm measures" had been taken, the "mean and cunning niggers" showed little enthusiasm to work at the station!

This is not history. It is now. In Alice Springs, Arrernte people still fight to protect their sacred sites from bulldozers and developers. Aboriginal land rights legislation is still in jeopardy. At their national convention in Brisbane in January 1991, the Young Liberals voted to withdraw support from the concept of land rights, arguing that Aboriginal people had "no concept of private ownership of land" and "did not attempt to convert the land into property through improvement, exploitation or settlement, therefore the land did not belong to anyone."

It is the old struggle between those who want to bend the world to their will and those who ask only for autonomy in their one homeplace. Throughout Central Australia, Aboriginal people are setting up outstations in traditional country, reconnecting with the land. It is sometimes called the homelands movement. It touches a universal chord. Hardly a day passes that you do not read in the newspapers of people striving to reclaim their homelands, resisting the military-industrial might of the modern state. The Kurds, the Palestinians, the Basques, tribal peoples everywhere.

Sometimes we tend to forget that the politics of freedom is rooted in a universal human need for somewhere in the world you can come into your own.

In the landscape around Tyuretye I remembered the desert places I had been. It isn't just the tricks of changing light that animate the rocks and suggest the forms of living things. It is the way you come to learn, living with Aboriginal people, that the landscape is never devoid of meaning, even when it is deserted. The landscape is a social map whose legend you must learn. The human body and the body of the land share a common language. Person and place coalesce. Whatever happens to the one, happens to the other.

It is dusk. Among the slabs and stones around me, rock wallabies have appeared. As if the stones themselves have come to life.

I am thinking how one must resist thinking that words can capture the nature of what is.

TWELVE

Place is security, space is freedom: we are

attached to the one and long for the other.

There is no place like home.

—*Yi-Fu Tuan*

Warlpiri say that no journey brings you back to exactly the same place from which you set out. By this they mean that the place stays the same, but you will have returned to it from a different direction, accompanied by different people, having undergone experiences that may have changed you.

A year passed before Francine and I returned to Lajamanu. During that time our son, Joshua, was born, and I wrote a draft of my book about home. But I never doubted that I would go back to Central Australia, to see people again and subject my ideas to the test of further fieldwork.

It was late September and the heat was stifling. From Alice Springs we traveled north via the Stuart and Buchanan Highways to minimize the distance we would have to drive over dirt roads with our eight-week-old son.

We stopped frequently. Road trains, tourist buses, and Toyotas passed down the road and disappeared into the heat haze. Of the landscape we knew little.

> The road like a spear
> in the side of the sky,
> the asphalt like solder in the heat

Near Tennant Creek, we encountered flocks of budgerigars, flashing and darting limegreen like schools of tropical fish. They brought to mind the budgerigar Dreaming around Karntawaranyungu, far to the west. We camped our second night on the road at Kalkaringi where the sky was like hammered gold in the last light and the hills to the south were like loaves from an oven.

We reached Lajamanu at noon on the third day. We had no guarantee of a place to stay, but found a school-owned house to rent, a stone's throw from where our caravan, now derelict, was still parked in the long grass. Pieces of charcoal scattered about on the red dirt marked the site of our old hearth.

The house had a ceiling fan, refrigerator, electric stove, and fly screens over the windows. We counted ourselves fortunate. Daytime temperatures soared to 100 degrees Fahrenheit and the bush flies were an unremitting irritant. It would have been inconceivable to camp outdoors with Joshua.

After unpacking supplies, I strolled to the edge of the football oval. There was a hot wind blowing. Two mangy dogs loped and scampered along behind a woman with big hips and skinny legs. The scuffed ground was littered with fragments of plastic cups, playing cards, unspooled cassette tape, Coca-Cola cans, torn plastic bags, a battered hubcap, feathers, and horseshit.

A car lumbered down the street, slowed, ground gears, and came to a stop. I tried to identify the driver as he bawled out someone's name. A flock of gallahs flew overhead.

For some reason, the familiarity of things depressed me. When Billy Japaljarri crossed the road to greet me, bearded now, his lachrymose eyes under beetling brows searching me out, I found it hard to make conversation. This was the man who his peers called *warungka* (loony) to his face. In his youth, in the so-called Welfare Days, Billy would knock off work in the evening, go to his camp, undress, and don armbands, headband, feathers, loincloth, and hairstring belt. Then, with boomerangs in his belt and spears in hand, he would rave in the center of the settlement, spoiling for a fight. It was all sham, informed by the same mimetic and histrionic genius that made him one of the great Warlpiri dancers. It was the same antic humor Billy displayed when I asked him back to the house for a cup of tea and he peered at Joshua, then at me, then back at Joshua again, exclaiming at last with a small cough, "Eh, Jupurrurla! Eh, Napanangka! This your son?"

In the cool of the evening, Francine put Joshua in his sling and we walked over to where Billy had told us some people from Yuendumu were camped. They had come to Lajamanu for sorry business. There had been too many deaths, Billy had told us. "Lot of people bin pass away."

The sun was like amber, sinking through a haze of smoke from cooking fires and dust. The river gums were dark silhouettes. Dogs and kids were running between makeshift windbreaks of eucalypt branches and tin sheets. The older people sat clumped together, as if sculpted from the earth.

Francine quickly located Jedda and Pearl. The women cried out, beckoning Francine to them. I stood apart as they embraced and laughed, and "Sheshua" was enfolded in Jedda's ample arms.

Pearl turned back the mouth of a flour bag and pulled out a gray joey, all skin and bones. Jangala had shot its mother, Pearl explained, so she was giving the joey milk, looking after it, growing it up.

I went over to where Nugget Jangala and his wife, Ina Nungarrayi, were sitting beside a pile of rumpled blankets. I lowered myself to the ground and shook Nugget's hand. They were now living at Jila, Nugget said. There was plenty of bush tucker there, big mobs of kangaroo.

Zack Jakamarra emerged out of the dusk, improbably dressed in white jeans, a Stetson, and dark glasses. A handkerchief dangled from the pocket of his shirt.

Zack sat down and tugged the handkerchief from his pocket.

"I bin thinking about you, Jupurrurla," he said. Working a pinch of *jangkulypa* (a ball of tobacco mixed with white ash) free from the corner of his handkerchief, Zack wedged it behind his lower lip.

"It's good to see you, Jakamarra," I said.

"You should have come back sooner," Zack said. It turned out that Zack was planning to set up an outstation at Yulpawarnu now that a track had been blazed from Rabbit Flat. "We got to go there, look around that country," he said.

I was curious to know what Dreamings linked Zack to Yulpawarnu. He answered my questions by explaining that Yulpawarnu was all "mixed up," meaning the ownership of the place was shared among several skin groups, all "countrymen" (*walya warlalja*). As Zack named the five Dreamings associated with the site, Nugget twirled his fingers and looked quizzically at me.

"We've got a baby now," I told Zack. "Might be too hard, traveling with Jakarra." It was my first realization of how emotionally unprepared I was to spend weeks in the desert, separated from Joshua and Francine.

"You got to leave Jakarra here in Lajamanu," Zack said. "Napanangka's got to stay here and look after him."

A few days before leaving Alice Springs for Lajamanu, someone at the Central Land Council told me Ringer had died. The news had weighed on my mind during our trip north and when we turned off the Buchanan Highway at Top Springs and came onto the road which we had traveled so often with Ringer, I was overwhelmed by memories of him. Such memories are terrible, because you cannot help but seize upon their vividness as proof that the person *must* be alive, and you cannot reconcile the strong sense of their presence with the brute fact of their absence. Perhaps this is why Warlpiri abandon their camps when someone dies, placing a generation-long embargo on the name of the deceased, taking pains to erase all trace of that person's existence. You contrive to make inward and outward realities concur. At the same time, not to speak a name is to avoid singling out the individual whose loss you grieve, so assimilating him or her to mythical time, to the Dreaming. A particular death thus comes to implicate and evoke all the deaths which collectively define the lived past.

On our first day back in Lajamanu, I was standing outside the Wulaign office when Ringer's son, Gary, came up and shook my hand.

"Did you hear?" he asked.

"Yes, I heard," I said. "I'm sorry." At a loss to know what it was appropriate to say or do, I touched Gary's upper arm.

"You remember my father?" he asked, as if unsure that I had understood him.

"Yes, I remember," I said, finding it impossible to say how much I remembered, seeing Ringer's features in his son's face.

Later, Ringer's widow, Nora, came to the house. I brewed a pot of tea while Francine talked to her. She held Joshua on her knee. Her head was swathed in a scarf to hide her cropped hair and the scars she had inflicted on herself when Ringer died.

Nora lowered her eyes when I offered her tea and biscuits. Her face was clouded with grief. All the aplomb and confidence she had when Ringer was alive had drained from her. That she and Ringer had always been inseparable now made her solitude all the more heartrending.

Nora said she was still in sorry camp. Bereft of the possessions that linked her with her previous life, she was wholly dependent on others for clothing, firewood, and food. Francine promised we would bring her provisions from the store that evening. Nora brightened, reminding Francine that she liked chicken wings from the takeout counter, and diet drinks.

But the sorrow was there like a cloud. It had to be. As Warlpiri see it, it is imperative that a person exteriorize his or her emotions and not keep grief or grievances bottled up inside. Cutting or gashing oneself, sitting in sorry camp, abstaining from speech, covered with dust, unable to fend for yourself, are all powerful metaphors for mourning. The sorrow felt within is shown without, and if it is not then people of your moiety (your *makurntuwangu*) will abuse and wound you until appearance satisfies the demands of social reality. The question of whether or not such emotions are by our standards "genuine" does not arise. This is because the social reality of death is considered more significant than the personal experience of the bereaved. Accordingly, simulated emotions are more effective in expressing the *cultural* meaning of the event than actual feelings, which are idiosyncratic, variable, and capricious. What matters is not the inward depth of feeling, but blurring the distinction between the felt and feigned, so that outward appearance can pass as the measure and metaphor of sincerity. For many Westerners, the notion of authenticity is still entangled with an idealist cult of inwardness that is a bourgeois invention. This is why we often find it hard to come to terms with a notion of truth that is less a matter of measuring up to some inner personal standard of spiritual, physical, or intellectual excellence than of meeting social demands and keeping faith with the worldview of one's forebears. *Junga* in Warlpiri means true or straight in the sense that a path runs true or straight.

I was about to leave the house when Billy turned up at the door. There was a radio call for me at Wulaign.

I clambered over the broken fence between our yard and the Wulaign office, and took the call. It was from the switchboard operator at the Central Land Council in Alice Springs; she asked me to hold the line while an emergency message was relayed to me.

The static and sizzle of the two-way radio made it difficult to decipher the panicked phrases from the middle of nowhere, but an unfamiliar voice told me his Toyota had broken down half-way between Emu Bore and Duck Ponds, stranding a group of Warlpiri men and the CLC field officers who were bringing them to Lajamanu for a mining meeting. They had a second vehicle but it could not hold everyone. Could I drive out and meet them and help bring some of the people back to Lajamanu? Over.

I jotted down the details, then parrotted them back to ensure I had got them right. Over.

"Right!" came the exasperated reply. "Over."

I was angry. I hadn't yet checked the equipment in my Toyota. It was four in the afternoon and I was being asked to drive over a degraded bush track I had never traveled before, to rescue someone who had no business being on the track in the first place.

"I'll leave as soon as I can," I said. "Over."

Back at the house I hurriedly explained to Francine where I was going and why. "I should be back by midnight," I said. I grabbed some maps, two plastic containers of drinking water, drove to the garage and fueled up, then turned in the direction of Nugget's camp.

I asked Nugget if he knew the track from Lajamanu to Tennant Creek. I said it was an emergency. I didn't know the road. I needed someone to guide me.

Nugget climbed to his feet and told Ina he was going. The dour expression on her face did not change.

Nugget struggled up into the Land Cruiser, gripping the handle above the door and swinging himself onto the seat. His left arm was all but useless. It was an injury he carried from his youth. He had fought and killed an old man at The Granites after being wrongly accused of stealing the old man's wife. Nugget had nonchalantly told me the story last year, and also showed me the furrow across the top of his skull—a scar from a long narrow fighting shield (*mirta*)—that recalled another fight at Lajamanu when Nugget speared and killed his assailant.

Nugget made a circular movement with his forefinger to indicate that I should turn the vehicle around and head southeast.

For an hour or so the going was not bad. The track ran straight over the hard earth, through waist-high spinifex. Going at this rate, I figured it would take no more than three hours before we met the vehicle coming from Emu Bore.

The sun was going down as we approached the Buchanan Hills. Immense eroded buttes and ramparts, fired by the furnace light of the sun, covered a vast area of the spinifex plain. It was the first time I had seen them.

I stopped the Toyota and offered Nugget some water. When he had drunk his fill, I took back the bottle and slaked my own thirst.

"Kurlungarlinpa," Nugget said.

In my haste to leave Lajamanu, it had not occured to me that we would drive through this region. Kurlungarlinpa was one of the great sites where, in years gone by, people gathered from far flung places for initiation.

"Did you ever come here, to Kurlungarlinpa?" I asked.

"Everyone came here," Nugget said. Perhaps it was the location of Kurlungarlinpa at the intersection of several tribal areas that brought people together to collaborate in initiations and forge alliances through intermarriage.

I asked Nugget where he hailed from.

He had been conceived and born at Kulpulurnu, somewhere in the trackless sandhill country to the south. As a boy he had accompanied his father to the cattle station at Mt. Doreen, where they worked for the white men. Then they walked NNW to Kirtinkirtinpa, place of the black-tailed native hen, and on to The Granites where they also worked on and off for the whites.

"Where did Ina come from. Was it up this way?" I asked.

"*Walku*," Nugget said. Kulpulurnu and Kurlungarlinpa were nonetheless linked through intermarriage: Jangala from Kulpulurnu regularly married Nungarrayi women from Kurlungarlinpa. The two places were *jurdalja* to each other, which is to say they were related affinally. These ties of marriage gave people hunting and gathering rights in each other's countries, and bound them in amity. As Nugget put it, "We raise their kids up. We can't hurt those ones because we married with them."

"So Ina is not from Kurlungarlinpa?" I asked.

"*Walku*," Nugget said.

To explain how he came to marry Ina, Nugget asked me if I remembered the old man we had gone to see last year.

"The old man who died?"

"Yuwayi."

I remembered the old man's bony shanks and scaly skin, the welts on his chest, the blanket slipping from his shoulders as his son helped him sit up. When he died, Jakamarra was reckoned to be the oldest man in Lajamanu. He was born near Karrku, place of red ocher. His father died without ever seeing a white man. "Died in the bush," Nugget said. Jakamarra then walked to The Granites about the time that white men were beginning to dig for gold there. He camped with his classificatory fathers, the Jupurrurlas, and was adopted and initiated by Jarrjina Jukurrpa Jupurrurla and Pirntapala Jupurrurla, both hare wallaby men from Kunalarunyu.

Nugget referred to Jakamarra as *malirdi*, his wife's mother's brother. But he also called him *kirda*, "father," because it was Jakamarra who circumcized him, who "grew him up" and "made him a man." Because the circumcizer inflicts pain, severing the foreskin, cutting cicatrices across the initiate's chest, piercing the nasal septum, it is thought only appropriate that he give the young initiate a start in life by bestowing a wife upon him. So Jakamarra gave his sister's daughter (*namirni*) to Nugget.

I was struck by the irony. The marriage which had been intended to cement a bond between Nugget and his mentor was one of the most volatile in the Tanami. Periods of morose calm would be interrupted by slanging matches and drunken dog fights which, the year before, had forced Nugget and Ina out of the West Camp at Yuendumu. I did not like to ask, but wondered whether they had gone to Jila (Ina's country) to live because they had outstayed their welcome everywhere else.

Though loathe to break off our conversation, I told Nugget we should press on.

As Kurlungarlinpa fell behind I rued having not had time to ask Nugget more about the place. It was, I knew, where the *ngarrka* (initiated men) Dreaming began, the track running south to a place near The Granites where a Dreaming site had recently been damaged by some whitefellas. I had pressed Nugget for details but he said we should wait until we were back in Lajamanu; the proper custodians of the site would give me the full story.

The sun melted into the horizon. Long shadows stretched across the red earth, forming dark pools in the pocked and rutted track ahead.

As the sun went down, the track became more and more difficult to follow. Gouged and lacerated by runoff from the rains, it was in places nothing more than a welter of braided sidetracks and sand bogs; elsewhere it ended in jagged bedrock. Half the time we were bush-bashing, our headlights picking out spectral trees among the unceasing spinifex. The farther we drove, the more my sense of urgency was undermined. And as my concentration flagged, I threw sidelong glances at Nugget and shouted questions at him about Kurlungarlinpa.

An instant of inattention was it all it took. The track become a gully with deep ruts on either side of a ridge of hard earth. In a moment, both differentials scraped and grounded on the ridge, and the tires lost purchase. It was an absurd situation: the Toyota high and dry, its four wheels spinning uselessly, and the darkness falling around us.

I had no torch, no spade, no matches. I made several attempts to jack the vehicle to give me room to work, but the ground offered no toehold for the jack. I thought of using the foot pump to increase the tire pressure, but wasn't convinced this would make much difference. There was nothing to do but try to chip away at the compacted earth under the rear differential housing. Slithering under the vehicle with a tire lever, I began the backbreaking task. Nugget helped as best he could, scooping the dirt away.

As soon as we had cleared a space under the rear differential, I tried to do the same in front, but it was far less accessible and I found it impossible to exert any leverage with the tire lever. Telling Nugget to jump in, I attempted to reverse the Toyota off the ridge. We scraped backward about a yard and grounded again. I saw little point in trying again.

Switching off the headlights, I shared the water bottle with Nugget. He was worried. We were more than 100 miles from Lajamanu. How would we get back? I assured him that we might be stranded for the night, but Francine would send someone out for us in the morning. It was also likely that the second CLC Toyota would soon meet up with us, coming from Emu Bore. We had a wire tow rope, and another four-wheel-drive would easily pull us off the ridge.

Nugget's anxieties were not so easily allayed. He wanted a fire. He complained about "the rubbish road" over which we had come. He said that no one in their right mind would come this way across the desert. He tried to persuade me to have another go at digging the vehicle out.

I suggested we sit a while and take stock of our situation. We sat together in the darkness, under the stars. The Milky Way arched high overhead. "*Wulpararri,*" Nugget said, when I asked him for its Warlpiri name. It was a celestial Dreaming track that belonged to the Jungarrayi/Nungarrayi-Japaljarri/Napaljarri subsections. The stars were the *kuruwarri,* strewn and seeded along the way.

It got me thinking about the motif of the journey, which crops up again and again in Warlpiri myth: the dialectic of coming out (*wilypimani*) and going back in (*yukami*), which at once suggests the passage from birth to death, from day to night, from waking to sleep.*

I was keenly aware of how differently I felt this year from last. At Paraluyu a year ago I had gazed into one of the few true wilderness areas left on earth, and felt as I suppose cosmonauts do when they gaze for the first time into deep space. But now my horizons had contracted.

To grasp this experience in Warlpiri terms it is necessary to evoke both pathway (*yirdiyi)* and camp (*ngurra)*—the complementary icons of line and circle. Whereas, last year I had yearned to travel far afield, seeking open horizons, now it was the enclosing circle, so often associated in Warlpiri thought with the belly or sacred site (*miyalu),* which had taken precedence.

* Reading this paragraph in June 1994, Japangardi commented, "Wilypi pardimirni kujaka manu kujaka yukamirra"—"like the sun or stars rising and setting."

It had been Joshua's birth which had brought about the change in me. As Francine neared full term, we both found ourselves withdrawing from the world, growing intolerant of intrusions and distractions. We began to harbor our resources, focus our energies, as if in preparation for the gruelling labor ahead. It seemed to me that rituals that begin with isolation and confinement simply give cultural form to a natural imperative. To endure the most critical moments in life— birth, illness, death—we must disengage from the world about us; we must be in touch with ourselves.

In the birthing center, this inwardness became intense. I remember at first light, after hours without sleep, hearing the sounds of traffic outside, a world away, while we, in a dimly lit room with little awareness of the passage of time, labored to bring our child into the world. In days to come, reflecting on the experience, Francine would say she was often in a daze, an emotional vacuum, aware of what she was doing but at the same time utterly detached. It was not unlike the experience of watching someone you love dying—the same sense of the world falling away, of oneself falling away from the world, and of all one's awareness condensed by pain into a black hole. At such times, the world at large is diminished and loses its hold, eclipsed by the viscerally immediate world of oneself. It is always a shock, going outdoors again after a birth or a death, to find that the world has not changed along with you, that it has gone on unaffected and indifferent.

The experiences of birth and death have something else in common: they are devastating to one's sense of autonomy. They happen *to* us. After Joshua was born, Francine confessed that her greatest anxiety had been that her body was out of her control. "There was nothing I could do to influence the situation; for as long as it lasted, it determined me; for that reason, I had no sense that it would end." At such times, one's only freedom lies in forgetting the ego, opening up, letting go.

This yielding also reinforces the sense that one has passed from the mundane world into another zone of existence. As sleep takes one into dreaming.

The compression of experience at *times* of birth and death has an exact analogue in the way we regard the *places* we hold dear to us and make central to our lives. We speak of intense experience in terms of mass. Images of bedrock and stone stand for what is real, while water, air, and sand suggest what is ephemeral. *Homeplaces are the spatial correlatives of the moments that have changed our lives.* These places of orientation, from which we perpetually start out and to which we perennially return in our imaginations, are steeped in the memory of births and deaths.

But the difference between a homeplace and the space of the world is, like the difference between critical and mundane time, one of degree rather than kind.

This lesson was chalked on the blackboard of the night sky above me. Gazing at the sky with images of Warlpiri myth in mind, I could understand how the relative density of *kuruwarri* along the Milky Way corresponded to the relative frequency of movement along a Dreaming track. Where people journeyed less often, the *kuruwarri*, like the stars, was dispersed and sparse.

I lay back on the hot earth, looking into the depths of the sky. The night ached with the shrilling of cicadas. But it seemed to me that the sound had its source not in the desert but in the heavens, a sibilant stitching that I imagined to be the stars themselves singing.

My reverie was broken by Nugget, urging me to get up and look toward the eastern horizon. At first I saw nothing, then I made out the faint pulsing of light a long way off. It was the CLC mob coming to meet us.

THIRTEEN

Man does not relate to the world as subject

to object, as eye to painting; nor even as actor

to stage set. Man and the world are bound

together like the snail to its shell.

—Milan Kundera

══

There were times in Lajamanu when it seemed that everything I was doing had been presaged by a dream.

The second night after Joshua's birth, I woke with my eyes burning with tears. I felt emotionally overwhelmed, physically drained. In the dream I had been moving with intense concentration and difficulty toward some obscure goal. Although I had the sensation of moving over land, I was making the motions of swimming breaststroke. Once, I was vaguely aware of the presence of a friend hampering my movements. But I reached a place of red earth, where shards poked through an arid surface and a withered sapling stood. Someone else I knew now appeared on the scene, saying how marvelous it was that, despite all odds, I had reached the place where the tree was growing. Then he said that the tree was from elsewhere; it had been transplanted to the place where I now stood.

When I woke I was able to explain to myself many details of the dream—the friend who hindered my progress had once expressed skepticism about my proposal to research the meaning of home in Central Australia, and the second figure was a teacher whose lectures on Sumer and Egypt had fired my undergraduate enthusiasm for anthropology. But I could not account for the emotions which left me so exhausted, or the image of the tree in need of water, unless it was some oblique reference to my own uprooted life.

It so happened that when I returned to Lajamanu, it was a tree that determined the course of my fieldwork: the same tree Francine and

I had visited with Nola Nungarrayi the previous year, and Nola had mourned as her father.

During the rains six months before, a road train had become bogged on the Tanami road, not far from where the tree was growing. A grader sent to unbog the vehicle uprooted and destroyed the tree. The whitefellas responsible had shrugged the matter off as an accident, expecting Warlpiri to forgive and forget. But for the Warlpiri it was a grievous and unforgiveable act of vandalism. The tree was not only the father of Nola and her surviving siblings, it marked a site on an important Dreaming track from Kurlungarlinpa, and bore the name of a Dreaming ancestor. Nola's brother and other custodians of the site demanded financial compensation, and enlisted my support in making their claim.

Once word got around that I was investigating the destruction of the site where the tree had stood, I had only to mention "that *watiya*" (that tree), and faces would darken with sorrow and anger. Billy Japaljarri looked at me as if I were *warungka,* and should not need to ask.

"We all sad for that *watiya,*" he said. "Everyone is getting angry (*makamakajarrijalu*), specially the *kirda* and *kurdungurlu.*"

The *kirda* (custodians) of the site were Jungarrayi/Nungarrayi and Japaljarri/Napaljarri. The principal *kurdungurlu* (ritual managers) were the affinally related subsections: respectively, Jampijinpa/Nampijinpa, and Jupurrurla/Napurrurla.

Late one afternoon I sat down with Clancy Japaljarri under a bough-shade at the edge of the football oval. Clancy had good reason to lament the destruction of the tree. He had inherited its name: Yunku-yirranu. Yunkuyirranu was his father's father.

"That wasn't a tree," Clancy said, "it was a person. A person's Dreaming (*yapa kirlangu jukurrpa*). It was the life-essence (*pirlirrpa*) of a person. When those whitefellas knocked down that tree they hurt the Dreamings and ceremonies there."

Like us, Warlpiri speak of trees and people as having trunks and limbs. Metaphorically, descent is a downward branching or radiation of roots (*jalpurr-karrimi*). Some Dreaming tracks are depicted as the tendrils of a vine (in Lily Hargreaves Nungarrayi's paintings of the *ngarrka* Dreaming, for example, the track is a *ngalypi* "snake" vine), or thought of as the roots of yams, extending for miles beneath the ground. Trees are also metaphors for the protective shade of one's family. They stand for kinship over time: branching overhead, yet rooted in home soil. But such genealogical images have more force for Warlpiri, perhaps, than for Westerners, as Francine and I had seen a year ago when Nola Nungarrayi wept at the sight of her father's broken limb.

In his epic work on Arrernte oral tradition, T. G. H. Strehlow notes recurring allusions to sacred trees in songs which celebrate the *pmara kutata*—the "everlasting home" from whence a person, and his or her totemic forebears, originated. Such sacred trees are incarnations of totemic ancestors, and charged with the life-force of the Dreaming. But, asks Strehlow, how can trees which live no more than a hundred years symbolize immortal Being? The answer is that new trees continue to spring up from the ground in which the old trees grew, so sustaining the continuity of the Dreaming. I wondered whether such a view provided consolation to Warlpiri people in the loss of the long-lived Yunkuyirranu?

I put the question to Clancy.

He said: "If you spoil a sacred place (*maralypi jukurrpa*), you destroy the people that belong to that place." His argument was that the loss of the life (*pirlirrpa*) of the tree entailed a corresponding loss of life among those who called the tree "father." Both the tree and those who were *kirda* for the tree shared the same Dreaming essence. This was why the *kirda* for the damaged site were so worried. They felt that someone would sicken and die now that the tree was dead. Their anxiety was compounded by a suspicion that perhaps they had not done everything in their power to safeguard the site. They felt sick in their stomachs at what had happened, filled with a sense of inner worthlessness (*maju-jarrijalu miyaluju*). The remorse went so deep that there had been talk of people singing themselves to death.

Clancy kept using the word *wajawaja-mani,* which suggested not only the loss of the tree but the loss of a link to the past. I tried to get him to be explicit.

"We feel the same way when a person passes away," Clancy said dolefully. "We pity that person, we feel great sadness for them." Clancy touched his abdomen to show me where these emotions were most deeply felt. He paused for a moment, then added: "I'm sad now. I can't show my children that tree. My father told me that Dreaming . . . but I can't show it to my son."

I turned the talk to how people could make good the loss of the tree, how it was possible to prevent harm befalling those who traced their kinship to it.

On this question, Clancy was adamant. Miming the stabbing action of a spear, he made as if to eviscerate himself. Just as the belly (*miyalu*) was the seat of a person's life-force, so a sacred site was the *miyalu* of the land where the life-force of a people was concentrated. The white-fella who had disembowelled the sacred site should suffer in kind, paying for his error with his own life. That was the Law.

"Has anyone tried to kill that whitefella?" I asked.

"*Walku.*"

"Did anyone try to sing him?"

"I don't know."

"So what's to be done?"

"We got to hurt those whitefellas, so they're more careful in future. We got to make them pay."

The principle of *lex talionis* was clear. In the opinion of many Warl-piri, the thing most precious to whites, more dear than life, was money. To hit them where it hurt, one would have to exact financial retribu-tion. "We say money is the whitefella Dreaming," Clancy said. "They make a lot of money, they want a lot of money, so if they have to fork out money, that teaches them a lesson."

"How much are you asking them to pay?"

Clancy named a sum. Given everything that he had told me, it seemed a paltry amount.

At the end of my first week's work I took stock of what I had gleaned from talking to various men and women about the tree. Clearly, each person's sense of self was metaphorically fused with a sense of place. People identified themselves and others in terms of the homeplaces to which they belonged. Or, more exactly, *relationships* between people were articulated as relationships between places. The metaphor which expressed and effected this fusion of person and place was kinship. For instance, Billy Japaljarri had taken pains to point out to me that the person and place known as Yunkuyirranu was his *warringiyi* (father's father). Tom Jupurrurla, a ritual manager for the site, called it his *ngamirni* (mother's brother), and Cliff Jampijinpa, another ritual man-ager, called it his *jamirdi* (mother's father). "Yunkuyirranu, my *jamirdi,* went south from Kurlungarlinpa," he said, "All my *jamirdi,* they bin go through there, all his brothers."

These remarks suggested to me that the identity of Yunkuyirranu, who I had previously known only as Nola's father, merged with the identity of scores of other men who had borne the same name and whose spirits dwelt at the Yunkuyirranu site.* The same was true of

---

* It turned out that Nola's father had not died beneath the tree but somewhere near Yuendumu. It was because his spirit and the tree were so closely identified that Nola had glossed over the fact that her father had actually passed away elsewhere.

the tree itself. Though said to have been growing at that site since the Dreaming, numerous trees must have sprung up and died there since time began. Just as the distinction between place and person gets blurred, so the recent past shades into mythical time.

I had also learned that responsibility for sacred places was couched in the idiom of kinship. One woman impressed upon me the importance of understanding that the worry she felt over the tree was the same as the worry a mother feels for a neglected child. Kinship implied an onus to protect and look after those in one's care, and identical terms—*warla-mardarni* and *warrawarra-kanyi*—applied to obligations to the country to which one is linked through kinship, as well as to one's kin. One must hold on to the country, sustain its life through ceremony, visit its sacred places, keep an eye open for strange tracks that might imply trespass, see that the land never comes to harm.

But I felt I was scraping the surface, failing to understand the roots of the beliefs which people shared with me, deploying the same well-worn phrases. The Dreaming is often said to be inside (*kaninjarni*) the country, buried beneath its surface, hidden in the darkness of caves or the shadows, as dreams are latent in the minds of men. If I was to grasp anything in depth, if I was to know what underpinned or grounded the beliefs people espoused, I would need to know more of the myths of the Dreaming.

I had returned to the house for respite from the heat of the day. Francine was bathing Joshua, trying to keep him cool. The soft whirring of the ceiling fan was punctuated by the desultory cawing of crows outside.

When Wilson Japangardi came to the door he did not knock, but stood uneasily on the threshold with his back turned to the screen door. His Stetson was pulled down over a tangle of black, glossy hair. The tail of his red tartan shirt was hanging out. He wore no shoes. He looked abashed, and when I went to the door and asked him in he turned his head and pursed his lips, indicating the dubious shade of a eucalypt in the yard.

I followed him out to the tree, and we sat cross-legged, facing each other. For the first time I noticed Wilson's dead left eye. He lit a cigarette. He was struggling with embarrassment.

He told me that he'd been employed by the local school for a while as a translator, but his daughter had fallen ill and he'd had to take her to Katherine. On his return to Lajamanu, the school principal sacked him. Now he was looking for work. He'd heard I was doing some research. He'd spent many years in Darwin and spoke good English. Was there any chance of my paying him to work for me?

We quickly negotiated terms, and I outlined what I was doing. Then I went over the ground I had already covered, asking Wilson to elaborate on the Warlpiri words and phrases which had cropped up in every account of the tree I had been given.

The tree was *tarruku* (sacred), Wilson said. It was not really a tree, but the spirit of a man. The tree was the *yuwirnngi,* or Dreaming spirit, of Yunkuyirranu. "Everyone grieved for that old man (*marijarrijarlula*)," Wilson said. "That tree was a person Dreaming. Everyone bin reminded of that Yunkuyirranu. Everyone felt sorrow."

I asked Wilson for the Warlpiri word for sorrow.

He reeled off several verbs: *mari-jarrimi* (to grieve for someone), *wajampa* (to grieve, to worry about), *luyurr-ngunami* (to be sad). As I wrote them down, Wilson commented quietly, "We got too many words for sorry."

Writing up my fieldnotes that night, I was once more confronted by the indeterminate relation between words and the world. Words do not invariably mirror inner feelings. The expectation that they should is an artifact of a particular Western tradition, not a universal. For Warlpiri, words state a *shared* disposition, and signal a *social* truth. When the tree was felled, what mattered was not so much whether an individual was grief-stricken, merely saddened, or utterly indifferent, but that the tree was from the Dreaming and that its destruction cut at the very roots of what it was to be Warlpiri.

Wilson came by the house next morning. I watched him through the window, sauntering along the road. Nothing in his demeanor suggested he had any intention of approaching the house. As circumspect as he had been yesterday, he loitered by the gum tree in the yard rather than come to the door and knock, waiting for me to join him.

He held a packet of Winfield cigarettes in his hand. He averted his good eye, as if waiting for me to issue orders. I said it might be useful to speak to some of the older men about the damaged site. What did he think?

The older men were now spending most nights in business camp, Wilson said, rehearsing song cycles in preparation for the forthcoming initiations. They slept during the day. But we could perhaps drive to Kalkaringi and talk to some of the men there.

So we drove north in the heat and dust, crossing the rubble waste-
land of Wave Hill and the bridge over the Victoria River where cocka-
toos rasped and flapped in the bedraggled gums and a hot wind
snatched at the dry leaves.

We drove first to Lumi Jupurrurla's house, but were told to look
for him at the store. Lumi was a gruff, taciturn man. He was sitting
under a mango tree outside the store. When Wilson walked over to
him and explained the reason for our visit, Lumi appeared indifferent
or uncomprehending. Then, without a word, he climbed to his feet
and got into the Toyota.

Wilson had already told me that Lumi was *kurdungurlu*, or ritual
manager, for the initiated men Dreaming. But if Lumi was going to
confide details of the Dreaming to us, *kirda* would also have to be
present. So we drove north to another settlement to pick up Joe and
Frank Jungarrayi. Joe had been born at Kurlungarlinpa. Frank was
known as a hard man whose fierce reputation went back to the time
of the Wave Hill strike.

Both Joe and Frank had participated in a ceremony held a couple of
months after the destruction of the tree. The whites responsible had
been asked to attend. The *kirda* and *kurdungurlu* for the site were eager
to impress upon them the gravity of what had happened. So they revealed some of the dances, painted designs, songs, and sacred objects
that belonged to that Dreaming. It was their way of showing the whites
that the site was steeped in the vital essence of the Dreaming, as were
the minds and memories of those who held that place in trust. In
giving voice and substance to what was ordinarily quiescent there—
things which the whites had been told about but had ignored—word
was made flesh, myth was made immediate, the Dreaming was made
real.

As soon as Wilson told Joe and Frank about my research, they said
we should all drive back to Lajamanu where we could talk in the
seclusion of the business camp.

"Is it all right for me to go there?" I asked.

"You're workin' for us," Wilson said, "you're OK."

A long swath had been cleared among the snappy gums. In the heat
of the afternoon, there were the remains of several fires and a row of
mattresses and crumpled bedding on the pocked earth. Pepper and
some other men were sitting in the shade, playing cards. Zack lay on
his back near the circle of cardplayers, his head resting on a powdered
milk tin, his gaunt face upturned, dead to the world and snoring.

The new arrivals settled among the cardplayers. Wilson and I sat behind them.

The air was like the air from a blast furnace on my back. A bird lisped and piped, fugitive in the snappy gums. I felt like an intruder.

I said nothing for a while, hoping that Wilson would take the initiative. When he asked me what I wanted to ask, I was at a loss for words. I flipped over the pages of my notebook, reviewing questions it now seemed impertinent to broach. In the end I asked Wilson to ask the men if they believed the whitefellas had understood what had been disclosed during the ceremony at the damaged site.

"I wasn't there," Wilson said, and relayed my question to Joe and Frank.

"Those *kardiya* alonga Granites, don't understand *yapa* side," Joe said.

"Those miners have to go through *yapa* first," Frank said. "Sometimes they don't ask . . . no one alongside them. When whites get the OK to come on, they think they are free to do what they like."

The anger cut deep. Japanangka turned from his cards. He was wearing a T-shirt in Aboriginal colors. His curly white hair was dirtied to rust, and the stubble on his chin was like mica. He too had taken part in the ceremony. "Did they catch that man who knocked that tree over?" he wanted to know. "Did they get 'im? What they goin' to do to him? They bin punish 'im yet?"

Pepper Jupurrurla saved me from having to come up with an answer. Tossing in his cards and struggling to catch his breath, he embarked on one of his long-winded explanations of the Law.

"In the old days you signaled with fire smoke if you wanted to cross other people's country. You waited until you were asked. Same if you shared in other people's ceremony. You got to be invited, you got to be asked. But in those days we couldn't stop those whitefellas. We had to be friendly, to get tobacco, matches, and tucker, so we tried to work along together. But they too strong for we . . ."

Billy Japaljarri chipped in. "Olden times people should have told 'im, but we didn't have the sense to talk to whitefellas in those days, Welfare days, long time ago, Native affairs time I mean . . ."

As Billy grappled with these slabs of white-defined history, Archie Jangala placed his hand on my shoulder and demanded my attention.

"You know that *watiya?*" Archie said. "When you bin knock 'im down, that not *watiya* like rubbish one. *Jukurrpa kujalpa yanu,* that was a Dreaming, traveling. That was really a man. When you see those big trees along the road, don't you knock 'im down, don't you touch 'im, those big trees. I tell you, Jupurrurla, I tell you really true."

"We got to put a stop somewhere," Joe said. "We know we bin robbed. Whitefellas have to wake up to themselves, to Aboriginal people. They got to work with Aboriginal people and try to make a deal with us when they're going through Aboriginal lands. Whitefellas have to go through Aboriginal people first."

Frank Jungarrayi tilted the Stetson back on his forehead. His voice was harsh and deliberate. "We gotta push 'im properly. We worry for that business all the time. We worry too much because they bin knock down sacred trees for us. Really worry. They got to pay up. We want that money now!"

Frank's vehemence triggered an angry chorus. The card game was over. Even Zack was awake and listening.

"This isn't bullshit," Joe rejoined. "We not just making this up."

"White people cheating us for money," Japanangka said. "Rubbish money. They gotta pay us properly."

Under this barrage, the last thing I felt like doing was playing devil's advocate. But I needed to know what the men thought about the whitefellas' plea that the destruction of the tree was a regrettable accident.

The men listened as I stated the non-Aboriginal case. Their expressions were obdurate and unimpressed. When I had finished, Frank was the first to speak. No longer belligerent, he now seemed at pains to help me understand something that was obvious to any Warlpiri. If a sacred tree simply grows old and dies, that is all right, Frank said. But if a person damages or cuts down such a tree, that person must pay with his or her own life.

"But what if that person did not know the tree was sacred?" I asked.

"Everyone knows!" Frank said. He reminded me that boys were taken on long initiatory journeys across the country and shown sacred places, instilled with knowledge of the Dreaming and responsibility for the land.

"But what of whites?"

"Those whitefellas knew about the tree," Frank said.

For Frank and the other men, knowledge was something you lived. It wasn't something you bore in mind but never acted upon. It wasn't something to which you simply paid lip service. And it certainly wasn't something abstract, which you wrote down on a piece of paper, filed away, and then forgot. This was why there was no excuse, no extenuating circumstance, for what had been done. Indeed, the destruction of the tree suggested not ignorance of its significance but negligence and indifference, the consequences of which were as ruinous and reprehensible as premeditated malice.

FOURTEEN

Home is where one starts from. As we grow older

The world becomes stranger, the pattern more complicated

Of dead and living.

—T. S. Eliot

⸻

That the men had been so outspoken at business camp said a lot about the meaning of initiation. In initiation rites the world over, the passage of human life from birth to death is played backward. When neophytes are symbolically killed and reborn, a natural course of events gives way to a culturally contrived sequence, creating the impression that men have mastery over life and death. This vicarious midwifery implies that men possess the power of women to bear children and influence the destiny of their sons. Whatever the psychological and social reasons behind this sleight of hand, it has the effect of making men the measure of all things. Rather than living passively as creatures of nature, men act purposefully and concertedly as creators of culture.

In business camp—*kirrirdikirrrarnu,* the place of the long road—Warlpiri men truly came into their own. This was their stamping ground. Here they called the shots and spoke their own language. Though they might have lost their land, names, and dignity when they entered the world of whites, here they were unchallenged masters. They chanted the songlines, singing up the country, and no one could deny them this authority. It was synonymous with *walya,* with the land itself.

The men's strength and self-assurance marginalized me. I became as circumspect and self-effacing as Wilson had been the day he came to the house and asked for work. It wasn't only the indefatigable chanting, the men sitting in close-packed circles, rhythmically clapping their hands against their thighs or clacking paired boomerangs—ac-

147

tivities in which I could not participate—it was the aggressive edge to the badinage, the sexual raillery, the mock fighting that alienated me. It was the male camaraderie of the pub: the assertion of maleness through a denigration of women, a rhetoric of exclusiveness which, ironically, was wholly dependent on allusions to the opposite sex.

Despite these temperamental shortcomings, my experience at business camp reinforced my conviction that a sense of home is grounded less in a place per se than in the activity that goes on in a place.

Whether the body is engaged in dancing or in mundane labor, concentrated activity is experienced as a quickened relationship between oneself and whatever one works upon. Inert matter—the ground under one's feet, the shield or spear one fashions—becomes infused with the energy and effort that goes into the work. The object comes to embody the life of the worker. This means that before Warlpiri recognize a metaphorical fusion between person and place, this fusion is felt in bodily praxis—making an artifact, hunting and gathering, lighting a fire, cooking a meal, performing ceremony. But such activities engage more than an individual's relationship with landscape or objects. Carried out in concert with others, generation after generation, and depending upon complex relationships of complementarity between men and women as well as between paired subsections, these activities unite the living with the living and the living with the dead. It is in this way that a place becomes charged with the energy and vitality of those who live and labor there. And it is the stepping up and concentration of activity during ceremony that lends a site the depth and density that makes it "sacred." As if the earth at that place were stamped and impregnated with the vital force of the activities carried out upon it.

In all societies, however, human handiwork tends to take on a life of its own. Human beings forget that the world is not simply given; it is also made and made over in everything they do. Speaking of our proclivity for reification (*vergegenständlichung*), Marx observed that "the process disappears in the product." A gap opens up between our activity of shaping the world and the end products of that activity, and we tend to disown the part we play in making the world what it is. Practical knowledge gives way to a purely theoretical knowledge, which tends to lose touch with the immediacies of lived experience. As I see it, one of the tasks of anthropology is to close this gap, exploring the practical and social underpinnings of abstract forms of understanding, disclosing the subject behind the act, and the vital activity that lies behind the fixed and seemingly final form of things.

148

My experiences in Central Australia had led me to explore the notion of home, not as something given but as something made, not as a bounded entity but as a mode of activity. The Warlpiri protest over the felling of the tree was a case in point. A sacred site had been desecrated, to be sure, but Warlpiri had also seen this clumsy action as a violation of their autonomy. It was as though land rights had never been won. As though whites took Warlpiri knowledge of their country with a grain of salt and gave mining activity priority over the activity of the Dreaming. The pursuit of gold, the white men's Dreaming, was seen as more urgent than the project of initiation, whose primordial design also ran like a seam beneath the earth.

One afternoon, I walked over to Archie Jangala's house with Wilson and Pepper Jupurrurla. It was infernally hot. There was not a breath of wind. No one in the street. Archie was sitting on his porch with his hunting dog asleep beside him. Archie squinted as we approached. He thought I was looking for Nugget, who had gone back to Jila days ago. But when Wilson explained in Warlpiri that we had come to see him, Archie gestured for us to sit down.

Archie reiterated what he'd told me before. Whitefellas were throwing their weight around, doing what they liked without asking, as if the country was theirs to come and go in as they pleased.

I wanted to know what could be done to redress the situation.

Archie rolled a cigarette and lit it. It was impossible not to inhale some of the acrid smoke. There would have to be payback (*kunkamani*), Archie said. "That tree held ceremony (*juju wirika mardani*)."

Wilson explained that people had been shamed by what had happened. *Kurnta* connotes both respect and shame. Only by taking action to exact retribution could a person lift the burden of shame from himself (*kurnta-jarrimika nyanu*). This was why people were demanding compensation. The whites had acted without any regard for Warlpiri values. Warlpiri people had been demeaned. By paying compensation, whitefellas would demonstrate respect, and everything would be "level," resolved, "square and square" (*jangku-jangku*).

But payback wasn't simply a matter of settling a score. It was a way of making good an existential loss.

Wheezing and struggling for breath, Pepper spelled out his idea of making the whitefellas tote water to the despoiled site where several small desert walnut trees were already springing up.

"We bin tell 'im really, we all worry for that *watiya*. That's not really a tree, that's the spirit of an old man. Those *kardiya* got to grow 'im up again, water 'im every time. If they carry water, grow that little one, look after 'im, all right, we'll be happy for that."

Through Wilson, I asked Archie and Pepper if the new trees sprang from the same *kuruwarri* as the tree that had been destroyed.

Pepper started to say something, but was racked by coughing.

"That *walya* is still there," Wilson said. "The tree got knocked down, but the *kuruwarri* is still in the ground." Wilson drew an analogy with a tree whose trunk is sawn through above ground: though felled, its roots remain intact, enabling the tree to grow up again. As in Ecclesiastes: "For there is hope of a tree, for if it be cut down, it will sprout again. Though the root thereof wax old in the earth, and the stock thereof die in the ground, yet through the scent of water it will bud, and bring forth boughs like a plant."

In the ultimate scale of things, the destruction of the tree was transitory. Damage to the bedrock had not been done. Time would make good the loss and heal the wounds. Even the insult and injury people had suffered would be forgotten once compensation was paid and whites had learned from their mistakes.

So ran the Warlpiri reasoning. But I could not share their faith that the Dreaming would always remain inviolable and immutable. Too many Australians were driven by a belief in scientific rationality, pursuing profit in the name of progress, plundering the earth's resources for what was called "the general good." An Industry Commission report, published in February 1991, described several World Heritage listings as "irrational," and argued that Aboriginal land rights were often an "impediment" to putting "land and sub-surface resources . . . to their socially optimal use." In dismissing the ways in which Aboriginals put their land to what *they* conceived to be socially optimal use, terms like "the General Good," "Reason," and "the National Interest" were invoked. What these words implied was that Aboriginal interests were incompatible with common sense and modern values. Aboriginals were behind the times, stuck in their ways, unable to adjust to the demands of progress and development. This strategy of identifying Aboriginals with *time* past implies that Aboriginals have no *place* in today's world. It is an old story. Whether celebrated romantically as living changeless lives in a timeless land, or condemned as regressive and inert, the message remains tragically constant: Aboriginals are the antitheses of ourselves.

How can Warlpiri overcome this kind of prejudice? How, for instance, can whites be made to understand what sacred sites mean to Aboriginal people?

The day after my conversation with Archie and Pepper, I sought out Zack Jakamarra. Wilson and Clancy strung along with me. All three men had traveled a lot in their time and knew a good deal about the white man's world.

We sat in the shade of the huge river gum at the edge of the football oval. This was also a tree "from the Dreaming"—but a place for men to sit, not women.

I asked the men what in the white man's world could compare to the destruction of the sacred tree, the destruction of a sacred site? Would it be the desecration of a church?

Clancy said no, the tree was more like a memorial. Like the pioneer memorials which whites had erected along the Stuart Highway. "What if Aboriginals knocked one of them over?" Clancy asked. "There'd be big trouble."

I asked Wilson what he thought of the analogy between a sacred site and a memorial.

Wilson waved the bush flies from his face.

The War Memorial in Canberra was like an Aboriginal sacred site, Wilson said. He visited it once—the Pool of Reflection, the Hall of Memory, the Roll of Honour.

But Zack said there was no comparison. "That monument bin made by people's hands," he said. "That tree bin born with the land."

Zack smoothed the ground with the palm of his hand, and marked the key sites along the track of the initiated men Dreaming.

The first circle he drew in the dirt was Kurlungarlinpa. Boys were brought here from far and wide to be initiated. The place was also known as Witi, a reference to the decorated poles used in initiation. In the Dreaming, Yunkuyirranu flew south from Kurlungarlinpa with two neophytes, one of whom hailed from Yinindiwalkuwalku away to the southwest, on Lake MacKay. The party landed at Kartikarti hill, where they made a fire and camped. Zack reminded me of our trip to Paraluyu last year when he had showed me the site of Kartikarti. From Kartikarti, Yunkuyirranu and the neophytes traveled south on foot. They camped at the soakage at Pulkulpukulpa, then walked on to Kirriwarringki where an old man, boss for that place, grew angry at their intrusion and threatened the travelers with a boomerang. The party continued on its way, passing through places whose names contained cryptic allusions to events in the Dreaming.

Zack's account of the Dreaming journey left a lot unsaid. Indeed, it was as abbreviated as the song cycle that recounted the travels of the initiated men (*ngarrka*). Well-versed in such mnemonic chants and charts, a man of knowledge like Zack could flesh out the details of the original journey, revealing the critical events and activities associated with each named place. But such knowledge was withheld from noninitiates and divulged piecemeal over the course of a person's life. Dreaming myths are allegories. The publicly accessible narrative always conceals a wealth of secret knowledge, just as the visible landscape holds hidden and secret designs beneath the surface.

Dreaming myths also vary from place to place and person to person. In a myth of the initiated men M. J. Meggitt recorded in the 1950s, the Dreamtime travelers visit several places in the mulga country (Ngarliya) to the southeast, ending their journey near Kunajarayi. That Zack mentioned places only in the Warnayaka area suggested that Meggitt's informant may have hailed from the Ngarliya area.

Women's and men's versions of the myth also differ. In a lengthy account of the initiated men Dreaming that Francine recorded, Lilian Napurrurla emphasized the important part women played in male initiation. In Lilian's version of the *ngarrka* myth, the male travelers are accompanied by their wives, and at the end of their journeying it is Yunkuyirranu's Nangala wife who flies her weary husband home to Kurlungarlinpa! Whenever the travelers camp, they perform initiation rites (Lilian referred to them as *kurdiji*—"shield"). It is the women who prepare the witi poles, tying bloodwood leaves to them with snake vines, keeping them in the shade or covering them with earth to prevent the foliage wilting. The witi dance is attended by men, women, and children, and takes place on the eve of circumcision. The long poles are tied to the legs of a dancer who mimics the seven league strides of the Dreaming ancestors. The dancer is also the man who will circumcise the neophyte, separating him from the world of women and noninitiates, bestowing a wife upon him, bringing him into the world of married men.

A myth is thus replete with allusions, only some of which are spelled out in any one telling. In this sense, myths are synonymous with the Dreaming itself—a distillation of ancestral experience that can be tapped in dreams, enacted in ritual, revealed in initiation, without ever exhausting its potentiality and plenitude. What remains constant in every acting out or retelling of the myth is that which is constant in human life: the perennial journey of Everyman through the world, going to and fro in the tracks of those who passed before. But though each person follows in the footsteps of his or her forebears, no two people will share the same experience of the world. The contingent circumstances of one's birth, initiation, marriage, and death, like differences of personality and gender, mean that what is inherited from the past will always be subtly transmuted by events, encounters, and experiences that remain particular to each individual.

This is why no wholly consistent, systematic knowledge of the Warlpiri world is possible. To create such a synthesis would ignore the multiplex character of lived experience and deny the contingencies that bear upon the shape of narrative and activity alike.

Much of what Zack told me about the sacred site I was bound never to divulge. But there was a metaphor he used often when speaking of initiation, which I regarded as equally applicable to the ethnographic project.

The word *yama* connotes the shade of a tree, as well as the shadow, image, or likeness of a person. When, in the Dreaming, Yunkuyirranu visited the site that bears his name, he left something of himself there. This vital essence or *kuruwarri* is like the shadow of a tree. To stand in the shade of the tree where Yunkuyirranu once stood is thus to come under his influence, to be steeped in the Dreaming there. The understanding generated by this process is seen as a "coming into being" (*palka-jarrimi*), a kind of birth.

"The little one was standing in the shade," Zack said. "A person's life-force was there (*Yapalpa karrija pirlirrpa*). Thus was the Dreaming born beneath that tree (*Jukurrpala nyanungu kujalpa palka-jarrija watiyarla*). His father gave birth to him (enlightened him) under that tree (*Kirda nyanurlulpa palka manu watiyarla*)."

I felt that I was beginning to understand the emotional power of places like the Yunkuyirranu site. Old Lumi Jupurrurla had once spoken of the site as *mukanypa nyayirni*—"really sacred." It was something "money can't buy." "That proper dear one," he told me, " 'im dear one." It was the same way one spoke of a person who was near and dear.

In the West we tend to polarize material and spiritual values, sometimes going so far as to say that Aboriginal values are "spiritual," by contrast with the materialistic values of the non-Aboriginal world. The terms are both inapposite. What gives value to a so-called sacred site is the generative activity that went on there in the Dreaming and is continued by people in the here and now.

We owe to Marx the insight that labor and begetting are *both* reproductive activities. In the metaphor of birth, Warlpiri recognize the same connection. Hunting and gathering, food-sharing, initiation and marriage, bearing and rearing children, are all expressions of a mode of activity which is *social and visceral*—the activity of bringing life into being and sustaining it.

The Warlpiri metaphor for this activity is of "growing up." To "grow up" (*wiri jarrimi*) implies a process of nourishing and strengthening. The metaphor holds good for rituals of increase, the activity of making boys into men, raising children, and keeping faith with the Law.

Home is a word for where these things happen, where birth and initiation take place, where life is upheld in the work of human hands.

My research on the destruction of the tree had led me to explore the nature of what is often glibly called the "sacred" in Aboriginal life. It had also confirmed for me that the meaning of home cannot be sought in the substantive, though it may find expression in substantive things like land, house, and family. Experientially, home was a matter of being-at-home-in-the-world. It connoted a sense of existential control and connectedness—the way we feel when what we say or do seems to matter, and there is a balanced reciprocity between the world beyond us and the world within which we move.

For many Aboriginal people, this sense of control, connectedness, and balance has been hard to maintain. I have seen people intimidated and tongue-tied, faces suddenly stricken with insecurity, when thrown into a situation where whites were in the majority or had the upper hand. Like Zack at the office at The Granites mine, his confidence faltering, or the people we took to the "flash" camping ground in Katherine, or Ringer when we had to leave him alone at the hospital. Given their history of being laid off work on cattle stations, forced into overcrowded settlements, subject to welfare routines, denied the means to make their own livelihood, losing traditional land, seeing sacred sites destroyed, humiliated by assimilationist dogma, watching their culture marketed abroad, many Aboriginal people have come to feel marginal, vulnerable, reviled, and inadequate in the white man's world. Powerless to decide anything for themselves, people have often lost heart, abnegated their will, and blamed their misfortune on the very people they have been obliged, historically, to depend upon for their survival.

Land rights and the legal affirmation of "native title" signal a historic change in Australia. But land is but a precondition for regaining one's freedom. On traditional land, people can regroup and take stock, unpressured by whites and free of many of the hassles of living in large communities. But in the end, home is not a place that is given, but an experience born of what one makes of what is given, and the work is always before us all of becoming "bosses for ourselves."

EPILOGUE

Authenticity comes from a single faithfulness:

that to the ambiguity of experience. Its energy is to be

found in how one event leads to another. Its mystery is not

in the words but on the page.

—John Berger

—

Meyer Fortes used to say that ethnographers are like workers in a vineyard. We grow the grapes that others turn into wine. He tended to disparage theorists as more preoccupied with the taste of the vintage than the demands of fieldwork.

I have always shared this concern for the gap that opens up between the experience of fieldwork and the reworked accounts of this experience that one produces after returning home.

Sometimes one feels that this transmutation involves a kind of betrayal.

The question arises time and time again: how can one keep faith with the people who adopted one into their world and transformed one's understanding? How can one reconcile the different conceptions of knowledge that obtain in the field and in academe?

After leaving Central Australia and returning to the United States, I found myself going back over the ground I had crossed and recrossed during the course of fieldwork. Rereading my copious, disjointed journal notes, recalling journeys Francine and I had undertaken with Warlpiri people, I began to see how events could be readily recast as narratives. I hesitated to go beyond this point. Narrative did not stray too far from the lived experience of fieldwork, and I wanted to avoid the radical reconstruction and systematization that mark academic writing. Nevertheless, whenever one retraces one's steps in the imagination, an inevitable transformation occurs. One gives thought to things one did without thinking. One replaces words actually said with a vocabulary of one's own choosing. Face-to-face reality is subverted by a second order—written reality. Life gets rendered as language.

This is not always an impoverishment or loss, comparable to the way successive copies of an authentic article increasingly corrupt the character of the original. Each telling of a story bears the impress of every previous telling, even as it outstrips its own past. Events get replayed as stories. Stories reshape the way we see events. And each event, like each remembering, overlays those which went before, just as successive phases of occupation become strata in a midden.

This palimpsest of moments in time may also be conceived spatially. Every story told is a break in a journey. We tell stories at the places we make camp and rest, taking stock of experiences which are now behind us, reviewing the terrain we have yet to cross. Each place and each telling yields a different view, because we who travel are always changing and the weather, seasons, and landscapes through which we pass are changing too. There is no one place that is so unambiguously central that all other places are tributary to it, no one story into which we can condense all the stories ever told.

Every rest is also a transition. A track erased by wind or rain. A crossroads where we pass imperceptibly from what has already taken place to that which is about to occur. There is no primordial moment that can be called an absolute beginning, no culminating moment that can be called the end. And there is no one recounting of experience that can be said to constitute a deeper or more perfect understanding of all the rest. To arrest any one moment and declare it determinative is to embrace the fiction that we can escape the limitations of time and circumstance—as snapshots freeze a moment forever, belying what unfolds and is continuous.

No human being is ever in a position to claim ultimate knowledge of Being. Abstraction is a misnomer. Understanding is born not of transcendence but displacement. Metaphysics must give ground to metaphor. Rather than seek to get above and beyond the world, we seek connections between experiences and activities that belong to different places *within* the world, metaphor moving us. Says Hannah Arendt, commenting on the thought of Theodor Adorno and Walter Benjamin, "Metaphors are the means by which the oneness of the world is poetically brought about." Metaphors mediate correspondences between parts of the world of experience that are not ordinarily seen as belonging together, such as the human body, the body of a community, and the body of the land. We make these connections, not in the name of objective truth, but through our endeavor to enter into the lives of others, to realize our humanity more abundantly in the world.

We were driving back to Lajamanu after a trip to Jila and Ngurripatu. At Pikanniny Bore we stopped to set down some of the people with whom we had been traveling. I noticed Mick Jupurrurla loitering in the background. He avoided looking in our direction. But it was unmistakably Mick, his jerky walk the outcome of a car smash years ago which crushed his leg and hip. I wondered if Mick was too ashamed to greet us because the last time our paths crossed he had been drunk and made a pass at Francine. It had been in jest, and Francine had understood this, and I had made a pass at Mick in return, and we had all bantered and fooled around for a while before going our separate ways. But maybe Mick had been too drunk to register that there had been no hard feelings.

I called him over. His face relaxed a bit as he hobbled up to the Toyota and peered in. His eyes were wild, his hair tousled and dirty, his jowls covered in black stubble.

I asked him how things were going.

"OK, brother," he said. "You going to Lajamanu?"

I asked him if he wanted a lift.

"Yuwayi," he said.

Mick climbed up into the cab beside Francine, still looking abashed. I found it difficult to reconcile his sobriety with the raillery and inanity that had marked our last encounter.

We didn't talk much, and it was relief to reach the place where we'd decided to break our journey.

We all got out of the Toyota to stretch our legs. The women said they were going off to look for goannas, and Francine went with them. This left Mick, Japaljarri, and me to light a fire and boil the billy.

We were sitting in the shadow of two enormous ghost gums. People often stopped here. There were several fire places on the stony ground and the usual litter of rusty tins and plastic bags.

After a while Japaljarri went off on his own with a can of corned beef and a loaf of bread.

Mick and I sat by the fire, drinking mugs of tea.

For several weeks I had been intrigued by an entry in our Warlpiri dictionary that defined the word *watiyakari* (literally tree-other) as "skin grouping." I asked Mick why skin names were so-called. Did

Warlpiri draw an analogy between the skin of persons and the bark of trees, or compare categories of persons to species of trees?

Mick said just as there are different trees, so there are different groups of people. All trees are *watiya,* but trees differ in appearance and character and therefore have different names.

I asked Mick if the life of trees and persons was comparable. Did one use the term *pirlirrpa* of trees?

At this point we lost each other. My Warlpiri and Mick's English were not up to this kind of talk. It quickly became clear that Mick had assumed I was interested in the big ghost gums, trees that (though I did not know it at the time) were associated with one of the most secret Warlpiri Dreamings.

Mick revealed that where we were sitting was a very important place. It was connected with male initiation. He indicated that I should open my notebook. Then he got me to write down several words and phrases that touched on central events in male initiatory myth and ritual.

He spoke in a hoarse whisper. I glanced over at Japaljarri who was sitting with his legs crossed, using a clasp knife to eat corned beef from the tin he had cut open.

Mick said it was hard to talk about business. It was very secret. We had to take care that no woman overheard us. Perhaps when we were back in Lajamanu he and Ringer could tell me more.

The following day, I was fueling the Toyota at the service station in Lajamanu when Mick sidled up to me.

He was obviously distressed. He kept casting glances back up the road and running his hand through his matted hair. I had to "rub out that word," he whispered, and made a scrubbing gesture as if erasing a design in the sand. He had not slept last night for worrying. He could get shot for telling me about that word. He had no right to tell me anything about men's business without the approval of other initiated men. Maybe when I came back in a year's time, maybe then, but now wasn't the right time.

I told Mick I did not want to know about men's business. The easiest way for me to avoid inadvertently disclosing secret knowledge was to keep myself in complete ignorance of it. But I would do as he wanted—destroy the pages of my notebook that contained the secret words.

Mick seemed reassured. He limped up the street while I went about filling the Toyota's second diesel tank.

Later that day, I fulfilled my promise to Mick. I tore the offending pages from my notebook and threw them into the fire.

The thing about experience is that unlike language it covers everything that is the case. This is why words alone can never do justice to experience. As John Dewey observed, "What is really 'in' experience extends much farther than that which at any time is *known*." Michael Oakeshott held a similar view of experience as "a single whole," admitting "no final or absolute division."

Theoretical discourse creates an illusion of finitude and boundedness. But, as Adorno points out, there is no real identity between experience and language. "No object is wholly known." No concept covers the thing conceived. Experience does not conform to our descriptions. Words do not mirror the world.

Some would say that discourse rescues us from the wilderness of the inchoate and the unthinkable. It orders, assuages, settles. But language also brings us back, time and time again, to the edge of a domain of nondiscursive practices where words fail, a world of experience "that has not been tamed and symbolized in language." Discourse, says Michel de Certeau, always excludes certain experiences from its field in order to constitute it. And it is "the memory of this remainder," that haunts us.

An anthropology of experience shares with phenomenology a skepticism toward determinate systems of knowledge. It plays up the indeterminate, ambiguous, and manifold character of lived experience. It demands that we enlarge our field of vision to take into account things central *and* peripheral, focal *and* subsidiary, illuminated *and* penumbral. Merleau-Ponty used a Gestalt model to remind us of the ways in which consciousness continually shifts between figure and ground. Whatever is brought forth, embodied, and made visible carries with it a sense of other things which are copresent but backgrounded, shadowy, and ephemeral. Every modality or moment of experience entails its contrary. What is real one moment seems mere appearance the next. William James compared the way that consciousness continually slips from one modality to another with the life of a bird, a ceaseless movement between flights and perchings. The flights stand for the transitive parts of experience; the perchings suggest the substantive parts. The metaphor of a stream within banks, or of the growth of a tree are equally apposite. As the flow of the stream is periodically broken by eddies and backwaters, so the grain of a tree is whorled and knotted at the points where branches grow.

Our very identity participates in this ambiguity.

A human life is never a seamless whole, a single story. Our imaginations set free in us other selves that seldom see the light of day. We lead several lives in the course of one. There is a perpetual discrepancy between who we are to ourselves and who we are to others. Sometimes we stand aloof, seeing the world from afar. Sometimes we forget ourselves and become lost in another. Sometimes we seem to be singular entities, at other times we experience ourselves as diffuse and various. Sometimes we are fully aware of our bodies. At other times we have little or no sense of our consciousness as embodied. And our experience covers both a sense of ourselves as individuals *and* as belonging to a collectivity.

Philosophers have argued over whether the self is unitary or manifold, whether there is anything about a *you* or a *me* that is as constant as the names we carry or the things we call our own. But a person is as various as the experiences he or she has undergone. There is no essential self, no constant that can be made the measure of who we really are. We are manifold figures, continually shifting our ground. When one side is in shadow, another is in light. A person is both one and many.

But often as not we disown much of what has happened in our lives, worlds we have thought and dreamed and endured. We shape a singular sense of who we are by playing down experiences that fail to fit some ideal form, passing them off as unreal or making them over to others who we then spurn as alien.

Social ideologies tend to focus on a single modality of experience, making it foundational to all others, according formal recognition to only one moment of the whole. It is the task of critical thought to counter this tendency by seeking to describe life in all its aspects rather than reduce experience to the one modality that has been given epistemological currency. Antinomies such as subject and object, body and mind, individual and group are, observes William James, "affairs not of what an experience is aboriginally made of, but of its classification."

What becomes foundational to knowledge in any society is a product of arresting the stream of consciousness and singling out certain experiences at the expense of others, which are pushed below the surface. For example, Warlpiri give ontological priority to the Dreaming over the individual person, while Westerners often emphasize an individual life as heroically standing out from history and social determinations. An even more telling example of this kind of differential emphasis is the way in which the body is conceptualized. For Warlpiri, scars borne on the body from initiation, accidents, fights, bereavement, child-bearing, and the vicissitudes of life are part and parcel of who one is, and a person's body odor is as expressive of his or her identity as a speech mannerism or gestural idiosyncracy. Such traits may also disclose a person's Dreaming. Outward form indicates inward nature, and nowhere is this more forcefully felt than in the metaphorical fusion of person and country. But what is distinctive about Warlpiri anthropomorphism is that the human body and the body of the earth are metaphorically fused in terms of internal, visceral physiology and not just in terms of external anatomy. Thus, a sacred site is a womb, the odor of a person's sweat may evoke the aromatic sap of a particular species of tree, and a deposit of white clay may be said to be the semen of a Dreaming ancestor. Relations between person and country are couched in terms of organic processes such as sleeping and eating, digestion and defecation, procreation and parturition that Western bourgeois poetics shuns in its attempt to separate humanity, animality, and physicality into discrete domains.

Similar separations underwrite scientific inquiry. Science privileges experiences that are amenable to conceptual grasp and rational control, eclipsing and disparaging experiences that are ambiguous and refractory. Consequently, sensible and bodily experiences lose out to experiences that can be rendered readily in words, covered by concepts, organized into coherent systems, and possessed as knowledge. Immediate experience comes to be regarded as a kind of raw material or crude ore—something which has value only when the pure metal of truth is extracted from it. What is not essential gets discarded as dross.

One would be tolerantly bemused if the only consequence of such epistemic cuts were that they afforded us the magical consolation of believing that life can be ordered by language. Unfortunately, these epistemic divisions underpin systems of radical social inequality. Devalued modes of experience come to be associated with devalued categories of people. The rational male arrogates to himself privileges that he denies to allegedly less rational women. The bourgeoisie make a cult of the ethereal, and denigrate the peasant or primitive as ruled by materiality and emotion. And the intellectual considers himself the superior of the artist and artisan.

Can anthropology resist these invidious discursive and social divisions?

It seems to me that one might begin with something like John Dewey's test for adequacy in philosophy, and ask: "Does it end in conclusions which, when they are referred back to ordinary life-experiences and their predicaments, render them more significant, more luminous to us, and make our dealings with them more fruitful? Or does it terminate in rendering the things of ordinary experience more opaque than they were before, and in depriving them of having in 'reality' even the significance they had previously seemed to have?"

Dewey's is a conception of knowledge that begins and ends within the lifeworld. Knowing is an imperative part of existence. It is not a means of getting us beyond, beneath, or behind the exigencies of mundane life. According to this view, reflective thought is a way of enrichment rather than control, of critique rather than mystification. It urges that we replace our craving to know how to know with a desire to know how to live. Knowledge then becomes a way of carrying us into more fruitful and caring relationships with others, rather than distancing ourselves from others in the name of objectivity. Such a view suggests a notion of knowledge as a process of coming to know (*erkennen*), rather than a body of received findings or set theories.

Fieldwork may therefore be understood, not in the Baconian sense of putting reality on the rack until it reveals objective truth, but as a method for putting oneself in the place of another, and extending one's social capabilities. The object of ethnographic fieldwork ceases to be the representation of the world of others; it becomes a mode of using our experience in other worlds to reflect critically on our own. Fieldwork is not primarily a matter of settling issues or reaching a set destination; it is a way of undertaking a journey, of broadening one's horizons. Meaning resides in the journeying, not the destination, and the authenticity of ethnographic knowledge depends on the ethnographer recounting in detail the events and encounters that are the grounds on which the very possibility of this knowledge rests.

Such a conception of fieldwork implies a conception of writing. Theodor Adorno speaks of "exact fantasy" to describe a genre of writing that is rigorously empirical, but, without "going beyond the circumference" of the empirical, rearranges constellations of experienced facts in ways that render them accessible and readable. It is a method of writing that repudiates the form of lineal and progressive argumentation. It is paratactic. No one element is subordinated to another. Perhaps the term "exact fiction" best describes such an approach to ethnographic writing. Hélène Cixous calls it "a coming into language." "At once a vocation and a technique. This mode of passivity is our way—really an active way—of getting to know things by letting ourselves be known by them. You don't need to master. To demonstrate, explain, grasp. And then to lock away in a strongbox. To pocket a part of the riches of the world. But rather to transmit: to makes things loved by making them known."

The empirical naturalism of John Dewey, like the radical empiricism of William James, suggests a "mosaic philosophy, a philosophy of plural facts," which aims to give all modalities of experience their due. As such, radical empiricism helps rejoin that which classical British empiricism put asunder. If we have been led to believe that knowledge and certitude can only be secured by building boundaries that divide experience into separate domains, then radical empiricism is a form of bridge building that opens up the possibility of traffic across boundaries. If we have thought to determine the course of life by building embankments and dams, then radical empiricism reminds us of the power and presence of the stream. Experiences of the transitive and substantive, the conjunctive and the disjunctive, the intelligible and the sensible, are placed on the same footing and accorded equal weight in any description of human life. The project of classical empiricism was to abstract binding and abiding rules from the flux of lived experience. Such a reduction of the whole to one of its parts was undoubtedly a way of commanding and controlling the world. By contrast, the aim of radical empiricism is care. Its analogue in social life is empathy. Its field is experience undergone rather than gone beyond. Knowledge is seen as a form of worldly immanence, a being-with-others, an under-standing.

In dismissing the idea that any one modality of experience can be made foundational for a theory of knowledge, radical empiricism tends to undercut the privileges of the intellectual and his class. Here is a philosophy which begins in mediaa res, with particular phenomena, with the things themselves. It resists all forms of holistic thinking on the ground that these are merely the masks which particular truths put on when they want to lay claim to power. "The whole is the false," observed Theodor Adorno, inverting Hegel's famous dictum (Das Wahre ist das Ganze).

I suspect that a similar view lay behind Zack's antipathy to Jampijinpa during our trip to Paraluyu. Zack objected to Jampijinpa's inveterate habit of speaking of Dreamings into which he had not been directly initiated, of essaying generalizations on the basis of his own limited knowledge. It reminded me of the way Kuranko informants used to caution me against converting opinions into general truths. Kuranko villagers are reluctant to hazard guesses as to what other people think or feel, partly because slander is a legal offence, partly because wrongfully impugning a neighbor has retributive consequences of a mystical kind, and partly because opinion is not the same as knowledge. *N'de ma konto lon,* I would be told ("I don't know what's inside"). Or *N'de sa bu'ro* ("I am not in his belly"). Such discretion is less characteristic of the Western intellectual tradition. As Sartre notes, the intellectual emerges with colonialism and imperialism. He is defined as someone who goes beyond the area of his own particular competence and, overlooking the extent to which his understanding reflects and serves the interests of his own class, presumes to speak for all humankind. At the same time, he inherits the mantle of the hierophant in his cabalistic quest for hidden truths and elusive essences.

To say that there is nowhere we can go but to and fro *within* the world is not to condemn us to relativism. To deny epistemological privileges to any one modality of experience clears the ground for evaluating various experiences and activities in terms of their social consequences. Instead of determining truth by an appeal to protocols of discourse or correspondence to the facts, the radical empiricist enters into debates with others over the social implications of different points of view, working to decide between them on practical, political, ethical, and aesthetic grounds. In sum, the intellectual participates in the conversation of humankind rather than seeking to arbitrate the truth. And the value of any idea lies in its power to assist in bringing into being the kind of world people democratically decide they want.

Driving back to Lajamanu, Mick occasionally broke his silence to point out certain Dreamings. An eroded escarpment, a stack of tumbled boulders, a dried-up water course were named and identified with paired skin-groupings. It was as if Mick wanted to impress upon us that he too knew this country. When Francine took the wheel, I got out my notebook and scribbled details of what Mick had told me. His response was an emphatic, "I don't need that writing, I got it all in here." And he tapped his temple with his forefinger as if to confirm the difference between lived knowledge and the lifelessness of the marks I had made on the page.

It was reminiscent of the way Zack once poured scorn on Warlpiri men who knew the desert only secondhand, for whom it was an abstraction like a map rather than ground of which one had direct experience, covered on foot in the course of hunting and foraging, steeped in the memory of critical events.

Zack's wisdom came of having weathered the vicissitudes of life. In his view, a man of knowledge (*pinangkalpa*) knew things firsthand. Just listening to what people say "only takes you halfway," he said. To know something properly, you have to see and do things for yourself. Gradually, then, understanding is born (*milya pingka-jarrimi*). I shared Zack's skepticism toward knowledge not grounded in direct experience, not tested in the world. I too resisted the authority of the text and the idea of pure theory, feeling, as Sherwood Anderson put it, that you "can't fake raising corn in a field," that "life comes back to the substance in the sod." But it was no use denying that we live in a world where, as Dewey remarked, we crave "cognitive certification" of immutable realities far more than we desire sensible involvement in the precarious and changing field of experience. Accordingly, the false-seeming certitude of written lists, registers, and genealogies often gives more advantage than wisdom born of direct experience.

Zack once told me what it meant to "hold this *walya*," to know the ground. He contrasted earthbound, embodied knowledge with the abstract and ephemeral knowledge of reading and writing. There is no more telling example of what he meant than a performance he once improvised for me of an episode from the two kangaroo Dreaming.

It was during our visit to The Granites together. The two kangaroo Dreaming runs close to The Granites, and Zack was explaining how he "ran" the track from Warlangurlu, southward to Ngurripatu.

I recognized the episode from a narrative Meggitt had published in 1966, and knew a similar story was widely distributed through the Western Desert, but nothing had prepared me for the extraordinary mimetic powers that Zack called upon to bring this episode to life.

One of the two traveling kangaroos had gotten bogged down in a flooded claypan. His companion, unable to extricate him from the mud, was obliged to journey on alone. At a place called Wulyuwulyu ("Western chestnut mouse"), he came upon a marsupial mouse cowering in the spinifex. The kangaroo decided to transform the mouse into a kangaroo, "a new mate."

"He bin grab 'im now," said Zack, already animated by the story. "He bin carry 'im along Mulyu ("nose/snout"), teach 'im there like in school. Big camp there. He make that little one really kangaroo now . . ."

Zack placed his forefingers alongside his ears to show me how the ears got bigger. He pulled at his nose, drawing it out into an imaginary snout. He stretched out his legs . . . the long, sinewy hind legs of a kangaroo.

I laughed.

Zack narrowed his eyes and cocked his head. He looked paternally upon his protégé as it hopped around, getting accustomed to its new body.

Zack said, "That kangaroo bin ask 'im: 'Can you eat grass?' Go around now, look for tucker, good tucker there. That little rat bin look around. Come back. 'How are you? You all right?' He bin ask 'im: 'Can you scratch?' Teach 'im, you see. Teach 'im about those things . . . lie down, get up, look around country. Learn 'im all that. Really make a kangaroo out of 'im now."

Zack repeated his antics, mimicking the little kangaroo as it took its first tentative steps, nibbling at the grass, venturing out on its own. "Growing 'im up, you know?"

Of course, Zack was in a sense "growing me up" too, as well as imparting to me something of the spirit of initiatory praxis. But in enacting this episode from his Dreaming, Zack was also revealing that knowledge is both mimetic and eidetic. He could not have actually embodied his Dreaming without possessing a keen firsthand knowledge of the behavior of these marsupials in the wild. I was reminded of what Pincher Jampijinpa once said to me about myth. "You learned them from the boomerangs." In other words, one grasped the meaning of a myth not with the mind alone but through sitting on the ground, close to other initiates, the impact of the singing felt bodily along with the rhythmic clapping of the boomerangs.

How these multiple layers of sensibility and intelligibility could be suggested in a written account was a challenge I wanted to meet. It was a test of the method of radical empiricism—showing that the value of knowledge lay in the mundane world, an ethics proven in practice rather than a morality espoused in words.

Michael Oakeshott suggests that what we like to think of as theoretical knowledge is more like a *post facto* rationalization of what we say and do than an explanation of it. What an ethnographer commits to writing and subsequently synthesizes as a series of theoretical propositions about social organization, symbolism, or belief, should not be thought of as rules that govern those various modalities of social existence. That is to say, what we make of the world when we reflect upon our experience of it is not essential to the world's workings. Speaking does not spring from a knowledge of grammar any more than good research is an outcome of methodological training, or good workmanship is guaranteed by reading how-to-do-it books. We fall too easily into the habit of elucidating general principles from observations made in the course of research, then hypostatizing these principles as "rules," which allegedly determine human activity from within culture itself or from within the unconscious mind. Oakeshott compares this misconception with the common error of thinking of a cookbook as a kind of "independently generated beginning from which cookery can spring." In fact cookbooks, like the rules and principles spelled out in anthropological theory, are "mere abridgements" of activity, abstracts of somebody's practical knowledge of how to cook. Because they "do not exist in advance of the activity, they cannot properly be said to govern it" or "provide the impetus of the activity." A rule, like a recipe, says Oakeshott, "is the stepchild, not the parent of the activity."

In its original sense, knowledge was not the disembodied result of thought but a bodily ability to do. Philologically related to words such as generation, genitals, genius, and knee, Indo-European words for knowledge suggest a vital capacity to bring life into being, a generative capacity—the knee encapsulating the notion that power is first and foremost procreative power. Phenomenology recovers this conception of knowledge in its insistence on the intentional character of consciousness. Unlike the behavior of Samuel Beckett's victims of Cartesianism, our behavior is not an outcome of conceiving or willing something in the mind that is then executed by the body taking orders from the mind. Consider Watt walking, for instance: "Watt's way of advancing due east, for example, was to turn his bust as far as possible towards the north, and at the same time to fling out his right leg as far as possible towards the south, and then to turn his bust as far as possible towards the south and at the same time to fling his left leg as far as possible towards the north . . . and so on, over and over again, many many times, until he reached his destination, and could sit down." Motility, Merleau-Ponty reminds us, "is not, as it were, a handmaid of consciousness, transporting the body to that point in space of which we have formed a representation beforehand." "Consciousness," says Merleau-Ponty, "is in the first place not a matter of 'I think that' but of 'I can.' Consciousness is 'a being-towards-the-thing through the intermediary of the body.'" It expresses interrelationships *between* self and other, subject and object, which do not have to be contrived because they are the very precondition of our human situation.

We should not need phenomenology to bring home to us the extent to which intellectualist conceptions of knowledge have helped alienate us from the world in which we actually live. Ethnography continues to provide the basis for a critique of Western metaphysics. One thing that made a deep impression on me when I lived and worked among the Kuranko was that knowledge was neither reduced to practical skills nor formulated as abstract principles. Knowledge was grounded in social being. It was a *vita activa,* a form of savoir faire, of knowing how to comport oneself socially with gumption, nous, and common sense. What was expected of me as an outsider was not that I should know what to put in a book about "The Kuranko," but that I should demonstrate in my everyday dealings with people a knowledge of how to greet them, how to sit with them, how to give and receive, how to work alongside, how to express compassion in times of adversity. The measure of understanding was thus unequivocally social. The same principle holds true in Maori New Zealand. Knowledge (*maatauranga*) draws upon notions of *oranga* (necessity for life) and *taonga* (cultural wealth), suggesting that it is like the land through which one's identity is affirmed—the matrix of both life and livelihood, the milieu in which the living and their ancestors are united as one body. Many *pakeha* intellectuals have still to understand that alienating this knowledge from its contexts of social use and publishing it in books on the pretext that it will be thus preserved for posterity is an outrage against the notion that knowing has no other value apart from sustaining the life of the community whose *taonga* it is. In fact, for many Maori people knowledge is so utterly embodied that its loss imperils the life of the group to which it belongs. In the words of Te Uira Manihera of Waikato, knowledge that goes out of a family is quickly dissipated among others. The knowledge loses its "sacredness" and its "fertility." "And knowledge that is profane has lost its life, lost its tapu." Ngoi Pewhairangi of Ngati Porou put it this way: "One thing hard for the Pakeha to understand is that our elders never allow us to sell any knowledge of anything Maori that is really tapu. To them it is priceless. Money can never buy knowledge and when they teach they tell people: 'This knowledge I am passing over to you must never be sold.'"

These allusions to Kuranko and Maori notions of knowing also point up a contrast between knowledge gained through disinterested scholarship, laboratory experimentation, ethnographic conversation and questioning and knowledge gained through direct bodily experience, trial, struggle, and suffering. As Michel Foucault observes, the model of scientific inquiry that gains currency in the late eighteenth century—with its emphasis on control, instrumentation, and rationality—contrasts sharply with a shadowy counter-tradition in which understanding is reached through ecstatic experiences, painful ordeals, and chance encounters. In this tradition, ascetic practices, drug use, initiatory hazing, childbirth, and near-death experiences define the "propitious moments" in which truth is revealed and apprehended.

That ethnographic knowledge is sometimes born of "limit experiences" is often masked in an attempt to give anthropology standing as a science. The oxymoronic term, "participant-observation," obscures the full force of the interplay between *l'enquête* and *l'épreuve*—cool inquiry and painful initiation—in ethnographic practice, and downplays the extent to which it is this turbulent merger of two countervailing traditions of knowledge which gives anthropology its singular character.

One may have an indirect knowledge of something, yet not know how to actually do anything. This was, I think, Zack's point. One may create a simulacrum of knowledge through speaking or writing, but put to the test this knowledge will prove wanting or useless. Warlpiri men shared knowledge with me because they expected this knowledge to be used to secure land rights, strengthen royalty claims, and improve their lot. For an anthropologist not to recognize the practical import and implications of knowledge is to play people false.

Australia has become a kind of proving ground for anthropology, a place where traditional academic goals are being transformed by Aboriginal demands for social justice, and for regaining and resettling traditional land. No ethnographer working in Australia can avoid the ethical and professional challenges entailed by these demands. In doing fieldwork, it is likely that one will devote as much time and energy to researching a land claim or assisting with bureaucratic submissions as collecting ethnographic data. The kinds of data one collects are increasingly determined by the pressing practical needs of one's host community or family. One becomes contractually bound and ethically beholden to the people with whom one lives and works to a degree that few anthropologists would have anticipated a generation ago.

This is a far cry from any conception of anthropology as a kind of "higher calling" that warrants the publication of photos of Aboriginal sacred objects or secret ceremonies without consent, and condemns Aboriginal life to museum display. Without a doubt, the European view that images of Aboriginal life as it "was" must be preserved at all costs in fact contributed to the destruction of that life. Land was alienated, rights were denied, and indifference fostered by the mistaken notion that contemporary Aboriginals did not "represent" precontact Aboriginals. Unfortunately, many whites still argue that they have equal rights to claim custody of the Aboriginal past because contemporary Aboriginal people are so completely different from their "traditional" forbears.

At the Strehlow Research Centre in Alice Springs, you descend a ramp into a subdued room. The lights are dim. There is a febrile intoning over an invisible speaker system, faking a spooky sense of the spiritual. But there is no evidence of human activity here. Only lifeless objects, stripped of their contexts and reinstated in the reverential space of "art." A photomontage is one of the first things you see. There are no named individuals. Only photos of "Aranda men," or "Aboriginal people." Labor has become capital. *Walya* has become a painted wall. Life has become death. Yet, despite all the protests and appeals by Arrernte people to have their sacred objects returned into their hands, the non-Aboriginal status quo argues for the higher need to preserve these defiled, de-contextualized objects as a national resource.

The same week I visited the Strehlow Research Centre *Time* magazine featured an article entitled "Lost Tribes, Lost Knowledge." Tribal people had been photographed as though they were waxworks in a museum diorama. William Coupon, who took the photographs, deliberately placed his subjects against canvas backdrops to effectively banish and neutralize any natural context. It was a telling example of our habit of seeing the human figure standing out against a background rather than being-in-the-world.

In our global village, where irony has become fashionable, hyperreality is celebrated without a hint of irony. Surrounded by self-referential signs, sound bites, and fetishized things, we have a long way to go if we are ever to regain a sense of that world of birth, death, initiation, pain, separation, and struggle, which precedes knowledge, that world "of which knowledge always *speaks,* and in relation to which every scientific schematization is an abstract and derivative sign-language, as is geography in relation to the country-side in which we have learnt beforehand what a forest, a prairie or a river is."

POSTSCRIPT

Not long after completing this book, I went back to Lajamanu. I wanted to sit down with the men I had worked with in 1990 and 1991 and review the manuscript. If it was going to be published, I had to have their approval.

It was a nerve-racking experience. I had no idea how I was going to effectively communicate the content of the book to men who could neither read nor write. I felt great trepidation about the way people would respond to my descriptions of them. And there was a possibility that people would, for personal or political reasons, not want the work published at all.

I drove in to Lajamanu late one afternoon, and found the old men sitting outside Archie Jangala's house. It was as if two days had passed since I'd last seen them, rather than two years. We shook hands. We rehearsed kinship ties. We remembered journeys we had made together.

I considered myself lucky; everyone I needed to see was there. Japanangka, "my brother-in-law," with whom I'd once traveled to Yirntardamururu, urged me to sit down with him. Pepper Jupurrurla had driven in from his outstation that very morning to buy supplies. And Wilson Japangardi was also there, not long returned to Lajamanu after a year and a half in Katherine. Zack Jakamarra lay stretched out on his back, his head resting on a flour tin. He'd finally made it to Thomson's Rockhole, he said. The time we'd tried to find it with Jangala, Jampijinpa, and Francine we had been less than half a mile away. It was right there, just over that ridge." Then I made out Nugget Jangala, tottering up the road to greet me. He and his wife had come to Lajamanu for sorry business. Could I take them back to Yuendumu when I went south?

Next day I met with Clancy Japaljarri, now on the Council, and talked with Pincher Jampijinpa, as preoccupied as ever by the problems of marketing his paintings. Both men seemed reluctant to discuss my book directly, and I did not press the matter, knowing nothing could be resolved in a day. But it was different with the older men.

Zack came straight to the point. He'd heard about my book. He knew I had come back to talk to people about it. "When we going to sit down and talk that business?" he asked.

I told him we could make a start at once.

Japangardi was as helpful as he had been on my previous trip. His reading skills were rudimentary, but he had an incisive mind and was sympathetic toward the book. He volunteed to read it right through. We would sit with the other men, and I would explain the "hard English" and make penciled corrections whenever they were called for. The men underscored the need for everyone to check his own story, though this would require consultation with *kurdungurlu*. Zack was as forthright as ever about getting things right, warning me from setting too much store by the younger men. "Those young blokes know nothing," he said. "They can tell you all right, but don't believe it!"

For five days, Japangardi and I worked six or seven hours a day, sitting outside Archie Jangala's house. In the morning we sat in the sun for warmth. In the afternoons we sat in the shade of a wattle tree. Men came and went, sometimes inquiring when we would need to talk to them, but Japangardi's concentration was unflagging. Even when he paused to stretch his aching back or roll a cigarette, he kept his focus on the manuscript, painstakingly working his way through the ethnographic chapters, reading them aloud. He revised many of the Warlpiri phrases in the text, and asked me to include others. He was so thorough that he even insisted on my explaining the Foucault epigraph on the critical nature of knowledge. And whenever a passage did not ring true—such as my account of a conversation with Pincher Jampijinpa about the fate of the soul (*pirlirrpa*)—Japangardi invited debate among the other men, and I was asked to amend the manuscript accordingly.

From start to finish, I had no inkling of whether or not my work would stand up to this exacting scrutiny. But sitting with Japangardi day after day, laboriously reading through the text, with the old men periodically sweeping a space clear in the red dirt in order to trace a songline or go over the names of sites, I accepted that my fate was in their hands. They were asking of me only what they asked of any initiated man: that he sit with those who knew, that he listen, that he prepare to be tested, that he get the facts right (*jungarni*).

Without Japangardi's help, it would have been impossible to get this feedback and, in the end, to be sure that the book had met with my informants' approval. Frequently, Japangardi had to resist distractions and brush aside other demands on his time. Without looking up, he would tell someone, "I got to finish this business for Jupurrurla. It's important." When the work was done, I asked him what he thought of it. It was good (*ngurrju*), he said, good that I had written a book about home. He told me that when Warlpiri got their land back and the Welfare Days came to end, it was like "coming out of the darkness." Then, commenting on his return to Lajamanu after a year and a half away, he said, "I was lost and then I found myself." "Home is where my family is," he said. "My family. My language. Sharing talk with these old men, hearing stories about what happened before I was born, what people were like when we were young, in the old days." Then he added, "We appreciate you coming back here, sitting down with us every day, sharing our talk (*yimi*)."

The night before I left Lajamanu, I went to say goodbye to Zack Jakamarra. The moon was like a great alabaster vessel, yellowed by the desert. I asked Zack if he was satisfied with the book.

"That's it now (*ngulajuku*)," he said. "You got it straight, my father. We bin straighten 'im out, like that concrete there." And he indicated the sharp sides and corners of an old concrete slab a few yards from where we were sitting—the foundations of a house that had never been finished.

NOTES

EPIGRAPH

VII   *Michel Foucault   The Use of Pleasure,* vol. 2 of *The History of Sexuality,* trans. R. Hurley (New York: Vintage, 1990), 8–9.

ACKNOWLEDGMENTS

IX   *"the one and only truth"* and *"an atmosphere"*   Vaclav Havel, "The end of the modern era," *New York Times,* 1 March 1992, E15.

ONE

1   *"Most serious thought in our time"*   Susan Sontag, "The Anthropologist as Hero," in *Against Interpretation* (New York: Dell, 1961).

1   *"we live not just our own lives"*   John Berger, *And our Faces, my Heart, Brief as Photos* (London: Writers and Readers, 1984), 67.

2   *Homeless in New York City*   David Gonzalez, "New York's Homeless Recall a No-Count Night," *New York Times,* 14 April 1991, 16.

2   *"like some green laurel"*   W. B. Yeats, "Prayer for my Daughter," in *The Collected Poems of W. B. Yeats* (New York: Collier MacMillan, 1989), 188.

2   *Salmon Rushdie on home*   "At the Auction of the Ruby Slippers," *Granta* 39 (1992): 247.

2   *Edward Said*   "Reflections on exile," *Granta* 13 (1984): 159.

2   *Blaise Cendrars, lines from "Hotel Notre Dame"*   Au Coeur du Monde, in *Trop c'est Trop* (Paris: Denoël, 1957) 33–34.

3   *Simone Weil   The Need for Roots,* trans. A. Wills (New York: Harper and Row, 1952), 43.

3   *Sigmund Freud   Civilization and its Discontents,* trans. James Strachey (New York: W. W. Norton, 1962), 38.

3   *Kenneth Read   The High Valley* (New York: Charles Scribner's, 1965), 58–

61, and *Return to the High Valley* (Berkeley: University of California Press, 1986), 114.

4 *Thomas Wolfe* *You Can't Go Home Again* (New York: Harper, 1934), 704–6.

4 *Diogenes* cited by Thomas McEvilley in *Art and Discontent: Theory at the Millenium* (Kingston, N.Y.: McPherson and Co., 1991), 179.

4 *Susan Sontag* "The Anthropologist as Hero."

5 *John Cage* "Composition as Process," in *Silence* (Middletown: Wesleyan University Press, 1961), 41, and "The Future of Music," in *Empty Words: Writings '73–'78,* (Middletown: Wesleyan University Press, 1979), 179.

5 *"If every event"* John Berger, *Once in Europa,* (New York: Pantheon, 1983), 77.

5 *Theodor Adorno* "The name of dialectics says no more, to begin with, than that objects do not go into their concepts without leaving a remainder, that they contradict the traditional norms of adequacy. Contradiction . . . indicates the untruth of identity, the fact that the concept does not exhaust the thing conceived." *Negative Dialectics,* trans. E. B. Ashton, (New York: Seabury Press, 1973), 5. Elsewhere, Adorno speaks of the task of proving, "by criticism of knowledge, the impossibility of a coincidence between the idea and what fulfils it." *Minima Moralia—Reflections from a Damaged Life* (London: Verso, 1978), 127.

5 *things counter, original, spare, strange* Gerard Manley Hopkins, "Pied Beauty," from *Poems of Gerard Manley Hopkins* (New York: Oxford University Press, 1961), 74.

5 "To omit a word always, to resort to *inept metaphors and obvious periphrases,* is perhaps the most emphatic way of stressing it." Jorge Luis Borges, "The Garden of Forking Paths," in *Labyrinths,* ed. D. A. Yates and J. E. Irby (New York: Penguin Books 1970), 53.

5 *William James* "Our fields of experience," *Essays in Radical Empiricism* (Cambridge: Harvard University Press, 1976), 35. "We ought to say a feeling of and": *Principles of Psychology,* vol. 1 (New York: Dover, 1950), 245–46. One might also remark Heidegger's view that an experientially authentic language would make verbs its grammatical subject.

6 *Hopi and Nootka* Benjamin Lee Whorf, "Language," in *Thought and Reality,* (Cambridge: MIT Press, 1956), 215–16.

6 *"To approach experience"* John Berger, *Pig Earth* (London: Writers and Readers, 1979), 6.

7 *Done with indoor complaints* . . . Walt Whitman, "Song of the Open Road," in *Leaves of Grass* (New York: Modern Library), 118–27.

TWO

10 *Police raid on Redfern* Tony Hewett, "Police 'spied' on Aborigines," *The Sydney Morning Herald,* 7 February 1990, 6. Deborah Cornwall and Tony Hewett, "Blacks call for inquiry into raids," *The Sydney Morning Herald,* 9 February 1990, 2.

11 *The Lost Children* Ed. Coral Edwards and Peter Read (Sydney: Doubleday, 1989).

12 *"Through many negatives to what I am"* Lawrence Durrell, "Alexandria," in *Collected Poems* (London: Faber and Faber, 1960), 72. "As for me I now move/Through many negatives to what I am."

13 *Négritude* Jean-Paul Sartre, *The Family Idiot: Gustave Flaubert 1821–1857,* vol. 2, trans. C. Cosman (Chicago: University of Chicago Press, 1987), 175.

14 *A Bastard Like Me* Charles Perkins (Sydney: Ure Smith, 1975), 13–14, 18.

14 *The polarization of "us" and "them"* William James, *Principles of Psychology,* vol. 1, 312.

15 *After 200 Years* Penny Taylor, ed., *After 200 Years: Photographic Essays of Aboriginal and Islander Australia Today* (Canberra: Australian Institute of Aboriginal Studies, 1988).

THREE

16 *Barry Lopez* "Landscape and narrative" in *Crossing Open Ground* (London: Picador, 1989), 64.

16 *Ugliest town* The person in Sydney who told me that Alice Springs was the ugliest town in the world must surely have read Robyn Davidson's *Travelling Light* (Sydney: Collins, 1989), 118.

19 *Besitzen* Heini P. Hediger, "The evolution of territorial behavior" in *Social Life of Early Man,* vol. 31 of Viking Fund Publications in Anthropology, ed. S. L. Washburn (New York: Werner Gren Foundation, 1961), 36–37.

19 *Nancy Munn* *Walbiri Iconography: Graphic Representation and Cultural Symbolism in a Central Australian Society* (Chicago: University of Chicago Press, 1986), xiv–xvi. Most middle-aged and older Warlpiri remember Nancy Munn (Nangala) and the location of her camp at Yuendumu, but few are aware of her writings on the Warlpiri.

23 *Francis Kelly Jupurrurla and the Warlpiri Media Association* See Eric Michaels, *For a Cultural Future: Francis Jupurrurla Makes TV at Yuendumu,* vol. 3 of Art and Criticism Monograph Series (Malvern: Artspace, 1987).

24 *Coniston killings* David J. L. McClay, "Surviving the Whiteman's World: Adult Education in Aboriginal Society" (Ph.D. diss., University of Queensland, Australia, 1988), 164–66.

26 Fred Myers *Pintupi Country, Pintupi Self* (Washington: Smithsonian Institution Press, 1986), 48–51.

26 *The unconscious as the unknown* In exploring an "ontology of the unthought," Michel Foucault speaks of the unconscious as an "obscure space," an "element of darkness," which lies both inside and outside thought. "The unthought (whatever name we give it) is not lodged in man like a shrivelled-up nature or a stratified history; it is, in relation to man, the Other: the Other that is not only a brother but a twin, born, not of man, nor in man, but beside him and at the same time, in an identical newness, in an unavoidable duality." *The Order of Things* (London: Tavistock, 1970), 326.

26 *John Dewey* *Experience and Nature* (London: Allen and Unwin, 1929), 44.

28　*"A house is a good thing"*　From M. Heppell, ed., *A Black Reality: Aboriginal Camps and Housing in Remote Australia* (Amata, South Australia: Aboriginal Studies Press, 1979), 152.

28　*History of Hooker Creek (Lajamanu)*　David J. L. McClay, "Surviving the Whiteman's World: Adult Education in Aboriginal Society," (Ph.D. diss., University of Queensland, Australia, 1988), 188–205.

36　*Kuruwarri and kurruwalpa*　"In Walbiri thought there is a close relation between graphic forms and the country, or ground (*walya*), since the term *guruwari* can be used in a general sense to refer to any visible mark left by an ancestor in the country, and in addition, *guruwari* in the abstract aspect of "ancestral powers" are lodged in the country." Nancy Munn, *Walbiri Iconography: Graphic Representation and Cultural Symbolism in a Central Australian Society* (Chicago: University of Chicago Press, 1986), 119. For further details see also *Walbiri Iconography*, 29–31, and M. J. Meggitt, *Desert People: A Study of the Walbiri People in Central Australia* (Sydney: Angus and Robertson, 1962), 272–74.

36　*Pirlirrpa*　Jampijinpa's conviction that the spirit returns to the place whence it came confirms the findings of M. J. Meggitt (*Desert People,* 329) and Françoise Dussart, "Warlpiri Women's Yawulyu Ceremonies: A Forum for Socialization and Innovation" (Ph.D. diss., The Australian National University, Canberra, 1988), 61. However, when reviewing this section of my book with senior men in Lajamanu in June 1994, I was told in no uncertain terms that after lingering among the living for a while the spirit dissipates into the ether. The men insisted that if the bones go into the ground, then, logically, the spirit should go into the air. When I suggested that this view might owe more to Christian teaching than pre-contact knowledge, I was assured that this was not the case. Tony Swain reports a similar disparity of views in *A Place for Strangers: Toward a History of Australian Aboriginal Being* (Cambridge: Cambridge University Press, 1993), 119.

FIVE

41　*Honey-Ant Men's Song*　R. M. W. Dixon and Martin Duwell, ed., *The Honey-Ant Men's Song and Other Aboriginal Song Poems* (St. Lucia: University of Queensland Press, 1990), 52–69.

48　*Names*　Françoise Dussart includes a detailed and perceptive account of Warlpiri naming practices in her Ph.D. thesis "Warlpiri Women's Yawulyu Ceremonies: A Forum for Socialization and Innovation" (The Australian National University, Canberra, 1988). On *kumunjayi,* see also D. Nash and J. Simpson, "No-name in Central Australia," *Chicago Linguistic Society* 1, no. 2 (1981): 165–77.

49　*Robert Tonkinson*　"The Jigalong people, now far from their homelands, say that they are unable to return because they have lost the skills necessary for prolonged survival in the desert and have grown too used to European food. The dream-spirit has thus assumed a vital role in their lives by providing the only convenient means of communication with their homeland, and has enabled them to maintain contact and identity with ancestral and other spirit beings, totemic creatures and so on." "Aboriginal dream-spirit beliefs in a contact situation: Jigalong, Western Australia," in *Australian Aboriginal Anthropology,* ed. R. M. Berndt (Nedlands, W.A.: University of Western Australia Press, 1970), 276–91.

SIX

50 *Ingmar Bergman The Magic Lantern,* trans. Joan Tate (Harmondsworth: Penguin Books, 1988), 208.

50 *T. E. Lawrence Seven Pillars of Wisdom* (Poole: Dorset Press, 1988), 29.

50 *Edmond Jabes* Cited in John Berger, "A Story for Aesop," in *Keeping a Rendezvous* (New York: Pantheon, 1991), 63–64.

50 *Antoine de Saint-Exupéry Wind, Sand and Stars (Terre des Hommes),* trans. Lewis Galantiere (London: Heinemann, 1954), 113, 116, 92.

50 *W. H. Auden The Enchafèd Flood, or The Romantic Iconography of the Sea* (Charlottesville: University Press of Virginia, 1950), 17.

58 *Fred R. Myers Pintupi Country, Pintupi Self: Sentiment, Place and Politics Among Western Desert Aborigines* (Washington: Smithsonian Institution Press, 1986), 48.

58 *Herodotus and historie* Margaret T. Hodgen, *Early Anthropology in the Sixteenth and Seventeenth Centuries* (Philadelphia: University of Pennsylvania Press, 1964), 22.

58 *Hannah Arendt The Human Condition* (Chicago: The University of Chicago Press, 1958), 184.

SEVEN

60 *Samuel Beckett All That Fall* (New York: Grove Press, 1957), 7.

62 *Placing ourselves and the Other in different times we thus deny coevalness.* Johannes Fabian's *Time and the Other* (New York: Columbia University Press, 1983) offers a brilliant critique of the ways different models of time have given spurious legitimacy to notions of racial and social difference in anthropology. By *"denial of coevalness,"* Fabian means *"a persistent and systematic tendency to place the referent(s) of anthropology in a Time other than the present of the producer of anthropological discourse"* (p. 31, italics in text).

62 *How Westerners identify self* On the transformed social landscape of Europe that breaks the old constancies of space and kinship, making identity more a matter of *who* one is than *where* one hails from, see J. Frykman and O. Löfgren, *Culture Builders: A Historical Anthropology of Middle-Class Life* (New Brunswick: Rutgers University Press, 1987), 63–91.

70 *Kurdungurlu* Jupurrurla's remarks lend support to linguist David Nash's arguments concerning the meaning of the term *kurdungurlu.* David Nash, "An Etymological Note on Warlpiri kurdungurlu," in *The Languages of Kinship in Aboriginal Australia,* Oceania Linguistic Monograph no. 24, ed. J. Heath, F. Merlan, and A. Rumsey (Sydney: University of Sydney, 1982), 141–59. It should also be noted that a person can become *kurdungurlu* for places whose ceremony he gains a knowledge of and learns "to run," even though he has

no close uterine ties to these places. Thus, in Lajamanu, it is recognized that Zack Jakamarra's deep and detailed knowledge of Dreamings other than his own *effectively* makes him *kurdungurlu* for places with which he has no close uterine connection.

EIGHT

74 *Bruce Chatwin   What Am I Doing Here* (New York: Viking, 1989), 273.

74 *Wave Hill*   I have drawn several details about Aboriginal life at Wave Hill Station in the 1940s from Ronald and Catherine Berndt's *End of an Era: Aboriginal Labour in the Northern Territory* (Canberra: Australian Institute of Aboriginal Studies, 1987), chapter 3. Other details concerning the Wave Hill strike and the Pastoral Era have been borrowed from Pamela Lyon and Michael Parsons, *We Are Staying: The Alyawarre Struggle for Land at Lake Nash* (Alice Springs: Central Land Council, I. A. D. Press, 1989).

84 *Pincher Jampijinpa, "A house is just like a big jail"*   The source of this comment is Paddy Patrick Jangala, in *Stories from Lajamanu* (Department of Education, N. T. Division, photocopied, undated), no pagination.

85 *International tennis tournament*   ATP Tour World Championship, Frankfurt, 17 November 1990.

85 *Athapaskan Indians*   Hugh Brody, *Maps and Dreams* (Harmondsworth: Penguin Books, 1983), 60.

85 *Eskimos*   Ann Fienup-Riordan, *Eskimo Essays: Yup'ik Lives and How We See Them* (New Brunswick: Rutgers University Press, 1990), 12.

85 *Emile Durkheim   The Elementary Forms of the Religious Life,* trans. J. W. Swain (Glencoe: The Free Press, 1954), 95–96.

85 *Home as private abode and domestic space*   See Witold Rybczynski, *Home: A Short History of an Idea* (Harmondsworth: Penguin Books, 1987), 51–75.

86 *John Berger   And Our Faces, My Heart, Brief As Photos* (London: Writers and Readers Publishing Cooperative, 1984), 55.

86 *Gaston Bachelard   The Poetics of Space,* trans. M. Jolas (Boston: Beacon Press, 1969), 3–37.

86 *Primo Levi   Other People's Trades,* trans. R. Rosenthal (London: Michael Joseph, 1989), 5.

86 *Being as dwelling*   Martin Heidegger, *Poetry, Language, Thought,* trans. A. Hofstadter (New York: Harper and Row, 1975), 146–47. Karl Marx: See Maurice Godelier, *The Mental and the Material,* trans. M. Thorn (London: Verso, 1986), 19. Sigmund Freud: *Introductory Lectures on Psycho-Analysis,* trans. J. Riviere (London: Allen and Unwin, 1922), 249.

86 *Germaine Greer   Daddy, We Hardly Knew You* (London: Hamish Hamilton, 1989), 70.

87 *"The Homeless Mind"*   Peter Berger, Brigitte Berger, and Hansfried Kellner, *The Homeless Mind* (Harmondsworth: Penguin Books, 1973).

87 *Theodor Adorno   Minima Moralia* (London: Verso, 1975), 38–39.

NINE

88 *Derek Walcott Omeros* (New York: Farrar Straus Giroux, 1990), 63.

92 *Sacred sites as "gold"* Cf. Fred Myers, *Pintupi Country, Pintupi Self* (Washington: Smithsonian Institution Press, 1986), 64–66.

92 *Lasseter* Billy Marshall-Stoneking, *Lasseter in Quest of Gold* (Sydney: Hodder and Stoughton, 1989).

98 *Colin Chapman* Letter to Sweeney, 26 May 1943. Australian Archives, N. T., CA 1076 Welfare Branch, CRS: F3 Item 21/59.

98 *Aboriginal living conditions at The Granites in the 1930s and 1940s* Australian Archives, N. T., CA 1115, CRS: F126 Item 29; CA 1070, CRS: F1 Item 43/65; and Item 44/172.

99 *David Grossman The Yellow Wind,* trans. H. Watzman (London: Picador, 1989), 68–69.

100 *Cosmopolitan* Alice Kosner, "How to Recharge a Stale Relationship," November 1987.

100 *"A Toyota's just tin and iron"* Adapted from a comment cited in David McClay, "Surviving the Whiteman's World: Adult Education in Aboriginal Society" (Ph.D. diss., University of Queensland, Australia 1988), 279.

100 *Names of Warlpiri at The Granites:* Australian Archives, N. T., CA 1070, CRS: F1 Item 42/299.

102 *"My country is the place"* Cited by Norman B. Tindale, *Aboriginal Tribes of Australia* (Berkeley: University of California Press, 1974), 18.

105 *Davidson at Paraluyu* Allan A. Davidson, *Journal of Explorations in Central Australia, 1898–1900* (Adelaide: Government Printer, 1905), 58–59.

108 *Olive Pink Northern Territory Newsletter* (July 1975): 4–9; (September 1975): 5–8.

109 *"Tragedy Track"* C. H. Madigan, *Central Australia* (Melbourne: Oxford University Press, 1944), 239; Michael Terry, *Hidden Wealth and Hiding People* (New York: Putnam, 1934), chapter 16; F. E. Baume, *Tragedy Track: The Story of The Granites* (Sydney: Frank C. Johnson, 1933), 49–50.

109 *Finding one's way in the desert* Cf. David Lewis, "Observations on Route Finding and Spatial Orientation Among the Aboriginal Peoples of the Western Desert Region of Central Australia," *Oceania* 46, no. 4 (1976): 249–82. "[T]he commonest usage in giving directions, and the one which appears to reflect Aboriginal territorial identification most directly, is by the informant, and perforce the questioner, *visualising themselves at some (often distant) point of reference, from where directions are given* . . . If you ask where a place is you will be given directions from some other place, not from where you are" (ibid., 255).

110 *Views of the desert* Ernest Giles, *Australia Twice Traversed: The Romance of Exploration, Being a Narrative Compiled from the Journals of Five Exploring Expeditions,* vol. 2 (London: Sampson Low, Marston, Searle and Rivington, 1889), 320. Michael Terry, *Hidden Wealth and Hiding Places* (New York:

Putnam, 1934), 200. The descriptions of "desert sickness" and of Aboriginals are taken from Baume, *Tragedy Track,* chapters 6 and 20 respectively.

ELEVEN

112   *T. S. Eliot* "Little Gidding," *Four Quartets* (London: Faber, 1959), lines 240–43.

114   *"the place where they live"* Raymond Carver, "Miracle," in *Carver Country: The World of Raymond Carver* (New York: Charles Scribner's, 1990), 92.

116   *"Man alone exists. Rocks are, but they do not exist"* Martin Heidegger, "The way back into the ground of metaphysics," in *Existentialism: From Dosto-evsky to Sartre,* selected and introduced by Walter Kaufmann (New York: Meridian Books, 1956), 214.

117   *Trauma of the unresponsiveness of matter* George Devereux, *From Anxiety to Method in the Behavioral Sciences* (The Hague: Mouton, 1967), 18–34.

117   *First contact in the New Guinea Highlands* Bob Connolly and Robin Ander-son, *First Contact: New Guinea's Highlanders Encounter the Outside World* (New York: Viking, 1987), 43–47.

117   *Lionel C. G. Gee General Report on Tanami Goldfield and District* (Adelaide: Government Printer, 1911), 19.

118   *"moments of the whole"* Theodor Adorno, *Minima Moralia* (London: Verso, 1978), 246.

118   *William James The Principles of Psychology,* vol. 1, (New York: Dover, 1950), 294.

119   *Merleau-Ponty on the primacy of the social Phenomenology of Perception,* trans. Colin Smith (London: Routledge, 1962), 362.

120   *Montaigne on "inconstancie" The Essayes of Michael Lord of Montaigne,* trans. John Florio (London: 1908), 1–11.

120   *Jadran Mimica Intimations of Infinity: The Mythopoeia of the Iqwaye Counting System and Number* (Oxford: Berg, 1988), 160.

120   *The Tallensi concept of home* Meyer Fortes, *The Web of Kinship among the Tallensi* (London: Oxford University Press, 1949), 185–86.

121   *Gaston Bachelard The Poetics of Space,* trans. Maria Jolas (Boston: Beacon Press, 1969), 8.

121   *Yi-Fu Tuan Space and Place* (Minneapolis: University of Minnesota Press, 1977), 22, 29.

121   *Pure Land Buddhism* Allan G. Grapard, "Flying Mountains and Walkers of Emptiness: Toward a Definition of Sacred Space in Japanese Religions," *History of Religions* 2, no. 3 (1982): 195–221.

122   *Anjelica Huston* Brad Darrach, "Jack Nicholson finds his Queen of Hearts at last," *Women's Day,* 26 August 1985, 4.

122   *Tennessee Williams The Night of the Iguana,* Act 3. Quoted by Yi-Fu Tuan in *Space and Place,* 139.

124   *T. G. H. Strehlow Songs of Central Australia* (Sydney: Angus and Robertson, 1977). *Pmara kutata,* pp. 547–48; destruction of the Unmatjera sacred site, pp. 586–87.

125   *Young Liberals National Convention Waikato Times,* 8 January 1991, 7.

TWELVE

126   *Yi-Fu Tuan* *Space and Place* (Minneapolis: University of Minnesota Press, 1977), 3.

130   *On the cultural versus personal authenticity of emotions* Fred Myers, *Pintupi Country, Pintupi Self* (Washington: Smithsonian Institution Press, 1986), 104–7.

134   *On the dialectic of coming out and going back in* And the iconography of circle and line: Nancy Munn, "The Spatial Presentation of Cosmic Order in Walbiri Iconography," in *Primitive Art & Society,* ed. Anthony Forge (New York: Oxford University Press, 1973), 193–220.

THIRTEEN

137   *Milan Kundera* *The Art of the Novel,* trans. Linda Asher (New York: Harper & Row, 1988), 35.

139   *Sacred trees* T. G. H. Strehlow, *Songs of Central Australia* (Sydney: Angus and Robertson, 1971), 574–76.

FOURTEEN

147   *T. S. Eliot* "East Coker," *Four Quartets* (London: Faber, 1959), lines 190–92.

150   *Industry Commission* *Mining and Minerals Processing in Australia, Volume 1, Report* (Canberra: Australian Government Publishing Service, 25 February 1991), xi–xxi.

152   *Ngarrka myth* M. J. Meggitt, "Gadjari among the Walbiri Aborigines of Central Australia," *Oceania* 37, no. 2 (1966): 124–31.

EPILOGUE

156   *John Berger* *Keeping a Rendezvous* (New York: Pantheon, 1991), 216–17.

156   *Meyer Fortes on ethnography* I am recalling here part of a conversation I had with Meyer in Canberra in the summer of 1974–75. In 1978 Meyer published "An Anthropologist's Apprenticeship" and used A. J. Ayer's distinction between pontiffs and journeymen to reiterate this contrast between the heady, ethereal world of theory and the reality of "fieldwork in the empirical mode." He liked to think of himself as a journeyman, whose eyes "are on his material, not on higher things." B. J. Siegel, A. R. Beals, and S. A. Tyler, eds., *Annual Review of Anthropology* 7 (Palo Alto: 1978), 1–30.

157   *"As snapshots freeze a moment forever"* An echo of John Berger's observation that "All photographs are ambiguous. All photographs have been taken out of a continuity. If the event is a public event, this continuity is history; if it is personal, the continuity, which has been broken, is a life story" (John Berger and Jean Mohr, *Another Way of Telling* (London: Writers and Readers Publishing Cooperative, 1982), 91.

157   *"Metaphysics must give ground to metaphor"* Hannah Arendt's remarks on the role of metaphor in the thought of Walter Benjamin are relevant here:

In his concern with directly, actually demonstrable concrete facts, with single events and occurences whose "significance" is manifest, Benjamin was not much interested in theories or "ideas" which did not immediately assume the most precise outward shape imaginable. To this very complex but still highly realistic mode of thought the Marxian relationship between superstructure and substructure became, in a precise sense, a metaphorical one. If, for example—and this would certainly be in the spirit of Benjamin's thought—the abstract concept *Vernunft* (reason) is traced back to its origin in the verb *vernehmen* (to perceive, to hear), it may be thought that a word from the sphere of the superstructure, or, conversely, that a concept has been transformed into a metaphor—provided that "metaphor" is understood in its original, nonallegorical sense as *metapherein* (to transfer). ("Introduction" to Walter Benjamin, *Illuminations,* trans. H. Zohn (New York: Schocken Books, 1969), 13.

"Metaphors are the means by which the oneness of the world is poetically brought about" ("Introduction," 14). For a comprehensive exploration of this way of understanding metaphor, see my essay "Thinking Through the Body," in *Paths Toward a Clearing* (Bloomington: Indiana University Press, 1989), 137–55.

160   *"What is really 'in' experience"*   John Dewey, *Experience and Nature* (New York: Dover, 1958), 20.

160   *Experience as "a single whole"*   Michael Oakeshott, *Experience and its Modes* (Cambridge: Cambridge University Press, 1933), 10.

160   *"No object is wholly known"*   Theodor Adorno, *Negative Dialectics* (New York: Continuum, 1973), 14.

160   *Michel de Certeau on the field of the nondiscursive*   "The Arts of Theory," in *The Practice of Everyday Life,* trans. Steven Rendall (Berkeley: University of California Press, 1984), 61.

160   *Merleau-Ponty on Gestalt models and the ambiguity of experience*   Phenomenology of Perception, trans. Colin Smith (London: Routledge, 1962), 3–12.

160   *William James and the image of the life of a bird*   Principles of Psychology, vol. 1 (New York: Dover, 1950), 243.

161   *Sometimes we are fully aware of our bodies*   As Drew Leder observes, while the Cartesian split between body and mind is epistemologically untenable, it nevertheless resonates with aspects of our experience in which the body disappears from consciousness. *The Absent Body* (Chicago: University of Chicago Press, 1990), 155.

161   *Sense of oneself as an individual* and *belonging to a collectivity*   Theodor Adorno points out that these contrasted modalities of self experience are mutually entailed. "Neither one exists without the other—the particular only as defined and thus universal; the universal only as the definition of something particular, and thus itself particular. Both of them are and are not." "Subject and Object," in *The Essential Frankfurt School Reader,* ed. A. Arato and E. Gebhardt (New York: Urizen Books, 1978), 510.

161   *William James on the antinomies of subject and object, etc.*   "The Place of

Affectional Facts in a World of Pure Experience," in *Essays in Radical Empiricism* (Cambridge: Harvard University Press, 1976), 71.

163 *Dewey's test for adequacy in philosophy* *Experience and Nature*, 7.

163 *Knowledge as a process of coming to know* (erkennen) Adorno's view of knowledge and experience is summarized by Gillian Rose in *The Melancholy Science: An Introduction to the Thought of Theodor W. Adorno* (London: Macmillan, 1978), 150.

163 *Meaning resides in the journeying, not the destination* I am reminded here of Wittgenstein's remarks in the preface to his *Philosophical Investigations*. Noting how impossible he had found it to force his remarks "in any single direction against their natural inclination," he observes that "this was, of course, connected with the very nature of the investigation. For this compels us to travel over a wide field of thought criss-cross in every direction. The philosophical remarks in this book are, as it were, *a number of sketches of landscapes which were made in the course of these long and involved journeyings.*" *Philosophical Investigations*, trans. G. E. M. Anscombe (Oxford: Blackwell, 1968), ix. (Italics added).

163 *Adorno on "exact fantasy"* "The Actuality of Philosophy," *Telos* 31–34 (1977–78): 131. For an account of Adorno's paratactic style, see Gillian Rose, *The Melancholy Science*, 13.

164 *Helénè Cixous on "coming into language"* *Coming to Writing and Other Essays*, ed. D. Jenson, with an introductory essay by S. R. Suleiman (Cambridge: Harvard University Press, 1991), 57.

164 *William James on "mosaic philosophy"* "A World of Pure Experience," in *Essays in Radical Empiricism* (Cambridge: Harvard University Press, 1976), 22.

165 *the things themselves* Heidegger's phenomenology of *die Sachen selbst*. *Being and Time* (San Francisco: Harper, 1962), 50. The phrase echoes Husserl's exhortation "Back to things themselves." *Logical Investigations* (London: Routledge and Kegan Paul, 1970).

165 *"The whole is the false"* Theodor Adorno, *Minima Moralia* (London: Verso, 1974), 50.

165 *Sartre on intellectuals* "A Plea for Intellectuals," in *Between Existentialism and Marxism*, trans. J. Matthews (London: Verso, 1974), 228–85.

166 *cognitive certification* John Dewey, *Experience and Nature* (New York: Dover, 1958), 126.

166 *The two kangaroo myth* C.f. M. J. Meggitt, "Gadjari Among the Walbiri of Central Australia," *Oceania* 36, no. 4 (1966): 44, and A. Capell, "The Walbiri Through Their Own Eyes," *Oceania* 23, no. 2 (1952): 131–32. Capell notes that he recorded his version of the myth at Yuendumu from Minjina, "with a wealth of eloquence that only a recording machine could have preserved, and of action which would have demanded a ciné camera" (ibid., 130).

168 *Michael Oakeshott on practical knowledge* *Rationalism in Politics and Other Essays* (London: Methuen, 1962), 90–91. Oakeshott's work antedates Bourdieu's comparable critique of the notion of rule by ten years [Pierre Bourdieu, *Esquisse d'une théorie de la pratique, précédé de troi études d'ethnologie kabyle* (Geneva: Librairie Droz, 1972)].

168   *The philology of "knowledge"*   R. B. Onians, *The Origins of European Thought* (Cambridge: Cambridge University Press, 1951), 174–86. See also H. A. Bunker and B. D. Lewin, "A Psychoanalytic notation on the root GN, KN, CN," in *Psychoanalysis and Culture,* ed. G. B. Wilbur and W. Muensterberger (New York: International University Presses, 1965), 363–67.

168   *Behavior is not an outcome of will*   R. May, *Love and Will* (London: Fontana, 1972), 225.

168   *Watt walking*   Samuel Beckett, *Watt* (Paris: Olympia Press, 1958), 32.

169   *Merleau-Ponty on motility*   *Phenomenology of Perception,* 139. On consciousness as "I can": ibid., 137.

169   *Maori metaphors of knowledge*   Anne Salmon, "Theoretical Landscapes: On Cross-Cultural Conceptions of Knowledge," in *Semantic Anthropology,* ed. D. Parkin (London: Academic Press, 1982), 82–83. Comments by Te Uira Manihera and Ngoi Pewhairangi are from Michael King, ed., *Te Ao Hurihuri: The World Moves On* (Wellington: Hicks Smith & Sons, 1975), 7, 10.

170   *L'enquête and l'épreuve*   Foucault's distinction is brilliantly elucidated by James Miller in *The Passion of Michel Foucault* (New York: Simon and Schuster, 1993), 269–73.

171   *"Lost Tribes, Lost Knowledge"*   *Time,* 23 September 1991, 4, 56–66.

172   *That world "of which knowledge always speaks"*   Maurice Merleau-Ponty, *Phenomenology of Perception,* ix.

Michael Jackson was born and raised in New Zealand but
has lived in Sierra Leone, England, France, Australia, and
the United States. He is the author of four collections of
poetry, two novels, and four anthropological mono-
graphs, and has won numerous awards for his writing,
including the Commonwealth Poetry Prize in 1976, the
Curl Essay Prize in 1977, the New Zealand Book Award
for Poetry in 1981, and the Amaury Talbot Prize for
African Ethnography in 1989. He lives in Bloomington,
Indiana, with his wife and son, and teaches anthropology
at Indiana University.

———

Library of Congress Cataloging-in-Publication Data
Jackson, Michael, 1940–
At home in the world / Michael Jackson.
Includes bibliographical references.
ISBN 0-8223-1561-0. — ISBN 0-8223-1574-2 (pbk.)
1. Walbiri (Australian people)—Social conditions.
2. Philosophy, Walbiri.   3. Home—Philosophy.
4. Homelessness—Philosophy.   I. Title.
DU125.W3J33   1995
306'.089'9915—dc20   94-36881 CIP